Instructor's Manual to Accompany

ADVANCED ENGINEERING MATHEMATICS

SIXTH EDITION

C. Ray Wylie
Professor Emeritus, Montana State University

Louis C. Barrett
Professor Emeritus, Furman University

The McGraw-Hill Companies, Inc.

New York St. Louis San Francisco Auckland Bogotá
Caracas Lisbon London Madrid Mexico City Milan Montreal
New Delhi San Juan Singapore Sydney Tokyo Toronto

McGraw-Hill

A Division of The McGraw-Hill Companies

Instructor's Manual to Accompany
ADVANCED ENGINEERING MATHEMATICS
Sixth Edition

ISBN   0-07-072207-2

1 2 3 4 5 6 7 8 9 0   BKM   BKM   9 0 9 8 7 6 5

Contents

Chapter 1

Section 1.1

2. (a) 0

   (b) 0

   (c) $2\pi \sinh \pi$

4. (a) π

   (b) $-3\pi/2$

   (c) $\pi/6$

6. (a) 2

   (b) 8/3

   (c) 1

8. (a) 3π

   (b) $\pi + \ln 2$

   (c) $-2\pi + \ln 2$

10. $N(t) = \begin{cases} n & \frac{2n}{3} \le t < \frac{2(n+1)}{3}; \quad n = 0,1,2,\ldots,11 \\ 12 & t = 8 \end{cases}$

where $N(t)$ is the number of times the truck has been loaded at the end of t hours.

12. (a) odd

   (b) even

   (c) neither

14. (a) Both the sum and difference are even; both the sum and difference are odd; neither is even or odd if neither function is a zero function.

   (b) The product is even; the product is even; the product is odd.

16. (a) $[\cosh x + \ln |x|] + \sinh x$

(b) $|x - 1| = f_{\text{even}} + f_{\text{odd}}$, where

$$f_{\text{even}} = \begin{cases} -x & x \le -1 \\ 1 & -1 \le x \le 1 \\ x & 1 \le x \end{cases} \quad \text{and}$$

$$f_{\text{odd}} = \begin{cases} 1 & x \le -1 \\ -x & -1 \le x \le 1 \\ -1 & 1 \le x \end{cases}$$

(c) $f(x) = f_{\text{even}} + f_{\text{odd}}$, where

$$f_{\text{even}} = \begin{cases} 1 & x < 0 \\ 2 & x = 0 \\ 1 & 0 < x \end{cases} \quad \text{and}$$

$$f_{\text{odd}} = \begin{cases} -1 & x < 0 \\ 0 & x = 0 \\ 1 & 0 < x \end{cases}$$

18. y, z dependent; x independent

20. u, v dependent x, y independent

Section 1.2

2. First-order, ordinary, linear

4. Fourth-order, ordinary, nonlinear

6. Second-order, ordinary, linear

8. Second-order, partial, linear

10. Second-order, partial, nonlinear

12. Second-order, partial, linear in x; linear in u, the equation is nonlinear.

14. First-order, ordinary, linear

16. Nonlinear in x, linear in y

18. Nonlinear in x, and in y

Section 1.3

12. $m = -1, 1$

14. All subintervals of $(-\pi, 0)$, $(0, \pi)$, $(\pi, 2\pi)$, and $(2\pi, 3\pi)$

16. $y = \frac{1}{2} \tan x$; defined on all subintervals of $(-\pi/2, \pi/2)$

18. $y = c + \ln \left| \frac{x}{(x-2)} \right|$

20. $y = c_1 + c_2 x + e^{-x} - \cos 3x$

22. $y = c_1 + c_2 x + c_3 x^2 + c_4 x^3 + 16 \sinh(x/2)$

24. $y = c_1 + c_2 x + \frac{1}{2} \mathrm{Tan}^{-1}(\frac{1}{2} \tan \frac{x}{2})$

26. $y = 1 - \ln (\cos x)$

28. $y = x \, \mathrm{Sin}^{-1} x + (1 - x^2)^{1/2}$

30. $y = 4x^3 - 3 \sin 2x + 2$

32. $c + \ln x$, where $c = a + \ln b$

34. $\frac{a'x+b}{c'x+1}$, where $a' = \frac{a}{d}$, $b' = \frac{b}{d}$, $c' = \frac{c}{d}$, $d \neq 0$;
or $\frac{a''x+b''}{x+d''}$, where $a'' = \frac{a}{c}$, $b'' = \frac{b}{c}$
$d'' = \frac{d}{c}$, $c \neq 0$

36. $B \cos x$, where $B = 2A \cos a$

38. $B \sin x + C \sin^3 x$, where $B = 3a + b$,
$C = -4a + c$

40. $B(3x + 4y + 5) + C(5x + 3y + 4)$, where
$B = -3a + b$, $C = 2a + c$

Section 1.4

2. General integral: $y^2 = 2x + c$; $y^2 = 2x + 10$;
$y = -\sqrt{2(x+5)}, -5 < x$

4. (a) $y = e^{-x^2/2} + c$

(b)

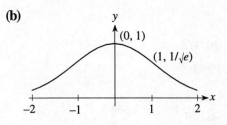

6. (a) $y = \begin{cases} c_1 x^3 & x \leq 0 \\ c_2 x^3 & x \geq 0 \end{cases}$

(b)

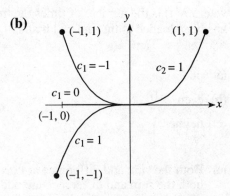

8. $y = c \cosh x$

10. $y = \begin{cases} c_1 x^2 - x & x \leq 0 \\ c_2 x^2 - x & x \geq 0 \end{cases}$

12. $y = c_n(1 - \cos\ x)\quad 2n\pi \leq x \leq 2(n+1)\pi$

Section 1.5

4. $(\cos x - \sin x)y'' + (2\cos\ x)\ y'$
$+ (\cos x + \sin x)y = 0$

6. $y'' + y' - 2y = 0$

8. $y''' - 2y'' - y' + 2y = 0$

10. $y'' - 4y = 0$

12. $(y^2 - y)\ y'' + (\ y')^2 = 0$

14. $y^2 y'' - 2t(y')^3 + 2y(\ y')^2 = 0$

16. $x(1 - x)\ y'' + (2 - x^2)\ y' + (2 - x)y = 0$

18. $y'' - y = 0$

20. No; $x^2 - \text{Tan}^{-1} ay + 2 = 0$ does not define y as a function of x because for all x,
$2 + x^2 > \frac{\pi}{2} > \text{Tan}^{-1} ay.$

22. (a) $yy' + x = 0$

   (b) $\left[1 + (y')^2\right]y''' - 3y'(y'')^2 = 0$

   (c) $xyy'' + x(y')^2 - yy' = 0$

   (d) $xyy'' + x(y')^2 - yy' = 0$

   (e) $(mx - y)y'' - m(y')^3 - (y')^2 - my' - 1 = 0$
   Special cases:
   $yy'' + (y')^2 + 1 = 0\ \ \text{if}\ m = 0$

$(x - y)y'' - (y')^3 - (y')^2 - y' - 1 = 0$
if $m = 1$
$xy'' - (y')^3 - y' = 0\ \ \text{if}\ m = \infty$

24. $(y')^2 - 2xy' + 2y = 0$

Section 1.6

2. $y = \sin \pi x + \pi \cos \pi x$ on $(-\infty, \infty)$; unique

4. $y = x\ln\ x - x - 1$ on $(0,\ \infty)$; unique

6. $y = x\,\text{Cos}^{-1}x - (1 - x^2)^{1/2} + 3/2$ on $-1 \leq x \leq 1$; unique

8. $y = \ln \sin\ x\quad 0 < x < \pi$; unique

10. $y = \begin{cases} c_1(x+1)^2 & x \leq -1 \\ c_2(x+1)^2 & x \geq -1 \end{cases}$; not unique

12. $y = \ln 2(x^2 - x)\quad x < 0$; unique

14. No solution

16. $y = \begin{cases} c_1 e^{-1/x^2} & x < 0 \\ 0 & x = 0 \\ c_2 e^{-1/x^2} & 0 < x \end{cases}$; not unique

18. Complete solution on $(-\infty, \infty)$:
$y = \tan^{-1} x + c_1 x + c^2$
Initial-value problem solution on $(-\infty, \infty)$:
$y = \text{Tan}^{-1} x - x$

20. Complete solution on $(0, \infty)$:
$y = e^x + 2x^2 \ln\ x - 3x^2 + c_1 x + c_2$

Initial-value problem solution on $(0, \infty)$:
$$y = e^x - ex + 2x^2 \ln x - 3x^2$$

22. Complete solution on $(-\infty, \infty)$:
$$y = 3\int_0^x e^{-t^2}\,dt + c_1 x + c_2$$
Initial-value problem solution on $(-\infty, \infty)$:
$$y = 3\int_0^x e^{-t^2}\,dt + x$$

24. (a) The solution over $x_1 \le x \le x_2$ is the trivial solution $y = 0$.

   (b) The solution curve is the subinterval $x_1 \le x \le x_2$ of the x axis.

   (c) Yes.

   (d) Theorem 1 applies.

26. $-\dfrac{26}{135} < x < \dfrac{26}{135}$

28. $-7/5 < x < -3/5$

Section 1.7

2. $xy^2 - x + \cos y = c$

4. $\cos x + ye^x - \frac{1}{3}y^3 = c$

6. $x^3 - 3x^2 y - y^2 = c$

8. $x^2 y^4 + x \sin y = c$

10. $-\ln|x| - \text{Sin}^{-1}x + xy^3 = c$

12. $\sin(x^2 + y) - xy^3 = c$

14. $x^2 y + \sinh xy = cy$

16. $y + x \ln xy = c$

18. $e^x + \ln|y| + y \ln x = c$

20. $y = (x+1)/x^2; \ 0 < x$

22. $y = \frac{1}{2}\left(\sqrt{68 - x^2} - x\right); |x| < 2\sqrt{17}$

24. $y = -\frac{1}{2}\left(x^2 + \sqrt{x^4 + 4\left(1 + x^3/3\right)}\right); x$ real

26. $y = 7\cosh(\ln x); \ 0 < x$

28. $y = -\dfrac{1}{2x}\left[e^x + \sqrt{e^{2x} + 8x\left(e - e^x\right)}\right]; 0 < x < x_0,$
where $x_0 \doteq 1.45989$ denotes the smallest positive zero of $e^{2x} + 8x(e - e^x)$.

32. For the equation $xy^2\,dx + (x^2 y + y)\,dy = 0$, Corollary 1 gives the solution $x^2 y^2 + y^2 = k$, which defines an explicit solution if and only if $k > 0$.

Section 1.8

2. $\frac{x}{y} + \frac{x^2}{2} + 2\ln|y| = c; \ u = 1/y^2$

4. $\ln|x| - \ln|y| - \frac{1}{xy} = c; \ u = 1/x^2 y^2$

6. $\ln\left|x^3 y\right| = y + c; u = 1/xy$

8. $x^2 + y = cx; \ u = 1/x^2$

10. $x + xy = cy; \ u = 1/y^2$

12. $x^2 + y^2 = cy$; $u = 1/y^2$

14. $x^2y^3 + y^2 = c$; $u = y$

16. $(1 + x^2)\ln|y| = c$; exact

18. $x^2y^2 + \cos\frac{x}{y} = c$; $u = 1/y^2$

20. $2y\cosh x = x + \sinh x \cosh x + c$; $u = \cosh x$

22. $x^3(1 - 3y) = c$; $u = x^2$

24. $cx^2 = y + \sqrt{x^2 + y^2}$

26. As an exact equation: $x^2y^2 - 2xy = c$. As solved via the integrating factor $1/x^2y^2$: $\ln|xy| + 1/(xy) = k$. The reconciliation of these results consists in observing that each of these solutions is of the form $f(xy) =$ constant and noting that the implication of either of these is simply $xy =$ constant. It is trivial to verify that $y = a/x$ does indeed satisfy the given differential equation.

Section 1.9

2. $y = ce^{-x^2}$

4. $y = \tan(x^3 + c)$

6. $y = ce^{y-x^2} - 1$

8. $x(y^2 - 9) = ce^{-x}$

10. $y = \ln\sqrt{2e^x + c}$

12. $y^2e^{2y} = cx$

14. $y = c/(1 - c\cos x)$

16. $y^2 = c/(1 - c\sin x)$

18. $y^2 - 1 = c(x^2 + 1)$

20. $y = \frac{x - c(x+1)}{1 + c(x+1)}$

22. $y = c(y+3)e^{3x^2/2}$ or $ky = (y+3)e^{3x^2/2}$

24. $\operatorname{Tan}^{-1}(x/3) + \operatorname{Sin}^{-1}(y/3) = c$

26. $x^2 - \ln(x^2 + 1) + \ln^2 y = c$

28. $y = cx^2 + k$

30. $y^2 = cx + k$

32. $y = ce^{x^2} + k$

34. $y = 0$

36. $y = 100e^{-2x}$

38. $y = 2(1 + x^2)$

40. $y = -\operatorname{sech} x$

42. $r = 13\csc^2\theta$, $0 < \theta < \pi$

44. $r = -(-\sin 2\theta)^{1/2}$, $\pi/2 \le \theta \le \pi$

46. $y = \begin{cases} \left(1-x^2\right)^2 & x \le -1 \\ 2\left(1-x^2\right)^2 & -1 \le x \le 1 \\ 0 & 1 \le x \end{cases}$

48. $y = \begin{cases} c_1 x^3 & x \le 0 \\ c_2 x^3 & 0 \le x \end{cases}$;

may take $c_1 = c_2 = 1$ to obtain $y = x^3$ as a particular solution on $(-\infty, \infty)$

50. c^2, yes; $\tan c$, no; $\sin c$, yes; e^c, yes; $\sinh c$, no; $\cosh c$, yes

52. $y = x + \frac{1-ce^{2x}}{1+ce^{2x}}$

54. $y = 4 - x - \frac{1}{x+c}$

56. $y = \begin{cases} x+1 & x \le 0 \\ e^x & 0 \le x \end{cases}$ has the required properties

Section 1.10

2. Homogeneous of degree -1

4. Homogeneous of degree $-1/3$

6. (a) Homogeneous of degree 2 in x and y

(b) $\{x, y, z\}$ degree 5; $\{y, z\}$ degree 2

8. The substitution $x = vy$ is preferable if in the equation $M(x, y)\,dx = N(x, y)\,dy$ the coefficient of dx is significantly simpler than the coefficient of dy, since simpler multiplica-tions are then involved.

12. No. Unlike each of the other terms, the term involving f is not a homogeneous function of degree 1 in the variables y and its first n derivatives.

14. $y^2 = x^2 - cx$

16. $x^3 = c(x^2 + y^2)$

18. $ye^{x/y} = c$

20. $y = x \sin\left(\ln|cx|\right)$

22. $x^2(4y^2 + x^2)^3 = c$; $c \ge 0$

24. $y = cx^2/(1 - cx)$

26. $y \cos\frac{x}{y} = c$

28. $\tanh\frac{y}{x} + \ln|cx| = 0$

30. $\ln|cx| + \mathrm{Tan}^{-1}\left(\sinh\frac{y}{x}\right) = 0$

32. $y^2 - xy + x^2 = c$. If $c > 0$, the curves are ellipses. If $c = 0$, the curve reduces to the single point $(0, 0)$. If $c < 0$, the curve has no real trace.

34. $123x^2 - 50xy + 3y^2 = c$. If $c \ne 0$, the curves are hyperbolas. If $c = 0$, the two lines $y = 3x$ and $y = 41x/3$ are obtained.

36. $(y-x)^3 = c(y + x)$. A family of cubic curves.

38. $ye^{y^2/(x^2+y^2)} = 2$

40. $x^3 = y^3(1 - \ln|y|^3)$

42. $y^3 = x^3(8 - \ln|x|)$

44. $\sin\frac{y}{x} = \ln\left|\frac{x}{2}\right| + 1$

46. $y = \frac{x}{2}(-1 + \sqrt{1 + 8x}); \ -1/8 < x$

48. $(y-3)^2 + 2(y-3)(x+2) - (x+2)^2 = c$

50. $(x - y + 1) = ce^{x+y}$

52. $\begin{cases} y+2 = c\left[(y+2)\ln|y+2| - x + 1\right] \\ (y+2)\ln|y+2| = x - 1 \end{cases}$

58. $\ln|c|(x^2 + y^2) = 4\,\mathrm{Tan}^{-1}(y/x)$

62. $x^3y^2 = c$

64. $y = -x + c/x^2$

Section 1.11

2. $y = x\,\ln|c/x|$

4. $y = \frac{1}{2} - \frac{1}{x} + \frac{c}{x^2}$

6. $y = x^2\ln|x| + cx^2$

8. $y = \sin x + c\cos x$

10. $y = e^{-x}[c + \ln(1 + e^x)]$

12. $y = \frac{x^2(x-1)}{2} + c(1-x)$

14. $y = e^{-x} + \frac{ce^{-x}}{x}$

16. $y = c\,\mathrm{sech}^2(x/2)$

18. $y = (c + x)/e^{xe^x}$

20. $x = ce^y + ye^y$

22. $x = (1 + ce^{-y})/y^2$

24. $y = c_1\ln|x| + c_2 + x + x^3/9$

26. $y = c\,\ln|\csc x - \cot x| + k - \cos x$

28. $y = (e^x + 3e^{-x})/2$

30. $y = \frac{4 + \cos 2 - \cos x}{x^2}$

32. $y = x - \sqrt{\frac{1+x^2}{2}}$

34. $y = (5x^2 + 1)^2 - \frac{1}{2}$

36. $y = e^x(10 + 2x - \sin 2x)$

38. $y = \frac{1 + \sin 2x}{2\sin x}$

40. $y = \frac{x^2+1}{4} + \frac{1}{1+x^2}$

42. $y = x^2 + 3/x$

44. $x = (\ln 2y)/(\ln y)$

46. $y = x^2 \operatorname{sech} x$

48. $x = \begin{cases} y^4 + 2y^3 & y \le 0 \\ y^4 - 2y^3 & 0 \le y \end{cases}$

50. $y = ce^{-\int P(x)dx}$

Section 1.12

2. $y = x/(x + c);\ y = 0$

4. $y^2 = x + cx^2;\ x = 0$

6. $1/y = -1/3 + c \exp\left(-\frac{3}{2}x^2\right);\ y = 0$

8. $y^2 = x - \frac{1}{2} + ce^{-2x}$

10. $\left(2x^2 + x\right)y^{1/2} = \frac{1}{2}x^2 + c;\ y = 0$

12. $y = x^2/(c - x);\ y = 0$

14. $x^2 y^2 + x^4 + 2x^2 = c$

16. $x^2 + y^2 + 1 = ce^{y^2}$

18. $x = \frac{\sin y}{c - 2y};\ x = 0$

20. $y = \frac{x^2}{2} - cx + c^2 \ln|x + c| + k$

22. $y^2 = x - \frac{1}{2} + e^{-2x}$

24. $x^3 + xy^2 = 10$

26. $y = \dfrac{1}{x^3(1 - \ln x)}$

28. $y = 2/(2x - x \ln^2 x)$

30. $y^\pi = x \tanh x$

32. $y^2 = \operatorname{Tan}^{-1} x$

34. $y = -1/x^2$

36. $y = x + 1/(ce^{-x} - 1)$

38. $y = 1 - x + 1/(c - x)$

40. $y = 1 + x/\left(1 - x + ce^{-x}\right)$

42. $c = 1:\ y_1 = 1 - x^2,\ y = 1 - x^2 + \dfrac{3}{k_1 e^{-3x/2} - 2}$

$c = -\frac{1}{2}:\ y_1 = -\frac{1}{2} - x^2,\ y = -\frac{1}{2} - x^2 + \dfrac{3}{k_2 e^{3x/2} + 2}$

The two solutions are equivalent under the relation $k_2 = -4/k_1$.

46. $y = mx + 1/4m;\ y^2 = x$

48. $y = mx - e^m;\ y = x \ln x - x$

50. $y = mx - e^{3m};\ y = \frac{x}{3}\left(\ln \frac{x}{3} - 1\right)$

Section 1.13

2. $y = \frac{cx^2}{2} + k$

4. $y = \frac{ce^{2x}}{4} - \frac{x}{2} + k$

6. $y = \frac{x^3}{3} - \frac{x^2}{4} + c\ln|x| + k$

8. $y^{-b} = ke^{-bcx}$

10. $y = -x + c\left(x + \frac{x^3}{3}\right) + k$

12. $y^2 = 1/(2x - 1)$

14. $y = \frac{1}{2} - (x + 2)^2/4$

16. $y = \sin^2 x + \sin x$

18. $y = \sinh x + \tanh x$

20. $x - y = y\,\mathrm{Tan}^{-1}y - \ln\sqrt{1 + y^2}$

Sec. 1.14

2. (a)

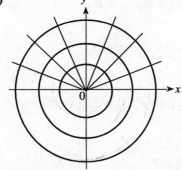

(b) Yes

(c) No. For every $c > 0$ or $c < 0$, the straight line defined by $y = cx$ is an orthogonal trajectory of the circles of K, but only part of such a line belongs to C.

(d) No. No circle of K passes through the origin.

(e) The coordinate axes in C; no curves of K.

4. (a) $a(x^2 + y^2 + 1) = x$

(b) The graph is the point $(1, 0)$, or else $(-1, 0)$, according as $h = 1$ or $h = -1$.

6. $2x^2 + 3y^2 = k$

8. $x(y^2 + x^2 \ln|kx|) = 0$

10. $y(x^2 + y^2 - ky) = 0$

12. $e^x(y\cos y + x\sin y) = k$

14. Circles through the origin with centers on the x axis: $x^2 + y^2 = cx$. Equation of the orthogonal trajectories: $(x^2 + y^2 - ky)y = 0$ Graphs and equations:

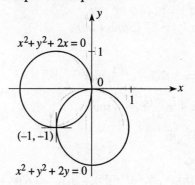

16. (a) $x(y - kx^3) = 0$

	Isotherm	Flux line
(b)	$x^2 + 3y^2 = 12$	$x = 0$
(c)	$x^2 + 3y^2 = 4$	$y + x^3 = 0$
(d)	$x^2 + 3y^2 = 4$	$y = 0$

(e) No isotherms, all flux lines.

18. (a) For every $c \neq 0$, the curve is a parabola with the x axis as its axis, and the origin as focus. For $c = 0$, the curve is the x axis.

(b) $y = 2xy' + y(y')^2$

(c) $y = 2xy' + y(y')^2$ but with the solution $y = 0$ excluded

(d) Yes

20. The related orthogonal families are defined by: $\mathrm{Rl}(z^3) = x(x^2 - 3y^2) = c$ and $\mathrm{Im}(z^3) = y(3x^2 - y^2) = k$

Section 1.15

2. $Q = 200(1 - e^{-t/20})$, 27.73 min

4. $Q = 2(100 - t) - 150[(100 - t)/100]^3$; 42.3 min; 70.4 lb; $Q_{max} = 89$ lb when $t = 33\frac{1}{3}$ min

6. 100 lb; $Q > 25$ for all $t > 0$

8. (a) $Q = 307(1 - e^{-t/4})$ gm

(b) $t = 4 \ln \frac{307}{113} \doteq 4$ min

(c) 307 gm

10. Lake Erie: $t_{1/2} \doteq 1.82$ yr, $t_{1/10} \doteq 6.05$ yr
Lake Ontario: $t_{1/2} \doteq 5.31$ yr, $t_{1/10} \doteq 17.63$ yr

12. $\frac{4}{3}Ry^{3/2} - \frac{2}{5}y^{5/2} = -r^2\sqrt{2g}\,t + \frac{16}{15}\sqrt{2}R^{5/2}$; $\frac{16\sqrt{2}-14}{15r^2\sqrt{2g}}R^{5/2}$; $\frac{16}{15\sqrt{g}r^2}R^{5/2}$

14. $\left[\left(y - \frac{h}{2}\right)^{3/2} - \left(\frac{h}{2}\right)^{3/2}\right] - \left[y^{3/2} - h^{3/2}\right]$
$= \frac{3r^2h\sqrt{2g}}{4R^2}t$, $\frac{h}{2} \leq y \leq h$

$2y^{1/2} = \sqrt{2h} - \frac{r^2\sqrt{2g}}{R^2}\left[t - \frac{2R^2(\sqrt{2}-1)\sqrt{h}}{3r^2\sqrt{g}}\right]$,
$0 \leq y \leq \frac{h}{2}$

$t_{h/2} = \frac{2R^2(\sqrt{2}-1)\sqrt{h}}{3r^2\sqrt{g}}$, $t_0 = \frac{R^2}{r^2}\sqrt{\frac{h}{g}}\left(\frac{2\sqrt{2}+1}{3}\right)$

16. $(2R - y)^{3/2} = R^{3/2} + \frac{3\pi r^2\sqrt{2g}}{4l}t$;
$\frac{4l}{3\pi r^2\sqrt{2g}}\left[(2R)^{3/2} - R^{3/2}\right]$

18. $y = kx^2$

20. $4Ry^{1/2} - \frac{2}{3}y^{3/2} = -k\sqrt{2g}\,t + \frac{10}{3}R^{3/2}$; $\frac{10R^{3/2}}{3\sqrt{2gk}}$

22. $y^{-1/2} = \frac{w\sqrt{2g}}{3\pi r^2}t + h^{-1/2}$; the tank will never be completely empty.

24. $Q \doteq 20\frac{1-e^{-0.024t}}{2-e^{-0.024t}}$

26. $Q \doteq 120\frac{1-e^{-0.00314t}}{4-3e^{-0.00314t}}$

28. $\frac{7Q}{20-Q} + \ln\left(1 - \frac{Q}{20}\right) = 0.133\,t$

30. $C = C_0 e^{-kt}$

32. $Q = 60\frac{1-e^{-0.00953t}}{2-e^{-0.00953t}}$; 45.9 min

34. $B = \dfrac{k_1 A_0\left[1-e^{-(k_1+k_2)t}\right]}{k_1+k_2}$; $\dfrac{A_\infty}{B_\infty} = \dfrac{k_2}{k_1}$

36. $T \doteq 20 + 80e^{-0.0693t}$;

$\quad\; T = 20[1 + 4(2^{-t/10})]°C$

38. 120.8°C

40. $Q = \dfrac{(T_0-T_1)4k\pi r_0 r_1}{r_0-r_1}$;

$\quad\; T = \dfrac{r_0 T_0 - r_1 T_1}{r_0 - r_1} - \dfrac{r_0 r_1(T_0-T_1)}{r_0-r_1}\dfrac{1}{r}$

42. $T = T_a - (T_a - T_0)e^{-at/P}$

44. Influx, 166 lb/min; efflux, 116 lb/min

48. **(b)** $r = \left[R\left(3\sqrt{\dfrac{g}{2}}t + \sqrt{R}\right)\right]^{2/3}$

50. In the notation of example 6
$\quad\; r = (-r_c)/[1-b\cos(\theta+\alpha)],\;\; b>1.$
The orbits are hyperbolas.

52. $w = h\cos(\theta+\alpha)$; $r = \dfrac{r_c}{1-b\cos(\theta+\alpha)}$; $b = -hr_c$

54. When $t = 80\; h$

56. $N = \dfrac{b}{a}\dfrac{N_0}{N_0 - \left(N_0-\frac{b}{a}\right)e^{bt}}$, where a and b are the
coefficients in the final form of the differen-
tial equation, $\dfrac{dN}{dt} = aN^2 - bN$. If $N_0 < b/a$, the
equation for N is correct for all values of t
and predicts that the population declines
mono-tonically to zero. If $N_0 > b/a$, the
equation for N is valid only for
$0 \le t < \dfrac{1}{b}\ln\left(\dfrac{N_0}{N_0-b/a}\right)$ and predicts that the

population becomes infinite as t approaches
the latter value.

58. The differential equation in this case would
be of the form $\dfrac{dN}{dt} = a_0 N^3 + a_1 N^2 + a_2 N$. This
is a separable equation which can be solved
through the use of partial fractions. A
solution for literal a_0, a_1, a_2, would be very
complicated.

60. $\ln\dfrac{N}{N_0} = \dfrac{b_1}{b_2}\left(1-e^{-b_2 t}\right) - \dfrac{d_1}{d_2}\left(1-e^{-d_2 t}\right).$

$\quad\;$ As $t \to \infty$, $\ln\dfrac{N}{N_0} \to \dfrac{b_1}{b_2} - \dfrac{d_1}{d_2}$

62. 81%

64. $P = P_0 e^{-0.01386t}$; 20.8yr; $\frac{3}{4}P_0$;

$\quad\; \frac{3}{64}P_0$; $29\times10^{-7} P_0$

66. $I = 10 \times 50^{(50-y)/200} \doteq 26.6e^{-0.0196y}$ cd / ft

68. $p = \dfrac{e^{kwy}-1}{k}$; 1.02

70. $11,111

72. $r = r_0(1 - 0.002063t)$; $t_{r_0/2} = 242$ days;

$\quad\; t_0 = 485$ days

74. $\dfrac{dr}{dt} = -\dfrac{k_1}{pr} - \dfrac{k_2}{3}\left(\dfrac{r^3-r_0^3}{r^3}\right)$ where k_1 is the

proportionality constant in evaporation law
and k_2 is the proportionality constant in the
condensation law.

76. **(a)** $v = 5 + (v_0 - 5)e^{-gt/50}$ ft/s

$\quad\;$ **(b)** $5 + \dfrac{250}{g}(e^{-g\,50} - 1)$ ft

78. $s = 2,560 - \dfrac{(480-t)^3}{43,200}$, $0 \le t \le 480$;

$s_{max} = 2,560$ ft

80. $\omega = \omega_0 e^{-kt/I}$; the flywheel never comes to rest.

82. $s = -16\,t^2 + 16t$; $s_{max} = 4$ ft ($= 1,764$ ft above the earth); the stone strikes the ground when $t = 11$ s; its velocity of impact is -336 ft/s

84. $y = 256t - 2,560(1 - e^{-t/8})$; $y_{max} = 55.0$ ft; the object strikes the ground at 54.8 ft/s when $t = 3.71\ s$

90. (a) $t = \sqrt{\dfrac{x_0 m}{2k}}\left[\sqrt{x_0 x - x^2} + \dfrac{x_0}{2}\cos^{-1}\left\{(2x - x_0)/x_0\right\}\right]$

(b) $t = \sqrt{\dfrac{x_0 m}{2k}}\left[\sqrt{x^2 - x_0 x} + \dfrac{x_0}{2}\cosh^{-1}\left\{(2x - x_0)/x_0\right\}\right]$

92. 7.0 mi/s

94. $s = \left[\dfrac{5}{12}g\,\sin\,\alpha\right]t^2$

96. $Q = \dfrac{E_0 C}{1 + \omega^2 R^2 C^2}\left\{\sin\omega t - RC(\cos\omega t - e^{-t/RC})\right\}$

98. $i = \dfrac{E}{R}(1 - e^{-Rt/L})$; $t_{1/2} = 0.693\,\dfrac{L}{R}$; E/R; E/R

102. $y = \dfrac{H}{w}\cosh\dfrac{wx}{H}$

104. $y^2 = 2cx + c^2$

106. $\omega = \dfrac{2}{r}\sqrt{hg}$

108. $r = \frac{1}{2}\left[(2r_0 + h)\exp\left\{\rho\pi h(2r_0 + h)x/w\right\} - h\right]$

86. (a) 1.78

(b) 1.41

(c) 1.04

(d) 0.69

(e) 0.55

(f) 0.52

(g) 0.51

88. (a) $x = \sqrt{\dfrac{m}{k}}v_0 \sin\sqrt{\dfrac{k}{m}}t$

(b) $x = \sqrt{\dfrac{m}{k}}v_0 \sin\sqrt{\dfrac{m}{k}}t + x_0 \cos\sqrt{\dfrac{m}{k}}t$

110. $r = v_1 t_0 e^{k\theta}$ where $k = \sqrt{(v_2{}^2 - v_1{}^2)/v_1{}^2}$

112. 585.4 kg

114. $y = c - (c - y_0)e^{-kAt/V}$

116. $x = \dfrac{(x_0 + y_0) + (x_0 - y_0)e^{-2kAt/V}}{2}$; $y = \dfrac{(x_0 + y_0) - (x_0 - y_0)e^{-2kAt/V}}{2}$

118. $k = 0.196$

120. (a) $u(x) = \dfrac{F}{E} \displaystyle\int_0^x \dfrac{ds}{A(s)}$

(b) $20\, F/E$

(c) $80\, F/\pi E$

Chapter 2

Section 2.1

2. All subintervals of $(-\infty, \infty)$

4. All subintervals of $(-\infty, 0)$ or $(0, \infty)$

6. $(0, 1)$

8. $(-\infty, 0)$ or $(0, \infty)$

10. $(0, e^2), (e^2, \infty)$

12. $(-1, 0), (1, 2)$

14. $\begin{cases} y = c_1 + c_2 \ln\left|\tanh \frac{x}{2}\right| + x; \\ 0 < |x| \end{cases}$

    (a) $y = c_1 + x;$

    (b) $y = \ln\left|\tanh \dfrac{x}{2}\right|$

20. $y = e^x$

22. $y = 1$

24. No, because the differential equation is not normal on an interval containing $x = 12$.

Section 2.2

2. $y_1 = 1/x$ on $(-\infty, 0)$ and $(0, \infty)$;
$y_2 = 1/(x-1)$ on $(-\infty, 1)$ and $(1, \infty)$;
$c_1y_1 + c_2y_2$ on $(-\infty, 0)$, $(0, 1)$ and $(1, \infty)$;
d.e. normal on all subintervals of $(-\infty, 0)$, $(0, 1)$ or $1, \infty)$;

4. $y_1 = x^2$ a solution on $(-\infty, \infty)$; $y_2 = 1/x$ on $(-\infty, 0)$ and $(0, \infty)$; $c_1y_1 + c_2y_2$ on $(-\infty, 0)$ and $(0, \infty)$: d.e. normal on $(-\infty, 0)$ and $(0, \infty)$.

6. $y_1 = \ln|x|$, $y_2 = x\ln|x|$, and $c_1y_1 + c_2y_2$ are all solutions on $(-\infty, 0)$ and $(0, \infty)$; d.e. normal on $(-\infty, 0)$, $(0, 1)$ and $(1, \infty)$.

8. $y_1 = e^x$ a solution on $(-\infty, \infty)$; $y_2 = \coth x$ on $(-\infty, 0)$ and $(0, \infty)$; $c_1y_1 + c_2y_2$ on $(-\infty, 0)$ and $(0, \infty)$; d.e. normal on any interval that does not contain $x = 0$ or $x = \frac{1}{2}\ln(\sqrt{5} - 2)$.

10. $y_1 = x$ a solution on $(-\infty, \infty)$; $y_2 = x\ln|\sec x|$ and $c_1y_1 + c_2y_2$ on $\left(\frac{2m-1}{2}\pi, \frac{2m+1}{2}\pi\right)$; d. e.. normal on any interval which contains none of the values $m\pi/2$, m an integer.

12. The first equation is linear, the second nonlinear.

14. The first equation is linear, the second is nonlinear.

16. (b) $c_1\cos x + c_2 \sin x, c_3\cosh x + c_4\sinh x$

    (c) Yes

20. The functions are linearly independent

22. The functions are linearly independent

24. The functions are linearly dependent; they satisfy the relation
$\cos 2x + \sin^2 x - \cos^2 x \equiv 0$

26. The functions are linearly independent.

28. The functions are linearly dependent; they satisfy the relation

$6 \ln(x - 1) + 3[2 \ln(x + 1)]$
$- 2[3 \ln(x^2 - 1)] \equiv 0.$

64. $y = c_1 x + c_2(1/x)$, $y = k_1 x + k_2 \frac{x^2+1}{x}$

30. The functions are linearly independent.

Section 2.3

32. Yes, $y(x)$ is a solution on $0 \le x \le b$ provided $a = 0$ or $a = b$; otherwise, $y(x)$ is not a solution because neither $y'(a)$ nor $y''(a)$ exists.

2. $7/2\pi$, 3

4. $5, 10\sqrt{2}$

42. e^{2mx}

6. $1/6\pi$, 5

48. **(a)** $y = c_1 x + c_2 e^{-x}$ on $(-\infty, -1)$ or $(-1, \infty)$

8. $y = c_1 \cos 5x + c_2 \sin 5x + 4 + \sin 10x$

(b) $y = c_1 + c_2 \ln|x|$ on $(-\infty, 0)$ or $(0, \infty)$

(c) $y = c_1(1/x) + c_2 x^3$ on $(-\infty, 0)$ or $(0, \infty)$

10. $y = c_1 \cos \frac{4x}{3} + c_2 \sin \frac{4x}{3} + 2 - 2e^x - 2 \cos 2x$

(d) $y = c_1 \sin^3 x + c_2 \csc^2 x$ on $\frac{n\pi}{2} < x < (n + 1)\frac{\pi}{2}$, n an integer

12. $y = c_1 \cos 6x + c_2 \sin 6x + 2 + 3x + x^2$

(e) $y = c_1 + c_2 \sin^3 x$ on $\frac{n\pi}{2} < x < (n + 1)\frac{\pi}{2}$, n an integer

14. **(a)** $x = r \cosh \phi = r \cosh(\omega t + \alpha)$
$y = r \sinh \phi = r \sinh(\omega t + \alpha)$

(f) $y = x^2[c_1 + c_2 \int x^{-4} e^{-x^2/2} dx]$ on $(-\infty, 0)$ or $(0, \infty)$

(b) $r \cosh(\omega t + \alpha)$, $r \sinh(\omega t + \alpha)$, $c_1 \cosh \omega t + c_2 \sinh \omega t$

50. Simply verify that $W(y_1, y_2, y_j) = 0$, $j = 1, 2$.

16. $c_1 \cosh 9x + c_2 \sinh 9x$

52. $y'' - 4y' + 13y = 0$

18. $c_1 \cosh 3x + c_2 \sinh 3x$

54. $x^2 y'' - x y' - y = 0$

20. $y = 78 \sinh x - 78 \sin x - 13x^3$

56. $x^2 y''(1 - \ln|x|) + x y' - y = 0$

22. $y = \sin x + \sinh x - 2x$

58. **(a)** $y_1 = \sec x$, $y_2 = \tan x$

(b) $W(y_1, y_2) = \sec x$

(c) $y = c_1 \sec x + c_2 \tan x$

24. $y = c_1 \cos \omega x + c_2 \sin \omega x$

Section 2.4

62. $y = c_1 e^x + c_2 e^{2x}$, $y = k_1(e^x + e^{2x}) + k_2(e^x - e^{2x})$

2. $y = c_1 e^{-x} + c_2 e^{2x} - \frac{e^x}{2}$

4. $y = c_1 + c_2 e^{-x} + e^{3x}$

6. $y = c_1 e^{-x} + c_2 e^{2x} - \dfrac{x}{2} + \dfrac{1}{4}$

8. $y = c_1 e^{-x} + c_2 x e^{-x} + x e^{-x} \ln|x|$

10. $y = c_1 e^{-2x} + c_2 x e^{-2x} - e^{-2x} \ln|x|$

12. $y = c_1 x + c_2 \dfrac{1}{x} + \dfrac{x \ln|x|}{2}$

14. $y = c_1 x + c_2 x^2 + x e^x$

16. $y = c_1 x + \dfrac{c_2}{x} - \left[\dfrac{1}{2} \ln|x| + \dfrac{1}{2x} - \dfrac{1}{2} \ln|x+1| \right] x$
$\qquad - \dfrac{1}{2x} \ln|x+1|$

18. $y = c_1 x + c_2 x^{5/2} + 6 x^{7/2}$

20. $y = c_1 + c_2 \ln|x| + x + \dfrac{x^2}{4}$

22. $y = e^{-x}(c_1 \cos x + c_2 \sin x - 1$
$\qquad + \{\sin x\} \ln|\sec x + \tan x|)$

24. $y = c_1 + c_2 \cos 2x + \dfrac{1}{16}\Big[\ln|\tan x|$
$\qquad + (\cos 2x) \ln \dfrac{\cos^2 2x}{(1+\cos 2x)|\sin 2x|} \Big]$

30. $Y = -2x e^x \ln|x|$

32. $Y = \ln|\csc x - \cot x| - x \sin x - (\cos x)\ln|\sin x|$

34. $Y = \ln|\sin x| - (\cos x) \ln\left|\tan \dfrac{x}{2}\right| - \dfrac{x^2}{2}$

36. $y = c_1 e^{-x} + c_2 e^{2x}$

38. $y = c_1 e^x + c_2 x e^{-x}$

40. $y = c_1 x + c_2 x^{-4}$

42. $y = c_1(x-1) + c_2(x^2 - x + 1)$

44. $y = c_1 e^{-x} + c_2 x e^{-x}$

46. $y = c_1 e^x + c_2 x e^x + c_3 x^2 e^x$

48. $y = c_1 x + c_2(x^2 - 1) + \dfrac{1}{x} - 2x(1 + \ln|x|)$

52. $y = c_1 e^x + c_2 e^{-x} + \dfrac{e^{2x}}{3}$

54. $y = c_1 + c_2(1/x) + \ln|x|$

56. $y = c_1 e^x + c_2 x e^x + \dfrac{1}{6} x^3 e^x$

58. $y = c_1 x + c_2 x e^{1/x} - 1$

60. Yes

Section 2.5

2. $y'' + y = 0$

4. $y''' = 0$

6. $y'' - 4y' + 5y = 0$

8. $y^{iv} + 4y'' = 0$

10. $y^{iv} + 2y'' + y = 0$

12. $\dfrac{2x}{1+x^2}$

14. $4(1 + t^2)$

16. $4x(1 + x^2)(1 + \ln[1 + x^2]^2)$

18. $4(1 - x^2)$

20. $\dfrac{4x(x^2-3)}{(1+x^2)^3}$

22. $n!$

24. For L to be defined, there must be an interval I over which the functions a_0, a_1, a_2, and f'' all exist; $Lf(x) = a_0(x)D^2f(x) + a_1(x)Df(x) + a_2(x)f(x)$.

28. Each of the expressions equals $-3 \cos x + \sin x$

30. $(D + 1)(D + x)e^x = 3e^x + 2xe^x$; $(D + x)(D + 1)e^x = 2e^x + 2xe^x$. These expressions differ because in permuting the operational coefficients, variables are moved across symbols of differentiation.

32. $r(x) = -1$

34. $y = c_1 e^x + c_2(x + 1)$

36. $y = c_1 + c_2 x$

38. $y = c_1 e^x + c_2 x e^x$

40. $y = e^{-x}(c_1 \cos 3x + c_2 \sin 3x)$

42. $y = c_1 e^{-\sqrt{5}x} + c_2 e^{\sqrt{5}x}$

44. $y = c_1 e^{-x/2} + c_2 x e^{-x/2}$

46. $y = c_1 e^x + c_2 e^{\pi x}$

48. $y = c_1 e^{-2\pi x} + c_2 x e^{-2\pi x}$

50. $y = e^{-3x/10}\left(c_1 \cos \dfrac{x}{10} + c_2 \sin \dfrac{x}{10}\right)$

52. $y = e^{-x/3}\left(c_1 \cos \dfrac{x}{5} + c_2 \sin \dfrac{x}{5}\right)$

54. $y = 2 \cos 2x + 3 \sin 2x$

56. $y = \dfrac{1}{5}(14 e^x + 6e^{-4x})$

58. $y = 4e^{-x/4} \cos \dfrac{x}{2}$

60. $y = 0$

62. $y = 3xe^{-3x}$

64. $y = e^{-x}(\cos 2x + \dfrac{1}{2} \sin 2x)$

66. $y_1 = (1 - x)e^x$, $y_2 = xe^x$

68. If $x_1 = x_0 + n\pi$, the conditions can be met if and only if $y_1 = (-1)^n y_0$. In this case the equations arising from the end conditions are dependent, and there is an infinite family of solutions meeting the given conditions.

70. $\lambda = n$; $y_n = A_n \cos nx$, A_n arbitrary

74. There are no nontrivial solutions satisfying the given conditions.

80. As $m_2 \to m_1$, y becomes an indeterminate of the form 0/0. This evaluates by L'Hospital's rule to xe^{m_1x}, which is a second, independent solution of the limiting equation.

82. (c) Suppose $p(D) = aD^2 + bD + c$; then the d.e. is $p(D)y = 0$, the characteristic equation $p(m) = 0$ has a repeated root r, $p(r) = p'(r) = 0$, and so $p(D)(xe^{rx}) = p(r)(xe^{rx}) + p'(r)e^{rx} = 0$. Hence, both e^{rx} and xe^{rx} are solutions of $p(D)y = 0$.

86. $y = -\dfrac{Ae^x + 2Be^{2x}}{x^2\left(Ae^x + Be^{2x}\right)}$

88. $y = \dfrac{(A-2B)\cos 2x + (2A+B)\sin 2x}{(A\cos 2x + B\sin 2x)\cos x}$

90. $y_1 = e^{px} \cos qx$, $y_2 = e^{px} \sin qx$

Section 2.6

2. $y = c_1e^x + e^{-2x}(c_2 + c_3x)$

4. $y = c_1e^{-x} + e^{2x}(c_2\cos x + c_3\sin x)$

6. $y = e^{-3x}(c_1 + c_2x) + c_3e^x$

8. $y = c_1e^{x/3} + c_2\cosh 3x + c_4\sinh 3x$

10. $y = c_1e^{-x} + e^{x/2}\left(c_2 \cos \dfrac{\sqrt{3}x}{2} + c_3 \sin \dfrac{\sqrt{3}x}{2}\right)$

12. $y = c_1e^{-3x} + c_2e^{-x} + c_3e^x + c_4e^{3x}$

14. $y = e^{-x}[(c_1 + c_2x)\cos 2x + (c_3 + c_4x)\sin 2x]$

16. $y = e^{-x/\sqrt{2}}\left(c_1 \cos\dfrac{x}{\sqrt{2}} + c_2 \sin\dfrac{x}{\sqrt{2}}\right)$
$+ e^{x/\sqrt{2}}\left(c_3 \cos\dfrac{x}{\sqrt{2}} + c_4 \sin\dfrac{x}{\sqrt{2}}\right)$

18. $y = c_1e^{2x} + c_2e^{3x} + e^{-x}(c_3\cos x + c_4\sin x)$

20. $y = c_1 + c_2x + (c_3 + c_4x)\cos\dfrac{x}{2}$
$+ (c_5 + c_6x)\sin\dfrac{x}{2}$

22. $y = e^{3x}(c_1 + c_2x + c_3x^2) + (c_4 + c_5x)e^x\cos 2x$
$+ (c_6 + c_7x)e^x \sin 2x$

24. $y = (c_1 + c_2x)e^{-5x} + (c_3 + c_4x)e^{5x}$
$+ e^{2x}[(c_5 + c_6x + c_7x^2)\cos 3x$
$+ (c_8 + c_9x + c_{10}x^2)\sin 3x]$

26. $y^{iv} + 13y'' + 36y = 0$

28. $y^{iv} - y''' - 2y'' = 0$

30. $[(D + 2)^2 + 1]^2 y = 0$

32. $(D + 1)^4(D^2 + 25)y = 0$

34. $y = \dfrac{1}{9}(4e^x + 6xe^x - 4e^{-2x})$

36. $y = 3 - e^{-x}$

38. $y = \sinh 5x - \cosh 5x = -e^{-5x}$

40. $y = \sin x - \sin 2x$

42. $y = \frac{1}{9}(32 e^{-x} - 23e^{2x} + 6xe^{2x})$

44. $y = x^2 + e^x$

46. $y = xe^{-x}(1 + \cos \pi x)$

48. $y(x) = e^{-2x} = \sum_{n=0}^{\infty} (-2x)^n / n!$

50. Only for the real values of λ which satisfy the equation $\tanh \lambda = \tan \lambda$.
$y_n = A_n(\sin \lambda_n \sinh \lambda_n x + \sinh \lambda_n \sin \lambda_n x)$
where λ_n is the nth one of the positive roots of the equation $\tanh \lambda = \tan \lambda$.

56. $e^{2x}, \cos x, \sin x; \; W(x) = 5e^{2x}$

Section 2.7

2. $y = e^{-2x}(c_1\cos x + c_2\sin x) + \frac{e^x}{5}$

4. $y = c_1 + c_2 e^{-x} + \frac{x^2}{2} + x$

6. $y = c_1 e^{-3x} + c_2 e^{-2x} - xe^{-3x}$

8. $y = e^{-x}(c_1 + c_2x + x \ln|x|)$

10. $y = c_1 e^{-x} + c_2 xe^{-x} + 1 - 6x^2 e^{-x}$

12. $y = c_1\cos x + c_2\sin x + \frac{x \sin x}{2} - \sin 2x$

14. $y = c_1 + c_2 e^{-3x} + \frac{\sin x - \cos x}{2}$

16. $y = c_1 e^{-2x} + c_2 xe^{-2x} + xe^{-x} - 2e^{-x}$

18. $y = c_1 e^x + c_2 xe^x + \frac{1}{6} x^3 e^x - \frac{1}{2} x^2 e^x$

20. $y = (e^{-x}\cos 2x)(c_1 + \frac{1}{4}\ln|\cos 2x|) + (e^{-x}\sin 2x)(c_2 + \frac{x}{2})$

22. $y = e^x(c_1 \cos 2x + c_2\sin 2x) + \frac{1}{5}x^2 + \frac{4}{25}x - \frac{2}{125} + \frac{1}{5}\sin x + \frac{1}{10}\cos x$

24. $y = c_1 e^{2x} + c_2 e^{3x} + \frac{7\cosh x + 5\sinh x}{24}$

26. $y = c_1 e^{x/5} + c_2 e^{2x/5} + 15 + 2x - 13xe^{2x/5}$

28. $y = e^{3x/10}(c_1\cos\frac{x}{10} + c_2\sin\frac{x}{10}) + \frac{4\cos 2x - 13\sin 2x}{37}$

30. (b) $A = 1$

32. $y = \sin 2x - 4 \cos 2x$

34. $y = -\frac{1}{2}e^{-2x} - x\,e^{-3x}$

36. $y = \frac{13}{2}e^{-2x} + 11xe^{-2x} + 2x - \frac{9}{2}$

38. $y = e^{-x}(3 \cos 2x + 4 \sin 2x) + 2 \cos x + \sin x$

40. $Y = \dfrac{\left(e^{\lambda t} - e^{at}\right) - (\lambda - a)te^{at}}{(\lambda - a)^2}$

42. $y = c_1 e^{2x} + c_2 e^{-2x} + c_3\cos 2x + c_4\sin 2x - \frac{1}{15}e^{x}$

44. $y = c_1 e^{-2x} + e^{2x}(c_2\cos x + c_3\sin x) + 3 \cos x - \sin x$

46. $y = c_1 + c_2 x + c_3 e^{-x} + c_4 xe^{-x} + c_5 e^{2x} + 5x^2 - x^3$

48. $y = c_1 e^{-x}\cos x + c_2 e^{-x}\sin x + \frac{1}{2} xe^{-x}\sin x$

50. $y = c_1 e^{-x}\cos \frac{x}{2} + c_2 e^{-x}\sin\frac{x}{2} + \left(e^{-x}\cos\frac{x}{2}\right)\ln\left|\cos \frac{x}{2}\right| + \frac{x}{2}\left(e^{-x}\sin\frac{x}{2}\right)$

52. $y = c_1 e^{x} + c_2 xe^{x} + \frac{1}{20}x^5 e^{x}$

54. $y = c_1 e^{x} + c_2 e^{2x} + c_3 e^{-3x} - \frac{1}{4}xe^{x} - xe^{2x}$

56. $y = c_1 e^{-x} + e^{-2x}(c_2\cos x + c_3\sin x) + \frac{1}{17}e^{2x}$

58. $y = c_1 e^{x} + e^{x}\left(c_2 \cosh \sqrt{3}x + c_3 \sinh \sqrt{3}x\right) + \frac{x}{2} - \frac{xe^{x}}{3}$

60. $y = e^x(c_1 + c_2 x) + c_3 e^{-x} + 1 + x + \dfrac{xe^{-x}}{4}$

62. $y = (c_1 + c_2 x + c_3 x^2)e^x - 2xe^x \ln|x|$

64. $y = c_1 \cos 2x + c_2 \sin 2x + c_3 x \cos 2x + c_4 x \sin 2x - \dfrac{1}{9}\sin x$

66. $y = c_1 e^{-x} + (c_2 + c_3 x)e^{2x} + 2e^x - 2xe^{-x}$

68. $y = c_1 e^{-x} + c_2 e^{-2x} + e^{-x}\ln|x| - e^{-2x}\displaystyle\int \dfrac{e^x}{x}dx$

70. $y = c_1 e^{-2x} + e^{-x}(c_2 \cos x + c_3 \sin x) - \dfrac{3}{8} + \dfrac{x}{4} + \dfrac{1}{5}\cos x$

72. $y = c_1 e^x + c_2 x e^x + c_3 e^{-2x} + c_4 x e^{-2x} + \dfrac{1}{18}x^2 e^x$

74. $y = c_1 + c_2 x + c_3 \cos x + c_4 \sin x + \dfrac{x^4}{4} - 3x^2 + 2x \cos x + x \sin x$

76. $y = e^x(c_1 \cos x + c_2 \sin x) + e^{-x}(c_3 \cos x + c_4 \sin x) + \dfrac{\cos x}{5} + \dfrac{\sin 2x}{20}$

78. $Y = x^{1/2} + \dfrac{1}{4}x^{-3/2} - \dfrac{3 \cdot 5}{4^2}x^{-7/2} + \dfrac{3 \cdot 5 \cdot 7 \cdot 9}{4^3}x^{-11/2} - \cdots$. This series diverges for all values of x.

80. The undetermined coefficients may be determined by substituting y into the differential equation and requiring the result to be an identity.

82. $Y = A \cosh 3x + B \sinh 3x$

84. $Y = Ax^2 + Bx^3 + Cxe^{-5x}$

86. $Y = Ae^{-x} + Bx^2 e^x$

88. $Y = x^2(c_1 + c_2 x)e^x + (c_3 + c_4 x)e^{-x} + x^2(c_5 \cosh 2x + c_6 \sinh 2x)$

90. $Y = c_1 + c_2 x e^{-x} + c_3 x e^x + c_4 x \cos 2x + c_5 x \sin 2x$

92. $Y = A \cos x + B \sin x + Cx^2 e^{-2x} \cos \pi x + Kx^2 e^{-2x} \sin \pi x$

94. $y = \cos x - 2 \sin x$

96. $y = (1 + x^3) e^x$

98. $y = 2(1 - x) \sin x + \frac{2}{3} x^3 - 4x$

100. $y = 2(1 - x) e^{-x} \cos 2x$

102. $y = 2(1 + \cosh x) \ln(1 + e^x) - x(2 + e^x)$

104. $y = (k_1 - 1) e^{-3x} + k_2 e^{-2x} - x e^{-3x}$, which agrees with (11) upon taking $k_1 - 1 = c_2$ and $k_2 = c_1$.

106. $A = \frac{a}{2}$

108. $Y = \frac{1}{2} \int_{x_0}^{x} f(s) \left[e^{x-s} - \cos(x - s) - \sin(x - s) \right] ds$

110. $Y = \frac{1}{6} \int_{x_0}^{x} f(s) \left[\sinh 2(x - s) - 2 \sinh(x - s) \right] ds$

112. $y = c_1 e^{-ax} + c_2 x e^{-ax} + \int_{x_0}^{x} f(s)(x - s) e^{-a(x-s)} ds$

114. $y = c_1 e^{ax} + c_2 e^{bx} + \frac{1}{a-b} \int_{x_0}^{x} f(s) \left[e^{a(x-s)} - e^{b(x-s)} \right] ds$

116. $Y = \int_{x_0}^{x} \frac{\sinh(x-s)}{s} ds$, where $x_0 x > 0$. Unlike the series obtained formally in Exercise 77, this expression for Y is meaningful for all x such that $x_0 x > 0$.

Section 2.8

2. $y = c_1 x^{-2} + c_2 x^3 - \frac{1}{6} \ln|x| - \frac{5}{36}$

4. $y = x(c_1 \cos \ln x^2 + c_2 \sin \ln x^2) + \frac{x}{4} + \frac{1}{5} \ln|x| + \frac{2}{25}$

6. $y = c_1 x + c_2 \frac{1}{x} + x^2$

8. $y = c_1 x + c_2 x \ln|x| + c_3 \frac{1}{x}$

10. $y = c_1 x^2 + c_2 x^2 \ln|x| + c_3 x^2 \ln^2|x|$

12. $y = (c_1 - \ln|x|) \cos \ln|x| + (c_2 + \ln \left|\sin \ln|x|\right|) \sin + \ln|x|$

14. $y = c_1 x^3 + x^{-2}(c_2 \cos \ln|x| + c_3 \sin \ln|x|) + \frac{1}{26} x^3 \ln|x|$

16. $y = c_1 x + c_2 x^2 + c_3 x^3 - \frac{1}{24} x^{-1}$

18. $y = c_1 x^{-1/3} + c_2 x^{1/3} + c_3 \cos 3 \ln|x| + c_4 \sin 3 \ln|x| + \cosh \ln|x|$

20. $y = c_1 x + c_2 x^{-1} + c_3 \sin 3 \ln|x| + c_4 \cos 3 \ln|x| + \frac{1}{39 x^2} - \frac{\ln|x|}{3}$

22. $y = x^2 + \sin (\ln x), \ x > 0$

24. $y = \pi \sqrt{x}, \ x > 0$

26. $y = \frac{x}{3}(1 + \ln x), \ x > 0$

28. $y = \frac{1}{3}(\frac{4}{3} - x + x^3 + \ln|x|), \ x < 0$

30. $y = 2x^{-3} - x^2 + x^2 \ln x^2, \ x > 0$

32. $y = 2(\sin 5 \ln|x| - x), \; x < 0$

34. $y = 1 + x^2, \; x > 0$

36. $y = c_1 x^{17} + c_2 x^{-1/5}$

38. $y = c_1 x^{1/11} + c_2 x + x^2$

40. $y = c_1(x-2)^{-3} + c_2(x-2)^2$

Section 2.9

2. $\dfrac{n(n+1)}{2}$

4. $\dfrac{n+1}{n+2}$

20. Define $u^* v(x) = \displaystyle\sum_{n=0}^{n} u_k(x) v_{n-k}(x)$

22. The exponential $e^{-x^2/2}$ and the series $(28a)$ represent the same function on $(-\infty, \infty)$.

24. $\dfrac{x}{x-1} = -\displaystyle\sum_{n=0}^{\infty} x^{n+1}$ and $\dfrac{1}{x-1} = -\displaystyle\sum_{n=0}^{\infty} x^{n}$

26. $\ln x = \displaystyle\sum_{n=0}^{\infty} \dfrac{(-1)^n}{n+1}(x-1)^{n+1}, \quad 0 < x < 2$

28. $\displaystyle\int_0^x e^{t^2/2} dt = \sum_{n=0}^{\infty} \dfrac{x^{2n+1}}{2^n n!(2n+1)}, \quad |x| < \infty$

30. $R = 2$

32. $R = 1/e$

34. $y = c_0 \sum_{k=0}^{\infty} \frac{(-1)^k}{(2k)!} (\lambda x)^{2k} + \frac{c_1}{\lambda} \sum_{k=0}^{\infty} \frac{(-1)^k}{(2k+1)!} (\lambda x)^{2k+1} = c_0 \cos \lambda x + \frac{c_1}{\lambda} \sin \lambda x$

36. (a) $y = 1 + \sum_{k=1}^{\infty} \frac{1 \cdot 4 \cdot 7 \cdots (3k-2)}{(3k)!} x^{3k} = 1 + \frac{1}{3!} x^3 + \frac{1 \cdot 4}{6!} x^6 + \frac{1 \cdot 4 \cdot 7}{9!} x^9 + \cdots$

(b) $y = x + \sum_{k=1}^{\infty} \frac{2 \cdot 5 \cdot 8 \cdots (3k-1)}{(3k+1)!} x^{3k+1} = x + \frac{2}{4!} x^4 + \frac{2 \cdot 5}{7!} x^7 + \frac{2 \cdot 5 \cdot 8}{10!} x^{10} + \cdots$

38. $y = c_0 + c_1 \sum_{k=0}^{\infty} \frac{x^{2k+1}}{k!(2k+1)} \quad |x| < \infty$

40. $y = c_0 \left[1 + \sum_{k=1}^{\infty} \frac{x^{4k}}{2^{2k} k! \{3 \cdot 7 \cdot 11 \cdots (4k-1)\}} \right] + c_1 \left[x + \sum_{k=1}^{\infty} \frac{x^{2k+1}}{2^{2k} k! \{5 \cdot 8 \cdot 13 \cdots (4k+1)\}} \right] \quad |x| < \infty$

42. $y = c_0 \sum_{k=0}^{\infty} \frac{(-1)^k (k+1)}{2^{2k}} x^{2k} + \frac{c_1}{3} \sum_{k=0}^{\infty} \frac{(-1)^k (2k+3)}{2^{2k}} x^{2k+1} \quad |x| < 2$

44. $y = c_0 (1 - \frac{x^2}{3}) + c_1 (x - \frac{x^3}{27})$

46. $y = c_0 \left[1 + \sum_{k=1}^{\infty} \frac{(-1)^k x^{3k}}{2 \cdot 5 \cdot 8 \cdots (3k-1)} \right] + c_1 \sum_{k=0}^{\infty} \frac{(-1)^k x^{3k+1}}{3^k k!} \quad |x| < \infty$

48. $y = c_0 \left[1 - \frac{3x^3}{2} \right] + c_1 \left[x - \frac{2x^4}{3} - 2 \sum_{k=2}^{\infty} \frac{1 \cdot 4 \cdot 7 \cdots (3k-5)}{3^k k!} x^{3x+1} \right] \quad |x| < 1$

50. $y = c_0 \sum_{k=0}^{\infty} \frac{(-1)^k x^{3k}}{3^k n!} + c_1 \left[x + \sum_{k=1}^{\infty} \frac{(-1)^k x^{3k+1}}{4 \cdot 7 \cdot 10 \cdots (3k+1)} \right] + c_2 \left[x^2 + \sum_{k=1}^{\infty} \frac{(-1)^k x^{3k+2}}{5 \cdot 8 \cdot 11 \cdots (3k+2)} \right] \quad |x| < \infty$

52. $y = 4 + 3x + 2x^2$

54. $y = \sum_{k=0}^{\infty} \frac{(-1)^k x^{3k}}{3^k n!} + \sum_{k=0}^{\infty} \frac{(-1)^k x^{3k+1}}{1 \cdot 4 \cdot 7 \cdots (3k+1)}$ $|x| < \infty$

60. $y_1 \doteq 1 - x^2 - \frac{1}{2}x^3 + \frac{1}{3}x^4$; $y_2 \doteq x - \frac{1}{2}x^3 - \frac{1}{4}x^4 + \frac{1}{8}x^5$

62. $y_1 \doteq 1 - 2x^3 - \frac{3}{10}x^5 + \frac{2}{5}x^6$; $y_2 \doteq x + \frac{1}{6}x^3 - x^4 + \frac{1}{40}x^5$

64. $y_1 \doteq 1 - \frac{1}{2}x^2 - \frac{1}{24}x^4 - \frac{1}{60}x^5$; $y_2 \doteq x - \frac{1}{2}x^2 - \frac{1}{24}x^4 - \frac{1}{60}x^5$

66. $y = c_0 \sum_{k=0}^{\infty} \frac{(x+1)^{3k}}{3^k k!} + c_1 \left[(x+1) + \sum_{k=1}^{\infty} \frac{(x+1)^{3k+1}}{4 \cdot 7 \cdot 10 \cdots (3k+1)} \right]$ $|x+1| < \infty$

68. $y = c_0 \sum_{k=0}^{\infty} \frac{2^{2k}(k!)^2}{(2k)!}(x-1)^{2k} + c_1 \sum_{k=0}^{\infty} \frac{(2k+1)!}{2^{2k}(k!)^2}(x-1)^{2k+1}$ $0 < x < 2$

70. (a) $\sqrt{5} \leqq R$

    (b) $2 \leqq R$

Section 2.10

2. (a) There are no singular points

    (b) $x = 0$, irregular; $x = 1$, regular

    (c) $x = 0$, regular

    (d) $x = 0$, irregular

    (e) $x = 0$, regular, $x = \frac{2}{3}$, irregular

    (f) $x = 0$, irregular; $x = -1$, irregular; $x = 1$, regular

4. (a) $\sum_{n=1}^{\infty} 2(-1)^{n+1}(x-1)^n$, $0 < x < 2$

    (b) $\sum_{n=1}^{\infty} (-3/2)n(n+1)x^n$, $-1 < x < 1$

6. $2r^2 + 3r = 0, x = 0$

8. $4r^2 + 4r + 1 = 0, x = 1$

10. $r^2 - 2r = 0, x = 0; \ r^2 - r = 0, x = 1; \ r^2 = 0, x = -1$

16. $y_1 = \displaystyle\sum_{n=0}^{\infty} \frac{(-1)^n n! 2^n x^{n+1}}{(2n+1)!}, \ |x| < \infty; \ y_2 = |x|^{\frac{1}{2}} \displaystyle\sum_{n=0}^{\infty} \frac{(-1)^n x^n}{n! 2^n} = |x|^{\frac{1}{2}} e^{-x/2}, \ 0 < |x| < \infty$

18. $y_1 = x^{1/3} \displaystyle\sum_{n=0}^{\infty} \frac{(-1)^n x^n}{n!} = x^{1/3} e^{-x}, \ 0 < |x| < \infty; \ y_2 = x^{-1/3}\left[1 + \displaystyle\sum_{n=1}^{\infty} \frac{(-1)^n (3x)^n}{1 \cdot 4 \cdots (3n-2)} \right], \ 0 < |x| < \infty$

20. $y_1 = \displaystyle\sum_{n=0}^{\infty} \frac{(-1)^n}{(n!)^2} \left(\frac{x}{2}\right)^{2n}, \ |x| < \infty; \ y_2 = y_1 \ln|x| - \displaystyle\sum_{n=1}^{\infty} \frac{(-1)^n H_n}{(n!)^2} \left(\frac{x}{2}\right)^{2n}, \ 0 < |x| < \infty$

22. $y_1 = |x| \displaystyle\sum_{n=0}^{\infty} \frac{(-1)^n x^n}{n!(n+2)! 5^n}, \ 0 < |x| < \infty;$

$\quad y_2 = |x|^{-1}\left[1 + \frac{1}{5}x + \displaystyle\sum_{n=3}^{\infty} \frac{(-1)^n \left(H_{n-2} + H_n - H_2 \right)}{(n-2)! n! 5^n} x^n \right] - \frac{1}{25} y_1 \ln|x|, \ 0 < |x| < \infty$

24. $y_1 = x^{-1} \cos(2 \ln|x|), \ 0 < |x| < \infty; \ y_2 = x^{-1} \sin(2 \ln|x|), \ 0 < |x| < \infty$

26. $y_1 = x, \ |x| < \infty; \ y_2 = |x|^{\frac{1}{2}}, \ 0 < |x| < \infty$

28. $y_1 = \displaystyle\sum_{n=0}^{\infty} \frac{x^n}{n!} = e^x, \ |x| < \infty; \ y_2 = e^x \ln|x|, \ 0 < |x| < \infty$

30. $y_1 = 1 - x, \ |x| < \infty; \ y_2 = y_1 \ln|x| - |x|^{-1}\left[\frac{1}{2} - 2x^2 + \displaystyle\sum_{n=3}^{\infty} \frac{x^n}{(n-2)(n-1)} \right], \ 0 < |x| < 1$

32. $y_1 = |x| \sum_{n=0}^{\infty} \frac{(-1)^n x^n}{n!} = |x| e^{-x}, \quad 0 < |x| < \infty; \quad y_2 = y_1 \ln|x| - |x| \sum_{n=1}^{\infty} \frac{(-1)^n H_n}{n!} x^n, \quad 0 < |x| < \infty$

34. $y_1 = x^{1/3} \sum_{n=0}^{\infty} \frac{(-1)^n x^n}{n!} = x^{1/3} e^{-x}, \quad 0 < |x| < \infty; \quad y_2 = x^{-1} \left[1 + 3x - \sum_{n=2}^{\infty} \frac{(-1)^n (3x)^n}{2 \cdot 5 \cdot 8 \cdots (3n-4)} \right], \quad 0 < |x| < \infty$

36. $y_1 = |x| \sum_{n=0}^{\infty} \frac{(-1)^n x^n}{(n!)^2}, \quad 0 < |x| < \infty; \quad y_2 = y_1 \ln|x| - |x| \sum_{n=1}^{\infty} \frac{2(-1)^n H_n x^n}{(n!)^2}, \quad 0 < |x| < \infty$

38. $y_1 = |x|^{1/2}, \quad 0 < |x| < \infty; \quad y_2 = |x|^{1/2} \ln|x|, \quad 0 < |x| < \infty$

40. $y_1 = \sum_{n=0}^{\infty} \frac{(-1)^n x^{n+2}}{n!(n+3)!}, \quad |x| < \infty;$

$y_2 = |x|^{-1} [2 + x + \frac{x^2}{2} - \sum_{n=4}^{\infty} \frac{(-1)^n (H_{n-3} + H_n - H_3) x^n}{(n-3)! n!}] + y_1 \ln|x|, \quad 0 < |x| < \infty$

42. $y_1 = 1 - x, \quad |x| < \infty; \quad y_2 = y_1 \ln|x| + \frac{5}{2} x - \sum_{n=2}^{\infty} \frac{(n+1) x^n}{2^n (n-1) n}, \quad 0 < |x| < 2$

44. $y_1 = x^3, \quad |x| < \infty; \quad y_2 = 1 + 3x^2, \quad |x| < \infty$

46. $y_1 = |x|^{1/2} \sum_{n=0}^{\infty} \frac{(-1)^n x^{2n}}{(2n+1)!}, \quad 0 < |x| < \infty; \quad y_2 = |x|^{-1/2} \sum_{n=0}^{\infty} \frac{(-1)^n x^{2n}}{(2n)!}, \quad 0 < |x| < \infty$

48. $y_1 = |x|^{1/2}, \quad 0 < |x| < \infty; \quad y_2 = 1 - x, \quad |x| < \infty$

50. $y_1 = 1 - x, \quad |x| < \infty; \quad y_2 = y_1 \ln|x| + 3x - \sum_{n=1}^{\infty} \frac{x^{n+1}}{n(n+1)(n+1)!}, \quad 0 < |x| < \infty$

52. $y_2 = e^x, \quad y_2 = 1 - x$

54. (a) $y = |x|^{-1/2}[a \sin x + b \cos x]$

56. $y_1 = |x|^a \cos x$, $y_2 = |x|^a \sin x$

58. $y_1 = \sum_{n=0}^{\infty} \frac{(3n+4)(x-1)^{n+1/3}}{3^n\, n!}$; $y_2 = 1 + \sum_{n=1}^{\infty} \frac{(n+1)(x-1)^n}{2 \cdot 5 \cdot 8 \cdots (3n-1)}$

60. $y_1 = (x-1)^{1/2}$; $y_2 = (x-1)^{1/3}$

62. (a)   irregular

   (b) $y_1 = x$, $|x| < \infty$; $y = x(a + b e^{5/x})$ a, b parameters

64.   The point at infinity is a regular singular point.

66.   The conditions $b_2 = a_1 b_1 / 2$ and $c_2 = b_1^2 / 4$ are sufficient to ensure that the given equation can be solved in terms of elementary functions.

68. $y = \frac{a \cos x + b \sin x}{\cosh(x/2)}$

70.   With $xP(x) = \sum_{n=0}^{\infty} P_n x^n$, $x^2 Q(x) = \sum_{n=0}^{\infty} Q_n x^n$, and $x^3 R(x) = \sum_{n=0}^{\infty} R_n x^n$, the indicial
   equation is $r^3 + (P_0 - 3)r^2 + (Q_0 - P_0 + 2)r + R_0 = 0$

72. $y = a \sum_{n=0}^{\infty} \frac{(-1)^n x^{n+2}}{n!(n+1)!(n+2)!}$

74. $y = a \sum_{n=0}^{\infty} \frac{(-1)^n (n+3)(n+4)}{(n+1)(n!)^2} x^{n+2}$

76. $y = a \left[x^2 + \sum_{n=1}^{\infty} \frac{(-1)^n x^{3n+2}}{4 \cdot 7 \cdot 10 \cdots (3n+1)} \right] + b \sum_{n=0}^{\infty} \frac{(-1)^n x^{3n+1}}{3^n\, n!} + c \left[1 + \sum_{n=1}^{\infty} \frac{(-1)^n x^{3n}}{2 \cdot 3 \cdot 8 \cdots (3n-1)} \right]$

Section 2.11

2. $y = 2\cos 4t - 2\sin 4t$

4. $y = 2\sin 14t$

6. $y = \dfrac{w}{k}\left(\cos\sqrt{\dfrac{kg}{w}}\,t - 1\right)$

8. $2\pi\sqrt{\dfrac{hw}{pg}}$ where p is the density of water

10. $r = a\cosh\omega t$

12. If the pellet starts from the midpoint of the tube with radial velocity $g/2\omega$ when the tube is horizontal, it will execute simple harmonic motion described by $r = \left(g/2\omega^2\right)\sin\omega t$. Furthermore, if the pellet starts with arbitrary displacement r_0 and initial velocity $-\omega r_0\ g/2\omega$ when the tube is horizontal, it will move according to the law

$r = r_0 e^{-\omega t} + \dfrac{g}{2\omega^2}\sin\omega t$ which is asymptotically simple harmonic.

14. The deflection $y(x, s)$ at x due to a unit downward load at s is given by

$$y(x,s) = \begin{cases} \dfrac{x^2(x-3s)}{6EI} & 0 \le x \le s \\ \dfrac{s^2(s-3x)}{6EI} & s \le x \le L \end{cases}$$

note that $y(x, s) = y(s, x)$

16. $y = \dfrac{-wx^2}{24EI}\left[(x-2L)^2 + 2L^2\right]$

18. $y(L) = \dfrac{-19L^5}{120EI}$

20. $y = \begin{cases} \dfrac{-kx}{48EI}\left(2x^3 - 6Lx^2 + 9L^3\right) & (1) \\ \dfrac{-kL}{48EI}(x-2L)\left(2x^2 - 8Lx + L^2\right) & (2) \end{cases}$

(1) $0 \le x \le L$
(2) $L \le x \le 2L$

22. $y = x - \dfrac{x^{m_1}}{m_1 L^{m_1-1}}$ where m_1 is the positive root of the equation $m^2 - m - 2\sqrt{2}\ F/\pi\,k^4 E = 0$ and k is the proportionality constant in the formula which defines the radius of the beam cross section as a function of x.

24. $\dfrac{1}{2\pi}\sqrt{\dfrac{3kg}{w+3W}}$ cycles per unit time

26. $\dfrac{1}{4\pi}\sqrt{\dfrac{3kg}{W}}$ cycles per unit time

28. $\dfrac{1}{2\pi}\sqrt{\dfrac{3kL^2 g}{wL^2 + 3Wl^2}}$ cycles per unit time

30. $\dfrac{1}{4\pi}\sqrt{\dfrac{kg}{W}}$ cycles per unit time

32. $\dfrac{1}{4\pi}\sqrt{\dfrac{kg}{W}}$ cycles per unit time

34. $\dfrac{1}{2\pi}\sqrt{\dfrac{2g(k_1+k_2)}{W_1 + 2W_2}}$ cycles per unit time

36. $y = a\cosh\sqrt{\dfrac{wg}{wL+W}}\,t + \dfrac{W}{w}\left(\cosh\sqrt{\dfrac{wg}{wL+W}}\,t - 1\right)$

38. $y = \left(a + \dfrac{W}{k}\right)\cosh\sqrt{\dfrac{kg}{kL+W+w+P/2}}\,t - \dfrac{W}{k}$

40. (a) $d^2 y/dt^2 - \sqrt{\dfrac{2wg}{2Lw+W_2+W_1}}\,y = \dfrac{(aw+W_2-W_1)g}{2Lw+W_2+W_1}$

(b) A complete solution is

$$y = A \cosh \sqrt{\frac{2wg}{2Lw+W_2+W_1}}\,t$$

$$+ B\sinh \sqrt{\frac{2wg}{2Lw+W_2+W_1}}\,t - \frac{aw+W_2-W_1}{2w}$$

Imposition of the initial conditions gives

$$y = \frac{aw+W_2-W_1}{2w}\left[\cosh \sqrt{\frac{2wg}{2Lw+W_2+W_1}}\,t - 1\right]$$

(c) To obtain the results of Example 3, take $W_1 = W_2 = 0$ in the solution of part (b).

(d) If $aw + W_2 = W_1$; in particular, if $a = 0$ and $W_1 = W_2$

(e) The particular solution of part (b) is valid until $y = L - \frac{a}{2}$, or else until $y = -(L + \frac{a}{2})$, according as $aw + W_2 - W_1$ is positive or negative.

42. The critical speeds are $\omega_n = \frac{n^2\pi^2}{L^2}\sqrt{\frac{EIg}{A\rho}}$.

The corresponding deflection curves are

$y_n = B_n \sin(n\pi x/L)$.

44. $\frac{1}{2\pi}\sqrt{\dfrac{3g\{(2W+w)L+4kl^2\}}{2L^2(3W+w)}}$ cycles per unit time

46. $\frac{1}{2\pi}\sqrt{\dfrac{k(I_1+I_2)}{I_1 I_2}}$ cycles per unit time

48. (a) $t = \frac{1}{2}\sqrt{\dfrac{l}{g}}\displaystyle\int_0^\theta \frac{d\theta}{\sqrt{\sin^2(\alpha/2)-\sin^2(\theta/2)}}$

Section 2.12

4. $y(x) = \begin{cases} \dfrac{3Px}{4T} & 0 \leqq x \leqq \dfrac{\ell}{2} \\[2mm] \dfrac{P(2\ell-x)}{4T} & \dfrac{\ell}{2} \leqq x \leqq \dfrac{3\ell}{4} \\[2mm] \dfrac{5P(\ell-x)}{4T} & \dfrac{3\ell}{4} \leqq x \leqq \ell \end{cases}$

6.

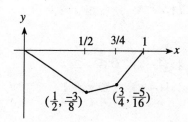

8. $y = \begin{cases} \dfrac{Px}{2T} & 0 \leqq x \leqq \dfrac{\ell}{4} \\[2mm] \dfrac{P(\ell-2x)}{4T} & \dfrac{\ell}{4} \leqq x \leqq \dfrac{\ell}{2} \\[2mm] -\dfrac{3P(\ell-2x)}{4T} & \dfrac{\ell}{2} \leqq x \leqq \dfrac{3\ell}{4} \\[2mm] \dfrac{3P(\ell-x)}{2T} & \dfrac{3\ell}{4} \leqq x \leqq \ell \end{cases}$

10. $y = \begin{cases} -\dfrac{\ell x}{8T} & 0 \leq x \leq \dfrac{\ell}{2} \\[2mm] \dfrac{4x^2-5\ell x+\ell^2}{8T} & \dfrac{\ell}{2} \leq x \leq \ell \end{cases}$

12. $y(x) = \begin{cases} \dfrac{x(x^2-\ell^2)}{6T}+\dfrac{Px}{2T} & 0 \leqq x \leqq \dfrac{\ell}{2}\ (1) \\[2mm] \dfrac{x(x^2-\ell^2)}{6T}+\dfrac{P(\ell-x)}{2T} & \dfrac{\ell}{2} \leqq x \leqq \ell\ (2) \end{cases}$

    (1) $y(\ell/4) = \dfrac{\ell}{128T}(16P-5\ell^2)$

    (2) $y(3\ell/4) = \dfrac{\ell}{128T}(16P-7\ell^2)$

14. $y(x) = \dfrac{\ell^2}{\pi^2 T}\sin\dfrac{\pi x}{\ell}$

16. $g(x,s) = \begin{cases} \dfrac{\sinh kx\ \sinh k(1-s)}{k\sinh k} & 0 \leq x \leq s \\[2mm] \dfrac{\sinh ks\ \sinh k(1-x)}{k\sinh k} & s \leq x \leq 1 \end{cases}$

18. $g(x,s) = \begin{cases} e^{-s}(e^x - 1) & 0 \leqq x \leqq s \\ 1 - e^{-s} & s \leqq x \leqq 1 \end{cases}$

20. $g(x,s) = \begin{cases} x(1-s) & 0 \leqq x \leqq s \\ s(1-x) & s \leqq x \leqq 1 \end{cases}$

22. $g(x,s) = \begin{cases} e^{2s}(e^x - e^{-2x})/3 & 0 \leqq x \leqq s \\ e^s e^x(e^s - e^{-2s})/3 & s \leqq x \leqq 1 \end{cases}$

24. (a) $g(x,s) = \begin{cases} \dfrac{\cos k(b-s)\sin kx}{k\cos kb} & 0 \leq x \leq s \\ \dfrac{\cos k(b-x)\sin ks}{k\cos kb} & s \leq x \leq b \end{cases}$

(b) $g(x,s) = \begin{cases} \dfrac{\sin k(b-s)\cos kx}{k\cos kb} & 0 \leq x \leq s \\ \dfrac{\sin k(b-x)\cos ks}{k\cos kb} & s \leq x \leq b \end{cases}$

(c) $g(x,s) = \begin{cases} \dfrac{\cos k(b-s)\cos k(x-a)}{-k\sin k(b-a)} & a \leq x \leq s \\ \dfrac{\cos k(b-x)\cos k(s-a)}{-k\sin k(b-a)} & s \leq x \leq b \end{cases}$

(d) $g(x,s) = \begin{cases} \dfrac{\sin k(b-s)[\sin k(x-a)+k\cos k(x-a)]}{k\sin k(b-a)+k^2\cos k(b-a)} & a \leq x \leq s \\ \dfrac{\sin k(b-x)[\sin k(s-a)+k\cos k(s-a)]}{k\sin k(b-a)+k^2\cos k(b-a)} & s \leq x \leq b \end{cases}$

26. $g(x,s) = \begin{cases} x(s-2)(1-x)/s^3 & 1 \leqq x \leqq s \\ x(x-2)(1-s)/s^3 & s \leqq x \leqq 2 \end{cases}$

28. $g(x,s) = \begin{cases} e^s \cos s\, e^{-x}\sin x & 0 \leqq x \leqq s \\ e^{-x}\cos x\, e^s \sin s & s \leqq x \leqq \pi/2 \end{cases}$

In this case, $g(x, s)$ is not symmetric. For the equivalent equation $e^{2x}y'' + 2e^{2x}y' + 2e^{2x}y = 0$, $g(x, s)$ is the symmetric function

$g(x,s) = \begin{cases} e^{-s}\cos s\, e^{-x}\sin x & 0 \leq x \leq s \\ e^{-x}\cos x\, e^{-s}\sin s & s \leq x \leq \pi/2 \end{cases}$

30. $g(x,s) = \begin{cases} \frac{(1-s)x}{s^3} + c(x^2 - x) & 0 \le x \le s \\ \frac{(1-x)x}{s^3} + c(x^2 - x) & s \le x \le 1 \end{cases}$

The differential equation is not normal on [0, 1].

34. $g(x,s) = \begin{cases} -\frac{1}{2}\left(\cos\frac{x}{2} + \sin\frac{x}{2}\right)\sin\frac{s}{2} & 0 \le x \le s \\ -\frac{1}{2}\left(\cos\frac{s}{2} + \sin\frac{s}{2}\right)\sin\frac{x}{2} & s \le x \le 2\pi \end{cases}$

$y(x) = (\cos x - 1)\cos\frac{x}{2} + (x + \sin x)\sin\frac{x}{2}$

36. $g(x,s) = \begin{cases} -\left(s - 8s^{-2}\right)\left(x - x^{-2}\right)/21 & 1 \le x \le s \\ -\left(x - 8x^{-2}\right)\left(s - s^{-2}\right)/21 & s \le x \le 2 \end{cases}$

$y(x) = 9x + 12x^{-2} - 21$

38. $g(x,s) = \begin{cases} \frac{1}{4}s^{-1/2}x^{-1/2}\ln x & 1 \le x \le s \\ \frac{1}{4}x^{-1/2}s^{-1/2}\ln s & s \le x \le 4 \end{cases}$

$y(x) = x^{-1/2}(\ln x - \ln 16)\ln x$

40. $\theta(x,s) = \begin{cases} \frac{x}{E_s J} & 0 \le x \le s \\ \frac{s}{E_s J} & 0 \le x \le \ell \end{cases}$

42. $g(x,s) = \begin{cases} \frac{(\ell-s)x}{E_s J\ell} & 0 \le x \le s \\ \frac{(\ell-x)s}{E_s J\ell} & s \le x \le \ell \end{cases}$

44. $\phi(x) = \frac{\omega^2 \rho(\ell - x)}{E_s g\ell}\int_0^x s\phi(s)ds + \frac{\omega^2 \rho x}{E_s g\ell}\int_x^\ell (\ell - s)\phi(s)ds$ $\quad \omega_n = \frac{n\pi}{\ell}\sqrt{\frac{E_s g}{\rho}}$ rad. per unit time

46. $y(x) = \begin{bmatrix} \frac{Px^2(4x - 9\ell)}{12EI} & 0 \le x \le \frac{\ell}{2} \\ \frac{P}{6EI}\left(\frac{\ell^3}{8} - \frac{3\ell^2 x}{4} + x^3 - 3\ell x^2\right) & \frac{\ell}{2} \le x \le \ell \end{bmatrix}$

48. (a) $y(x) = \begin{cases} \frac{x^2}{12EI}\left[P(2x-3\ell)-2Q(x-3\ell)\right] & 0 \leqq x \leqq \ell/2 \\ \frac{1}{48EI}\left[P\ell^2(\ell-6x)-8Qx^2(x-3\ell)\right] & \ell/2 \leqq x \leqq \ell \end{cases}$

(b) $Q = 64$

(c) $Q = 50$

(d) From $\ell/2$ to ℓ, the deflection curve is a straight line segment defined by

$y(x) = \frac{P\ell^2}{48EI}(\ell-6x)$ with endpoints $\left(\ell/2, -P\ell^3/24EI\right)$ and $\left(\ell, -5P\ell^3/48EI\right)$.

50. $y(x) = -\frac{x^5}{120EI} + \frac{\ell^2 x^3}{12EI} - \frac{\ell^3 x^2}{6EI}$

52. $y(x) = \begin{cases} \frac{Px^2}{12EI}(2x-3) - \frac{wx^2}{24EI}\left(x^2-4x+6\right) & 0 \leqq x \leqq \frac{1}{2} \\ \frac{P}{48EI}(1-6x) - \frac{wx^2}{24EI}\left(x^2-4x+6\right) & \frac{1}{2} \leqq x \leqq 1 \end{cases}$

$5P + 6w = 0$

54. $g(x,s) = \begin{cases} \dfrac{k\sin k(s-\ell)\sin kx}{2\sin k\ell} - \dfrac{k\sinh k(s-\ell)\sinh kx}{2\sinh k\ell} & 0 \leqq x \leqq s \\ \dfrac{k\sin ks\sin k(x-\ell)}{2\sin k\ell} - \dfrac{k\sinh ks\sinh k(x-\ell)}{2\sinh k\ell} & s \leqq x \leqq \ell \end{cases}$

where $k\,k\ell \neq n\pi$ and $EIk^4 = 1$

56. $g(x,s) = \begin{cases} \dfrac{\left(\ell^3+2s^3-3\ell s^2\right)x^3 - 3\ell s(\ell-s)^2 x^2}{6EI\ell^3} & 0 \leqq x \leqq s \\ \dfrac{\left(\ell^3+2x^3-3\ell x^2\right)s^3 - 3\ell x(\ell-x)^2 s^2}{6EI\ell^3} & s \leqq x \leqq \ell \end{cases}$

58. $y(x) = \begin{cases} \dfrac{-kx}{48EI}\left(2x^3-6\ell x^2+9\ell^3\right) & s \leqq x \leqq \ell \\ \dfrac{-k}{48EI}(x-2\ell)\left(2x^2-8\ell x+\ell^2\right) & s \leqq x \leqq 2\ell \end{cases}$

Chapter 3

Section 3.1

2. (a) $23 + 2i$

  (b) $8 - 6i$

  (c) $\frac{4}{41} + \frac{5}{41} i$

  (d) $-\frac{17}{10} + \frac{11}{10} i$

  (e) $\frac{43}{13} + \frac{59}{13} i$

  (f) $-\frac{51}{90} + \frac{33}{90} i$

4. (a) $\tan^{-1} \frac{3}{2} \doteq 56°19'$

  (b) $\tan^{-1} \frac{-7}{-9} \doteq 217°52'$

  (c) $\tan^{-1} \frac{-4}{1} \doteq -75°58'$

6. $x = 1, 3 \ y = -1, 3; z_1 = 1 - i, z_2 = 3 + 3i$

10. $r_1 = 2\left(\cos \frac{7\pi}{20} + i \sin \frac{7\pi}{20}\right) = 2e^{7\pi i/20}$

  $r_2 = 2\left(\cos \frac{15\pi}{20} + i \sin \frac{15\pi}{20}\right) = 2e^{15\pi i/20}$

  $r_3 = 2\left(\cos \frac{23\pi}{20} + i \sin \frac{23\pi}{20}\right) = 2e^{23\pi i/20}$

  $r_4 = 2\left(\cos \frac{31\pi}{20} + i \sin \frac{31\pi}{20}\right) = 2e^{31\pi i/20}$

  $r_5 = 2\left(\cos \frac{39\pi}{20} + i \sin \frac{39\pi}{20}\right) = 2e^{39\pi i/20}$

14. $e^{-7\pi/4}$

16. No. $i^i = e^{-(4n+1)\pi/2}$, $n = 0, 1, 2, \ldots$,

  No. $\left(\frac{1+i}{\sqrt{2}}\right)^i = e^{-(8n+1)\pi/4}$, $n = 0, 1, 2, \ldots$

20. The equality sign will hold if and only if $|x| = |y|$.

22. $1 + i$. No.

24. $\cos 5\theta = \cos^5 \theta - 10 \cos^3 \theta \sin^2 \theta$
$$+ 5 \cos \theta \sin^4 \theta$$
$$\sin 5\theta = 5 \cos^4 \theta \sin \theta$$
$$- 10 \cos^2 \theta \sin^3 \theta + \sin^5 \theta$$

26. (a) $\frac{2\sqrt{2}}{2} e^{11\pi i/12}$

  (b) $5120 e^{(\pi/3 + \phi)i}$, $\phi = \tan^{-1} \frac{4}{-3}$

  (c) $\frac{12\sqrt{2}}{13} e^{(5\pi/12 - \theta)i}$, $\theta = \tan^{-1} \frac{12}{5}$

  (d) $\frac{1}{1297} e^{-3\theta i}$

  (e) $\frac{5}{13} e^{(\phi - \theta)i}$, ϕ and θ as in Parts (b) and (c), respectively.

32. $w_n^{2^a} = w_{n/2}^{2^{a-1}} = w_{n/4}^{2^{a-2}} = w_{n/8}^{2^{a-3}} = \ldots$

46. Rule **d** implies rule **b**.

48. (a) It says that $i^2 = -1$

  (b) $(-i)^2 = -1$

  (c) i and $-i$

Section 3.2

2. $\pm\sqrt{3}$

4. $z = 1 + i$

6. $(x, y, z) = (1, 0, i)$

8. $x = -1, \pm\sqrt{2}$

10. $z = 1, -2i$

12. $\mathbf{u} \cdot \mathbf{v} = 56; \frac{1}{15}(5, -14, 2)$

14. $\mathbf{u} \cdot \mathbf{v} = -24; \frac{1}{14}(9, 5, 3, 9)$

16. $\mathbf{u} \cdot \mathbf{v} = 8; \frac{1}{10}(7, 5, 4, 3, 1)$

18. Orthonormal

20. Not orthogonal, $\mathbf{u} \cdot \mathbf{w} \neq 0$

26. $\mathbf{u} \cdot \mathbf{v} = 30 + 20i; \quad \overline{\mathbf{u}} \cdot \mathbf{v} = 30 + 30i;$
$\overline{\mathbf{v}} \cdot \mathbf{u} = 30 - 30i; \quad \ell_h(\mathbf{u}) = 7; \quad \ell_h(v) = 6;$
$\mathbf{u}, \mathbf{v}$ are not orthogonal.

28. $\mathbf{u} \cdot \mathbf{v} = 0; \overline{\mathbf{u}} \cdot \mathbf{v} = \overline{\mathbf{v}} \cdot \mathbf{u} = 0; \ell_h(u) = 4;$
$\ell_h(v) = \sqrt{2}; \mathbf{u}, \mathbf{v}$ are orthogonal in the hermitian sense.

30. $\mathbf{u} \cdot \mathbf{v} = 4 + 3i; \overline{\mathbf{u}} \cdot \mathbf{v} = 7i; \overline{\mathbf{v}} \cdot \mathbf{u} = -7i;$
$\ell_h(\mathbf{u}) = 2; \ell_h(\mathbf{v}) = 7; \mathbf{u}$ and $\mathbf{v}$ are not orthogonal.

32. No

34. $(-2b, b, c, b), b^2 + c^2 \neq 0$

36. (a) No
   (b) $(1, -1, -1, 1)$

38. (a) $z = i$
   (b) 0

40. $(4, \pi + 6i, 2 - \pi i, 4)$

Section 3.3

2. (a) $\begin{bmatrix} 0 & -3 & -8 \\ 3 & 0 & -5 \end{bmatrix}$

   (b) $\begin{bmatrix} 1 & 2 & 3 \\ 2 & 4 & 6 \end{bmatrix}$

   (c) $\begin{bmatrix} 1 & 2 & 3 \\ 2 & 4 & 8 \end{bmatrix}$

   (d) $\begin{bmatrix} 1 & -1 & 1 \\ -1 & 1 & -1 \end{bmatrix}$

4. $z = 2 + i, 2 - i$

6. $z = 2, -i$

8. (a) $A(BC) = (AB)C = \begin{bmatrix} 0 & 35 \\ 2 & 71 \end{bmatrix}$

   (b) $A(B + C) = AB + AC = \begin{bmatrix} 4 & 15 \\ 10 & 33 \end{bmatrix}$

   (c) $B(A - C) = BA - BC = \begin{bmatrix} -4 & -3 \\ 12 & -1 \end{bmatrix}$

   (d) $3(ABC) = A(3B)C = \begin{bmatrix} 0 & 105 \\ 6 & 213 \end{bmatrix}$

10. (a) Undefined

   (b) $\begin{bmatrix} 7 & -10 & 7 \\ -1 & 0 & -1 \end{bmatrix}$

12. (a) $\begin{bmatrix} 0 & 0 \\ 0 & 0 \\ 0 & 0 \end{bmatrix}$

   (b) Undefined

14. (a) A, B square, of the same order, and commutative

(b) $A = \begin{bmatrix} 1 & 1 \\ 1 & 1 \end{bmatrix}$ $B = \begin{bmatrix} 0 & 1 \\ -1 & 0 \end{bmatrix}$

16. $\begin{bmatrix} a & b \\ -b & a+b \end{bmatrix}$; a, b arbitrary complex numbers.

20. $x = -1/6$, $y = 5/6$

22. $x = y = 0$

24. (a) $\begin{bmatrix} -8 & 8i \\ -2 & 2i \end{bmatrix}$

(b) The sum is undefined.

26. 10

28. (a) $X = \begin{bmatrix} 5 & -2 \\ -7 & 3 \end{bmatrix}$

(b) $X = \begin{bmatrix} 5 & -2 \\ -7 & 3 \end{bmatrix}$

30. (a)

$\begin{bmatrix} 3 & 0 & 0 \\ 0 & 3 & 0 \\ 0 & 0 & 3 \end{bmatrix}$

(b)

$\begin{bmatrix} 5 & 0 & 0 & 0 & 0 \\ 0 & 5 & 0 & 0 & 0 \\ 0 & 0 & 5 & 0 & 0 \\ 0 & 0 & 0 & 5 & 0 \\ 0 & 0 & 0 & 0 & 5 \end{bmatrix}$

Section 3.4

2. (a) $(AB)^T = B^T A^T = \begin{bmatrix} 8 & -1 \\ 0 & 14 \end{bmatrix}$

(b) $(AB)^T = B^T A^T = \begin{bmatrix} 2 & 5 & 5 \\ 4 & 2 & -2 \\ 8 & 12 & 8 \\ -12 & -12 & -3 \end{bmatrix}$

6. (a) $A^T = \begin{bmatrix} 5 & -2 & 0 \\ -i & 2-3i & 4i \\ 3 & 4 & 1+i \\ 6i & -1 & 3i \end{bmatrix}$

$\overline{A} = \begin{bmatrix} 5 & i & 3 & -6i \\ -2 & 2+3i & 4 & -1 \\ 0 & -4i & 1-i & -3i \end{bmatrix}$

$A^* = \begin{bmatrix} 5 & -2 & 0 \\ i & 2+3i & -4i \\ 3 & 4 & 1-i \\ -6i & -1 & -3i \end{bmatrix}$

(b) $A^T = \begin{bmatrix} 0 & 6-5i & 5+6i \\ 0 & -1 & 8i \\ 4i & -i & 2i \\ 3 & 7 & 0 \end{bmatrix}$

$\overline{A} = \begin{bmatrix} 0 & 0 & -4i & 3 \\ 6+5i & -1 & i & 7 \\ 5-6i & -8i & -2i & 0 \end{bmatrix}$

$A^* = \begin{bmatrix} 0 & 6+5i & 5-6i \\ 0 & -1 & -8i \\ -4i & i & -2i \\ 3 & 7 & 0 \end{bmatrix}$

$A^T = \begin{bmatrix} 8 & 2i & 3i \\ 7 & -i & -2 \\ 1 & -3 & 2+i \\ -4 & 1-i & 5 \\ 2i & 6i & i \end{bmatrix}$

$$\overline{A} = \begin{bmatrix} 8 & 7 & 1 & -4 & -2i \\ -2i & i & -3 & 1+i & -6i \\ -3i & -2 & 2-i & 5 & -i \end{bmatrix}$$

$$A^* = \begin{bmatrix} 8 & -2i & -3i \\ 7 & i & -2 \\ 1 & -3 & 2-i \\ -4 & 1+i & 5 \\ -2i & -6i & -i \end{bmatrix}$$

10. (a), (b), (c), and (d)

12. (a), (b), (c), (d), and (e)

14. (b)

16. $DA = \begin{bmatrix} -6 & 3 & 0 & 9 \\ 0 & 0 & 0 & 0 \\ 0 & -4 & 6 & -8 \\ -7 & 6 & -4 & 1 \end{bmatrix}$

$AD = \begin{bmatrix} -6 & 0 & 0 & -3 \\ 27 & 0 & -10 & -9 \\ 0 & 0 & 6 & 4 \\ 21 & 0 & 8 & 1 \end{bmatrix}$

18. DA is undefined. $AD = \begin{bmatrix} 3 & 0 & -4 & -3 \\ 6 & 0 & 10 & 0 \end{bmatrix}$

22. No

24. Among infinitely many possibilities

$$\begin{bmatrix} 6 & 4 & 2 \\ 9 & 6 & 3 \\ -3 & -2 & -1 \end{bmatrix} \begin{bmatrix} 0 & 1 & -2 \\ -1 & 0 & 3 \\ 2 & -3 & 0 \end{bmatrix}$$

$$= \begin{bmatrix} 0 & 0 & 0 \\ 0 & 0 & 0 \\ 0 & 0 & 0 \end{bmatrix}$$

26. (a)

$$\begin{bmatrix} 4 & 6 \\ -12 & 10 \end{bmatrix}$$

(b)

$$\begin{bmatrix} 0 & 0 & 0 \\ 0 & 0 & 0 \\ 0 & 0 & 0 \end{bmatrix}$$

(c)

$$\begin{bmatrix} 12 & 0 & -8 \\ 8 & 12 & 0 \\ 0 & 8 & 12 \end{bmatrix}$$

28. $A^3 = \begin{bmatrix} -9 & 22 \\ -11 & 13 \end{bmatrix}$ $A^4 = \begin{bmatrix} -31 & 48 \\ -24 & 17 \end{bmatrix}$

$A^5 = \begin{bmatrix} -79 & 82 \\ -41 & 3 \end{bmatrix}$

32. Yes

36. Yes; for arbitrary A, the product of A and A^T is symmetric. See Exercise 34.

40. $D^2 A$

42. $\dfrac{dA}{dt} = -D \begin{bmatrix} \sin\lambda_1 t & 0 & \ldots & \ldots & 0 \\ 0 & \sin\lambda_2 t & \ldots & \ldots & 0 \\ & & \ldots\ldots\ldots & & \\ 0 & 0 & \ldots & \sin\lambda_n t \end{bmatrix}$, $\dfrac{d^2 A}{dt^2} = -D^2 A$

46. (a)

$$\begin{bmatrix} 1 & 0 & 0 & 0 & 0 & 0 \\ 0 & 0 & 1 & 0 & 0 & 0 \\ 0 & 0 & 0 & 0 & 1 & 0 \\ 0 & 1 & 0 & 0 & 0 & 0 \\ 0 & 0 & 0 & 1 & 0 & 0 \\ 0 & 0 & 0 & 0 & 0 & 1 \end{bmatrix}$$

(b)

$$\begin{bmatrix} 0 & 0 & 0 & 0 & 0 & 1 \\ 1 & 0 & 0 & 0 & 0 & 0 \\ 0 & 0 & 0 & 1 & 0 & 0 \\ 0 & 0 & 1 & 0 & 0 & 0 \\ 0 & 0 & 0 & 0 & 1 & 0 \\ 0 & 1 & 0 & 0 & 0 & 0 \end{bmatrix}$$

48.

$$\begin{bmatrix} 0 & 0 & 0 & 1 \\ 0 & c & 0 & 0 \\ 0 & 0 & 1 & 0 \\ 1 & 0 & k & 0 \end{bmatrix}$$

Section 3.5

2. (a) $3, 6$

4. $2^2, 2^3, 2^n$

8. (b) $4a^2b^2, c^2$

10. 0

12. $D_{10}(1) = D_{10}(-1) = 11$; no,

$D_n(x) = (x^{2n+2} - 1)/(x^2 - 1), \ x^2 \neq 1.$

16. If the three points are collinear the equation reduces to the equation of the straight line which, by hypothesis, contains the three points.

18. $(-1)^n(1 - n)2^{n-2}$

20. $\displaystyle\prod_{\substack{i,j=1 \\ i<j}}^{n} (a_i - a_j)$

26. (a) $f'(t) = -2$

(b) $f'(t) = \frac{1}{t} + \frac{2}{t^2}$

(c) $f'(t) = 4t^3 - 8t$

(d) $f'(t) = 0$

Section 3.6

2. (a)

$$\begin{bmatrix} 1 & 0 & 1/2 & 2 \\ 0 & 1 & -3/4 & -5/2 \\ 0 & 0 & 0 & 0 \end{bmatrix}$$

(b)

$$\begin{bmatrix} 1 & 0 & 1 & 0 & 3 \\ 0 & 1 & -1 & -1 & -2 \\ 0 & 0 & 0 & 0 & 0 \\ 0 & 0 & 0 & 0 & 0 \end{bmatrix}$$

(c)

$$\begin{bmatrix} 1 & 0 & 0 & 1 & -3 & -8 \\ 0 & 1 & 0 & -1 & 4 & 10 \\ 0 & 0 & 1 & 1 & -3 & -7 \end{bmatrix}$$

(d)

$$\begin{bmatrix} 1 & 0 & 1 & 0 & 3 \\ 0 & 1 & 0 & 0 & 2 \\ 0 & 0 & 0 & 1 & 1 \\ 0 & 0 & 0 & 0 & 0 \end{bmatrix}$$

4. There is no solution.

6.

$$\begin{bmatrix} x \\ y \\ z \\ w \end{bmatrix} = c \begin{bmatrix} 25 \\ -10 \\ 7 \\ 11 \end{bmatrix}$$

8.

$$\begin{bmatrix} x \\ y \\ z \\ w \end{bmatrix} = c_1 \begin{bmatrix} 1 \\ 1 \\ 0 \\ 0 \end{bmatrix} + c_2 \begin{bmatrix} 0 \\ 0 \\ 2 \\ 1 \end{bmatrix} + \begin{bmatrix} -2 \\ 0 \\ 1 \\ 0 \end{bmatrix}$$

10.

$$\begin{bmatrix} x \\ y \\ z \\ w \end{bmatrix} = \begin{bmatrix} 1 \\ 0 \\ -1 \\ 2 \end{bmatrix}$$

12.

$$\begin{bmatrix} x \\ y \\ z \\ w \end{bmatrix} = \begin{bmatrix} 5 \\ 4 \\ 3 \\ 2 \end{bmatrix}$$

14.

$$\begin{bmatrix} x_1 \\ x_2 \\ x_3 \\ x_4 \\ x_5 \end{bmatrix} = \begin{bmatrix} -1 \\ -1 \\ -1 \\ -1 \\ -1 \end{bmatrix}$$

16.

$$\begin{bmatrix} x_1 \\ x_2 \\ x_3 \\ x_4 \\ x_5 \end{bmatrix} = c \begin{bmatrix} 5 \\ -6 \\ 2 \\ 1 \\ 0 \end{bmatrix} + \begin{bmatrix} 1 \\ 1 \\ 0 \\ 0 \\ 0 \end{bmatrix}$$

22. See Theorem 4

26. They are linearly independent.

32. $4a + c = 4b$

Section 3.7

2. **(a)** All values except $-2, 3$

(b) All values of λ

(c) All values except $1, 2$

(d) No value of λ

(e) All values of λ

4. **(a)** $\lambda = -1, \quad \mathbf{x} = c \begin{bmatrix} 1 \\ -1 \end{bmatrix}, \quad c \neq 0;$

$\lambda = 4, \quad \mathbf{x} = k \begin{bmatrix} 2 \\ 3 \end{bmatrix}, \quad k \neq 0$

(b) $\lambda = \frac{4}{3}, \quad \mathbf{x} = c \begin{bmatrix} 1 \\ 2 \end{bmatrix}, \quad c \neq 0;$

$\lambda = 4, \quad \mathbf{x} = k \begin{bmatrix} 3 \\ -2 \end{bmatrix}, \quad k \neq 0$

(c) $\lambda = -1, \quad \mathbf{x} = c \begin{bmatrix} 1 \\ 0 \\ 1 \end{bmatrix}; \quad \lambda = 1, \quad \mathbf{x} = h \begin{bmatrix} 1 \\ 0 \\ -1 \end{bmatrix};$

$\lambda = 3, \quad \mathbf{x} = k \begin{bmatrix} 11 \\ 16 \\ -1 \end{bmatrix};$

$c, h,$ and k are arbitrary, nonzero constants.

(d) $\lambda = 1, \quad \mathbf{x} = c \begin{bmatrix} 1 \\ 0 \\ 2 \end{bmatrix} + h \begin{bmatrix} 0 \\ 1 \\ 2 \end{bmatrix}, \quad c^2 + h^2 \neq 0;$

$\lambda = \frac{19}{2}, \quad \mathbf{x} = k \begin{bmatrix} 4 \\ 4 \\ -1 \end{bmatrix}, \quad k \neq 0$

6. **(a)** $\begin{bmatrix} 1 & 0 & 0 & 0 \\ 0 & 1 & 0 & 0 \\ 0 & 0 & 1 & 1 \\ 0 & 0 & 0 & 0 \end{bmatrix}$ gives both forms.

(b) $\begin{bmatrix} 1 & 1 & -1 & 0 \\ 0 & 0 & 0 & 0 \\ 0 & 0 & 0 & 0 \\ 0 & 0 & 0 & 1 \end{bmatrix}, \begin{bmatrix} 1 & 1 & -1 & 0 \\ 0 & 0 & 0 & 1 \\ 0 & 0 & 0 & 0 \\ 0 & 0 & 0 & 0 \end{bmatrix}$

(c) $\begin{bmatrix} 1 & 0 & 1 & 0 \\ 0 & 1 & 2 & 0 \\ 0 & 0 & 0 & 0 \\ 0 & 0 & 0 & 1 \end{bmatrix}, \begin{bmatrix} 1 & 0 & 1 & 0 \\ 0 & 1 & 2 & 0 \\ 0 & 0 & 0 & 1 \\ 0 & 0 & 0 & 0 \end{bmatrix}$

(d) I_5 gives both forms.

8. **(a)** $(x_1, x_2, x_3) = \frac{1}{4}(5, 5, 2)$

   (b) $(x_1, x_2, x_3) = -(159, 205, 78)$

   (c) $(w, x, y, z) = (7, -1, 3, 2)$

   (d) $(w, x, y, z) = (5, 2, 0, -1)$

10. **(a)** $(x, y, z) = \frac{1}{11}(-12, 35, -4)$

   (b) $(x, y, z, w) = (1, 2, -1, 3)$

12. **(a)** $X = c_1\begin{bmatrix} -2 & 0 \\ -\frac{1}{2} & 0 \\ 1 & 0 \end{bmatrix} + c_2\begin{bmatrix} 0 & -2 \\ 0 & -\frac{1}{2} \\ 0 & 1 \end{bmatrix} + \begin{bmatrix} 0 & 4 \\ -\frac{1}{2} & 2 \\ 0 & 0 \end{bmatrix}$

   (b) No solution

   (c) $X = \begin{bmatrix} 0 & 1 & -2 \\ 1 & -2 & 3 \end{bmatrix}$

   (d) $X = c_1\begin{bmatrix} -1 & 0 \\ 0 & 0 \\ 0 & 0 \\ 1 & 0 \end{bmatrix} + c_2\begin{bmatrix} 1 & 0 \\ 1 & 0 \\ 0 & 0 \\ 0 & 0 \end{bmatrix} + c_3\begin{bmatrix} 0 & -1 \\ 0 & 0 \\ 0 & 0 \\ 0 & 1 \end{bmatrix} + c_4\begin{bmatrix} 0 & 1 \\ 0 & 1 \\ 0 & 0 \\ 0 & 0 \end{bmatrix} + \begin{bmatrix} -3 & 4 \\ 0 & 0 \\ 2 & -1 \\ 0 & 0 \end{bmatrix}$

14. **(a)** $X = \begin{bmatrix} -2 & 3 \\ 3 & 0 \end{bmatrix}$

   (b) $X = \begin{bmatrix} 3 & -4 & 2 \\ -2 & 4 & -2 \\ -3 & 4 & -2 \\ 2 & -4 & 2 \end{bmatrix}$

16. **(a)** $A^{-1} = \begin{bmatrix} 3 & 1 & -3 \\ -1 & 1 & 2 \\ -3 & 0 & 4 \end{bmatrix}$

   (b) $A^2 = \begin{bmatrix} 39 & -43 & 52 \\ -23 & 26 & -31 \\ 30 & -33 & 40 \end{bmatrix}$

   (c) $A^{-2} = \begin{bmatrix} 17 & 4 & -19 \\ -10 & 0 & 13 \\ -21 & -3 & 25 \end{bmatrix}$

   (d) $A^{-3} = \begin{bmatrix} 104 & 21 & -119 \\ -69 & -20 & 82 \\ -135 & -24 & 157 \end{bmatrix}$

   (e) $A^3 = \begin{bmatrix} 398 & -441 & 532 \\ -237 & 263 & -317 \\ 306 & -339 & 409 \end{bmatrix}$

18. The inverse of a nonsingular triangular matrix is a triangular matrix whose diagonal elements are the reciprocals of the corresponding diagonal elements of the original matrix.

20. Yes

26. **(a)** $\mathbf{x} = c\begin{bmatrix} 37 \\ 1 \\ -23 \end{bmatrix}$

   (b) $\mathbf{x} = c\begin{bmatrix} 1 \\ -2 \\ 1 \end{bmatrix}$

   (c) $\mathbf{x} = c\begin{bmatrix} 11 \\ -9 \\ 1 \\ 1 \end{bmatrix}$

28. Multiply the equation, symbolically, by A^{-1}, getting $A - 5I + 2A^{-1} = 0$

   Then $A^{-1} = \frac{1}{2}(5I - A) = \frac{1}{2}\begin{bmatrix} 4 & 2 \\ -3 & 1 \end{bmatrix}$

30. k, p, and n must satisfy the equation $-2k + 4p - n = 10$ and the inequalities

$$5 \leqq k \leqq 30$$
$$10 \leqq p \leqq 20$$
$$10 \leqq n \leqq 30$$

When they do, the required amounts of the three fertilizers are

$$x_1 = \lambda(40 - 2p), \quad x_2 = \lambda(20 + 4k - 3p),$$

$$x_3 = \lambda(-40 - 2k + 5p) \text{ where } \lambda \text{ is an}$$
arbitrary positive constant.

32. The percentage of only two of the three elements can be specified. If k and p are specified, they must satisfy the relation $4k + p = 50$, and the required amounts are either $x_1 = a(k - 5)$, $x_2 = a(10 - k)$ or $x_1 = b(30 - p)$, $x_2 = b(p - 10)$ and the amount of n is $.30x_1 + .10x_2$

If k and n are specified, they must satisfy the relation $4k - n = 10$, and the required amounts are $x_1 = j(k - 5)$, $x_2 = j(10 - k)$ or $x_1 = k(n - 10)$, $x_2 = k(30 - n)$ and the amount of p is $.10x_1 + .30x_2$.

If p and n are specified, they must satisfy the relation $p + n = 40$, and the required amounts are $x_1 = \ell(30 - p)$, $x_2 = \ell(p - 10)$ or $x_1 = m(n - 10)$, $x_2 = m(30 - n)$ and the amount of k is $.10x_1 + .05x_2$. a, b, j, k, ℓ, and m are arbitrary positive proportionality constants.

36.
$$\begin{bmatrix} 1 & 0 & 7 & 0 \\ 0 & 1 & 4 & 0 \\ 0 & 0 & 0 & 0 \\ 0 & 0 & 0 & 1 \end{bmatrix} \text{ and } \begin{bmatrix} 0 & 0 & 0 & 0 \\ -\frac{4}{7} & 1 & 0 & 0 \\ \frac{1}{7} & 0 & 1 & 0 \\ 0 & 0 & 0 & 1 \end{bmatrix}$$

38. Because the cofactors of the elements in either row cannot all be zero, as required by Theorem 3.

40.
$$\begin{bmatrix} x_1 \\ x_2 \\ x_3 \end{bmatrix} = c \begin{bmatrix} -1/2 \\ 3/4 \\ 0 \end{bmatrix} + \begin{bmatrix} 2 \\ -5/2 \\ 0 \end{bmatrix}$$

Section 3.8

2. (a) $\lambda_1 = 1$, $\mathbf{x} = c_1 \begin{bmatrix} 1 \\ 0 \\ -1 \end{bmatrix} + c_2 \begin{bmatrix} 1 \\ -1 \\ 0 \end{bmatrix}$, $c_1^2 + c_2^2 \neq 0$; $\lambda_2 = 5$, $\mathbf{x} = c_3 \begin{bmatrix} 1 \\ 2 \\ 1 \end{bmatrix}$, $c_3 \neq 0$

(b) $\lambda_1 = 1$, $\mathbf{x} = c_1 \begin{bmatrix} 1 \\ 1 \\ 1 \end{bmatrix}$, $c_1 \neq 0$; $\lambda_2 = 2$, $\mathbf{x} = c_2 \begin{bmatrix} 1 \\ 1 \\ 0 \end{bmatrix} + c_3 \begin{bmatrix} 1 \\ 0 \\ -1 \end{bmatrix}$, $c_2^2 + c_3^2 \neq 0$

(d) $\lambda_1 = 1,\ \mathbf{x} = c_1 \begin{bmatrix} 1 \\ 0 \\ 0 \end{bmatrix} + c_2 \begin{bmatrix} 0 \\ 1 \\ 0 \end{bmatrix} + c_3 \begin{bmatrix} 0 \\ 0 \\ 1 \end{bmatrix},\ \ c_1^2 + c_2^2 + c_3^2 \neq 0$

(e) $\lambda_1 = 1,\ \mathbf{x} = c \begin{bmatrix} e \\ -\pi \\ 0 \end{bmatrix},\ \ c \neq 0$

(f) $\lambda_1 = h,\ \mathbf{x} = c_1 \begin{bmatrix} 0 \\ 0 \\ 1 \end{bmatrix} + c_2 \begin{bmatrix} k \\ -1 \\ 0 \end{bmatrix},\ \ c_1^2 + c_2^2 \neq 0$

(g) $\lambda_1 = 0,\ \mathbf{x} = c_1(-4, 4, 2, 1),\ c_1 \neq 0;\ \lambda_2 = 3i,\ \text{for all}\ c_2 \neq 0,\ \mathbf{x} = c_2(1 - 3i, -1 - 3i, 4, 2);$

$\lambda_3 = -3i,\ \mathbf{x} = c_3(1 + 3i, -1 + 3i, 4, 2),\ c_3 \neq 0$

(h) $\lambda_1 = -2,\ \mathbf{x} = c_1(1, -1, 2, 0),\ c_1 \neq 0;\ \lambda_2 = 1 + i,\ \text{for all}\ c_2 \neq 0,\ \mathbf{x} = c_2(2 + i, 1, -2, 0);$

$\lambda_3 = 1 - i,\ \mathbf{x} = c_3(2 - i, 1, -2, 0),\ c_3 \neq 0$

(i) $\lambda_1 = -1/2,\ \mathbf{x} = c_1(0, 2, -1, 1),\ c_1 \neq 0\ \ \lambda_2 = 1/2,\ \text{for all}\ c_2 \neq 0,\ \mathbf{x} = c_2(1, 7, -3, 0)$

8. $\mathbf{v}_1 = \begin{bmatrix} x \\ y \end{bmatrix} = \begin{bmatrix} \sin\alpha \\ 1 + \cos\alpha \end{bmatrix}$

Slope of $\mathbf{v}_1 = \frac{1 + \cos\alpha}{\sin\alpha} = \cot\frac{\alpha}{2}$

$\mathbf{v}_2 = \begin{bmatrix} x \\ y \end{bmatrix} = \begin{bmatrix} -\sin\alpha \\ 1 - \cos\alpha \end{bmatrix}$

Slope of $\mathbf{v}_2 = \frac{1 - \cos\alpha}{-\sin\alpha} = -\tan\frac{\alpha}{2}$

Since the two slopes are negative reciprocals, the vectors (directions) are perpendicular.

10. (a) The equations of $T_2 T_1$ are $x_2 = x\cos\alpha - y\sin\alpha$ and $y_2 = -x\sin\alpha - y\cos\alpha$.

The invariant directions are defined by $\frac{y}{x} = -\tan\frac{\alpha}{2}$ and $\frac{y}{x} = \cot\frac{\alpha}{2}$, and these are perpendicular.

(b) The equations of $T_1 T_2$ are $x_2 = x\cos\alpha + y\sin\alpha$ and $y_2 = x\sin\alpha + y\cos\alpha$.

The invariant directions are defined by $\frac{y}{x} = \tan\frac{\alpha}{2}$ and $\frac{y}{x} = -\cot\frac{\alpha}{2}$, and these are perpendicular.

12. (a) $\lambda_1 = -1,\ \mathbf{v}_1 = \begin{bmatrix} 1 \\ 1 \end{bmatrix};\ \lambda_2 = 5,\ \mathbf{v}_2 = \begin{bmatrix} 2 \\ 1 \end{bmatrix}$

(b) $\lambda_1 = 2,\ \mathbf{v}_1 = \begin{bmatrix} 1 \\ -1 \end{bmatrix};\ \lambda_2 = 3,\ \mathbf{v}_2 = \begin{bmatrix} 4 \\ -3 \end{bmatrix}$

(b) $\lambda_1 = 2$, $\mathbf{v}_1 = \begin{bmatrix} 1 \\ -1 \end{bmatrix}$; $\lambda_2 = 3$, $\mathbf{v}_2 = \begin{bmatrix} 4 \\ -3 \end{bmatrix}$

(c) $\lambda_1 = 15$, $\mathbf{v}_1 = \begin{bmatrix} 2 \\ -6 \\ 4 \end{bmatrix}$; $\lambda_2 = 3$ is a repeated characteristic value, and two linearly independent

characteristic vectors correspond to it: $\mathbf{v}_2 = \begin{bmatrix} -3 \\ 1 \\ 6 \end{bmatrix}$ and $\mathbf{v}_3 = \begin{bmatrix} 2 \\ 0 \\ 1 \end{bmatrix}$

(d) $\lambda_1 = 3$, $\mathbf{v}_1 = \begin{bmatrix} 1 \\ 1 \\ 3 \end{bmatrix}$; $\lambda_2 = i$, $\mathbf{v}_2 = \begin{bmatrix} -5+3i \\ 1+i \\ 5-i \end{bmatrix}$; $\lambda_3 = -i$, $\mathbf{v}_3 = \begin{bmatrix} -5-3i \\ 1-i \\ 5+i \end{bmatrix}$

16. $\lambda_1 = 2$, $\mathbf{x}_1 = \begin{bmatrix} 3 \\ -1 \end{bmatrix}$; $\lambda_2 = 1/2$, $\mathbf{x}_2 = \begin{bmatrix} 0 \\ 1 \end{bmatrix}$

Chapter 4

Section 4.1

2. **(a)** $(D^2 - 1)x_1 + (3D^2 - D)x_2 + D^2 x_3 = 0$
   $(5D^2 - 1)x_1 - 6Dx_2 - (D^2 - 2)x_3 = 0$
   $(D^2 - 2D)x_1 + Dx_2 + (D^2 - 1)x_3 = 0$

   (b) $D^3 x_1 + D^2 x_2 + (tD - 1)x_3 = t$
   $(2tD^2 - 1)x_1 + Dx_2 + D^3 x_3 = -1$
   $(D^2 - e^t D)x_1 + 6t^2 x_2 - D^2 x_3 = 0$

4. **(a)** and **(c)**

6. x is a solution

8. x is not a solution; the last equation is not satisfied.

10. If twice the first equation is subtracted from the second, the result is
    $(D + 1)x_1 + (D + 2)x_2 + (D + 3)x_3 = 1$,
    which is clearly inconsistent with the third equation.

Section 4.2

2. $\begin{bmatrix} x \\ y \end{bmatrix} = c\begin{bmatrix} 2 \\ -3 \end{bmatrix}e^t + \frac{1}{2}\begin{bmatrix} 0 \\ 1 \end{bmatrix}e^{-t} + \begin{bmatrix} 9 \\ -15 \end{bmatrix}$

4. $\begin{bmatrix} x \\ y \end{bmatrix} = c_1\begin{bmatrix} 3 \\ -2 \end{bmatrix}e^{-t} + c_2\begin{bmatrix} 1 \\ -2 \end{bmatrix}e^{3t} - \frac{1}{8}\begin{bmatrix} 1+6t \\ -4t \end{bmatrix}e^{-t}$

6. $\begin{bmatrix} x \\ y \end{bmatrix} = c_1\begin{bmatrix} 1 \\ 3 \end{bmatrix}e^{-t} + c_2\begin{bmatrix} 4+3t \\ 9t \end{bmatrix}e^{-t} + \frac{1}{4}\begin{bmatrix} 2t-3 \\ 2t-5 \end{bmatrix}$

8. $\begin{bmatrix} x \\ y \end{bmatrix} = c_1\begin{bmatrix} 1 \\ -3 \end{bmatrix}e^{-t} + c_2\begin{bmatrix} 2 \\ -11 \end{bmatrix}e^{4t} + c_3\begin{bmatrix} 1 \\ -11 \end{bmatrix}e^{7t} + \begin{bmatrix} -1 \\ 3 \end{bmatrix}$

10. $\begin{bmatrix} x \\ y \end{bmatrix} = a\begin{bmatrix} 1 \\ 1 \end{bmatrix}\cos t + b\begin{bmatrix} 1 \\ 1 \end{bmatrix}\sin t + c\begin{bmatrix} 2 \\ -7 \end{bmatrix}\cos 2t + d\begin{bmatrix} 2 \\ -7 \end{bmatrix}\sin 2t + \begin{bmatrix} 23 \\ -73 \end{bmatrix}\cos 3t$

12. $\begin{bmatrix} x \\ y \\ z \end{bmatrix} = c_1 \begin{bmatrix} 1 \\ -2 \\ 1 \end{bmatrix} e^{-t} + c_2 \begin{bmatrix} 11 \\ 3 \\ -29 \end{bmatrix} e^{4t} + c_3 \begin{bmatrix} 1 \\ 1 \\ 1 \end{bmatrix} e^{-4t} + \begin{bmatrix} 0 \\ 2 \\ -1 \end{bmatrix} e^{-t}$

14. The system has no solution

16. $\begin{bmatrix} x \\ y \end{bmatrix} = c_1 \begin{bmatrix} 1 \\ -1 \end{bmatrix} + c_2 \begin{bmatrix} 1 \\ 0 \end{bmatrix} e^{t} + c_3 \begin{bmatrix} 0 \\ 1 \end{bmatrix} e^{t}$

18. (a) $\begin{bmatrix} x \\ y \end{bmatrix} = \begin{bmatrix} 3 \\ 3 \end{bmatrix} e^{-t} + \begin{bmatrix} -1 \\ 3 \end{bmatrix} e^{-5t} + \begin{bmatrix} -2 \\ 1 \end{bmatrix}$

(b) $\begin{bmatrix} x \\ y \end{bmatrix} = \frac{127}{16} \begin{bmatrix} 1 \\ 1 \end{bmatrix} e^{-t} + \frac{17}{16} \begin{bmatrix} 1 \\ -3 \end{bmatrix} e^{-5t} + \begin{bmatrix} -2 \\ 1 \end{bmatrix}$

20. $(5D - 4)x - Dy = 0; \ 3Dx + (D - 4)y = 0$

22. $a = c + d$ and $b = 2c$

24. (a) Any two independent equations of the family $(aD + b)x + (cD - b)y - (a + c)Dz = 0$ will form such a system.

(b) Any two independent equations of the family $(aD + b)x + (cD - a - b - c)y - (a + c)(D - 1)z = 0$ will form such a system.

28. $Q_1 = V\left[(s_1 - s)e^{-at/V} + s\right]; \ Q_2 = V\left[(s_2 - s)e^{-at/V} + \frac{a}{V}(s_1 - s)te^{-at/V} + s\right]$

Q_2 will reach an extreme value when $t = (s_1 - s_2)V/(s_1 - s)a$, which is physically meaningful if and only if $t \geqq 0$, i.e., if and only if $s_1 > s_2, \ s$ or $s_1 < s_2, \ s$.

30. $Q_1 = 100 + e^{-3t/40}\left[-100\cos\frac{\sqrt{3}}{40}t + \frac{100\sqrt{3}}{3}\sin\frac{\sqrt{3}}{40}t\right]; \ Q_2 = 100 + e^{-3t/40}\left[-\frac{200\sqrt{3}}{3}\sin\frac{\sqrt{3}}{40}t\right]$

$Q_3 = 100 + e^{-3t/40}[100\cos\frac{\sqrt{3}}{40}t + \frac{100\sqrt{3}}{3}\sin\frac{\sqrt{3}}{40}t]$

32. (b) $[(a_{22}D + b_{22})(a_{11}D + b_{11}) - (a_{12}D + b_{12})(a_{21}D + b_{21})]x = (a_{22}D + b_{22})f_1 - (a_{12}D + b_{12})f_2$
$[a_{22}(a_{11}D + b_{11}) - a_{12}(a_{21}D + b_{21})]x + (a_{22}b_{12} - a_{12}b_{22})y = a_{22}f_1 - a_{12}f_2$

34. (a) Yes

(b) Yes

(c) By substituting the solutions for x and y into the equations of the original differential system, and then equating to zero the net coefficients of the linearly independent functions that appear in each of these equations.

(d) Yes, providing the corresponding determinant of the operator coefficients is not identically zero.

38. (a) $x = c_1 e^{t/2} - 7e^t$, $y = c_1 e^{t/2} + 6e^t$, $z = 3e^t$

(b) $x = c_1 e^{t/2} + 2e^t - 4e^{2t/3}$, $y = c_1 e^{t/2} + 3e^t$, $z = e^{2t/3}$

(c) $x = c_1 e^{t/2} + 2e^t - 4e^{2t/3} + c - 2b - 2ct$, $y = c_1 e^{t/2} + 3e^t + 2b + c + 2ct$, $z = b + ct + e^{2t/3}$

40. (a) $a - c \neq 2$

(b) $a - c = 2$, $b \neq 2c + e + 2$

(c) $a - c = 2$, $b = 2c + e + 2$, $b + c \neq 0$

(d) $a = c + 2$, $b = c + 1$, $e = -c - 1$

42. (a) $\begin{bmatrix} x \\ y \end{bmatrix} = \begin{bmatrix} -2 - e^{-t} \\ 8 - 2e^{-t} \end{bmatrix}$

(b) $\begin{bmatrix} x \\ y \end{bmatrix} = c \begin{bmatrix} 4 \\ 1 \end{bmatrix} e^{-2t/5} + \frac{1}{7} \begin{bmatrix} 1 \\ 2 \end{bmatrix} e^t + \frac{1}{2} \begin{bmatrix} 0 \\ -1 \end{bmatrix}$

44. (a) $\begin{bmatrix} x \\ y \end{bmatrix} = c_1 \begin{bmatrix} 1 \\ -1 \end{bmatrix} e^t + c_2 \begin{bmatrix} 2 \\ 3 \end{bmatrix} e^{4t} - \begin{bmatrix} 2 \\ 0 \end{bmatrix} e^t - \begin{bmatrix} 0 \\ 3 \end{bmatrix} e^{2t}$

(b) $\begin{bmatrix} x \\ y \end{bmatrix} = c \begin{bmatrix} 2 \\ -3 \end{bmatrix} e^t + \begin{bmatrix} 0 \\ 1/2 \end{bmatrix} e^{-t} + \begin{bmatrix} 9 \\ -15 \end{bmatrix}$

46. (a) $\begin{bmatrix} x \\ y \end{bmatrix} = c_1 \begin{bmatrix} 3 \\ -2 \end{bmatrix} e^{-t} + c_2 \begin{bmatrix} 1 \\ -2 \end{bmatrix} e^{3t} - \frac{1}{8} \begin{bmatrix} 1 + 6t \\ -4t \end{bmatrix} e^{-t}$

(b) $\begin{bmatrix} x \\ y \end{bmatrix} = c_1 \begin{bmatrix} 1 \\ -2 \end{bmatrix} e^{-t/5} + c_2 \begin{bmatrix} 1 \\ 2 \end{bmatrix} e^{-t/15} + \begin{bmatrix} 20 \\ 20 \end{bmatrix}$

48. (a) $\begin{bmatrix} x \\ y \end{bmatrix} = c_1 \begin{bmatrix} 1 \\ -1 \end{bmatrix} e^t + c_2 \begin{bmatrix} 1 + 2t \\ -2t \end{bmatrix} e^t + \frac{1}{2} \begin{bmatrix} 2 \\ -3 \end{bmatrix} \cos t + \frac{1}{2} \begin{bmatrix} 0 \\ -1 \end{bmatrix} \sin t$

(b) $\begin{bmatrix} x \\ y \end{bmatrix} = c_1 \begin{bmatrix} 1 \\ 1 \end{bmatrix} e^t + c_2 \begin{bmatrix} 2 \\ 1 \end{bmatrix} e^{-t} + \frac{1}{2} \begin{bmatrix} 16 - \cos t + 3 \sin t \\ 12 + 2 \sin t \end{bmatrix}$

50. (a) $\begin{bmatrix} x \\ y \\ z \end{bmatrix} = c_1 \begin{bmatrix} 1 \\ 0 \\ 0 \end{bmatrix} e^{2t} + c_2 \begin{bmatrix} 3 \\ 2 \\ 1 \end{bmatrix} + c_3 \begin{bmatrix} 2+3t \\ 1+2t \\ t \end{bmatrix}$

(b) $\begin{bmatrix} x \\ y \\ z \end{bmatrix} = \left(c_1 \begin{bmatrix} 1 \\ 0 \\ 0 \end{bmatrix} + c_2 \begin{bmatrix} t \\ -1 \\ 0 \end{bmatrix} + c_3 \begin{bmatrix} t^2 \\ -2t-2 \\ 1/2 \end{bmatrix} \right) e^{2t}$

52. (a) Yes

(b) If and only if the determinant of the operational coefficients of S_{46} is of the second order.

Section 4.3

2. If and only if both A and $\mathbf{f}$ are continuous on I

4. (a) $\begin{bmatrix} x_1 \\ x_2 \end{bmatrix}' = \begin{bmatrix} 0 & 1 \\ -1 & 2t \end{bmatrix} \begin{bmatrix} x_1 \\ x_2 \end{bmatrix} + \begin{bmatrix} 0 \\ 1 \end{bmatrix} t^2$

(b) $\begin{bmatrix} x_1 \\ x_2 \end{bmatrix}' = \begin{bmatrix} 0 & 1 \\ 8 & -4 \end{bmatrix} \begin{bmatrix} x_1 \\ x_2 \end{bmatrix} + \begin{bmatrix} 0 \\ 1 \end{bmatrix} 5 \cosh 2t$

(c) $\begin{bmatrix} x_1 \\ x_2 \\ x_3 \end{bmatrix}' = \begin{bmatrix} 0 & 1 & 0 \\ 0 & 0 & 1 \\ 2\sinh t & 0 & -\tanh t \end{bmatrix} \begin{bmatrix} x_1 \\ x_2 \\ x_3 \end{bmatrix} + \begin{bmatrix} 0 \\ 0 \\ 1 \end{bmatrix} te^t \operatorname{sech} t$

(d) $\begin{bmatrix} x_1 \\ x_2 \\ x_3 \end{bmatrix}' = \begin{bmatrix} 0 & 1 & 0 \\ 0 & 0 & 1 \\ e^t & 2(1-e^{-2t}) & -(1+e^{-2t}) \end{bmatrix} \begin{bmatrix} x_1 \\ x_2 \\ x_3 \end{bmatrix} + \begin{bmatrix} 0 \\ 0 \\ 1 \end{bmatrix} 7e^{2t}$

(e) $\begin{bmatrix} x_1 \\ x_2 \end{bmatrix}' = \begin{bmatrix} 3 & -2 \\ 2 & -1 \end{bmatrix} \begin{bmatrix} x_1 \\ x_2 \end{bmatrix} + \begin{bmatrix} 1+2t \\ t \end{bmatrix} t$

(f) With $u_1 = x_1$, $u_2 = x_2$, and $u_3 = x_1'$: $\begin{bmatrix} u_1 \\ u_2 \\ u_3 \end{bmatrix}' = \begin{bmatrix} 0 & 0 & 1 \\ 0 & 3 & 1 \\ 2 & -3 & -1 \end{bmatrix} \begin{bmatrix} u_1 \\ u_2 \\ u_3 \end{bmatrix} + \begin{bmatrix} 0 \\ -\sin t \\ \sin t + \cos t \end{bmatrix}$

6. $y(t_0) = k_1, \ y'(t_0) = k_2, \ \ldots, y^{(n-1)}(t_0) = k_n$

8. **(a)** $y'' + e^t y' + e^{2t} y = e^{3t}$

(b) $y''' - t^2 y'' - t y' - y = \ln|t|$

10. **(a)** $y = c_1 + c_2 e^t + t e^t - e^t$

(b) $x_1' = x_2; \quad x_2' = x_2 + e^t$

(c) $\begin{bmatrix} x_1 \\ x_2 \end{bmatrix} = c_1 \begin{bmatrix} 1 \\ 0 \end{bmatrix} + c_2 \begin{bmatrix} 1 \\ 1 \end{bmatrix} e^t + \begin{bmatrix} t-1 \\ t \end{bmatrix} e^t$

(d) Use x_1 of Part **(c)**

12. **(a)** There is a unique solution over $(-\infty, \infty)$

(b) There is a unique solution over $(-\pi/2, \pi/2)$

(c) No solution

(d) There is a unique solution over $(0, 1]$

14. Suppose $a \neq 0$.

Section 4.4

2. **(a)** $\mathbf{x}_1, \mathbf{x}_2, \mathbf{x}_3$, constitute a basis on any interval that excludes $t = 1$ and $t = -1$.

(b) $w(t) = 1 - t^2$ is zero if $t = 1$ or $t = -1$; this does not contradict Theorem 3 because the differential system is not normal on any interval that contains either $t = 1$ or $t = -1$.

(c) $t = 0$

(d) Only (ii) and (iv) are solutions

8. **(a)** $x_1' = x_2$
$\quad x_2' = x_1$

(b) $x_1' = -x_2$
$\quad x_2' = x_1$

(c) $x_1' = \frac{1}{1+t^3}\left[t^2 x_1 - x_2\right]$
$\quad x_2' = \frac{2t}{1+t^3}\left[x_1 + t x_2\right]$

(d) $x_1' = [t x_1 - x_2]/t^2$
$\quad x_2' = x_2 / t$
$\quad x_3' = 2 x_3 / t$

(e) $x_1' = (\tan t) x_1$
$\quad x_2' = (\sec t) x_3$
$\quad x_3' = (\sec t) x_2$

(f) $x_1' = -\frac{1}{t e^t} x_2 + \frac{1}{e^{2t}} x_3$
$\quad x_2' = x_2 / t$
$\quad x_3' = x_3$

10. **(a)** $X = \begin{bmatrix} e^t & e^{-t} \\ e^t & 2e^{-t} \end{bmatrix}$

(b) $\begin{bmatrix} \frac{5}{3} e^{2t} + 2 \\ \frac{4}{3} e^{2t} + 3 \end{bmatrix}$

(c) $\begin{bmatrix} -t e^t + \frac{1}{2} e^t \\ -t e^t + e^t \end{bmatrix} + \begin{bmatrix} \frac{5}{3} e^{2t} \\ \frac{4}{3} e^{2t} \end{bmatrix}$

(d) $\begin{bmatrix} -3t - 1 \\ -4t \end{bmatrix} + \begin{bmatrix} 2 \\ 3 \end{bmatrix}$

(e) $\begin{bmatrix} -\frac{3}{2}\sin t - \frac{1}{2}\cos t \\ -2\sin t \end{bmatrix}$

12. A complete solution of the homogenous system is $c_1 \begin{bmatrix} t \\ 1 \end{bmatrix} + c_2 \begin{bmatrix} t^2 \\ 2t \end{bmatrix}$ and this is to be added to the particular integrals given below in Parts **(a)**, **(b)**, and **(c)** to form the required complete solutions.

(a) $\begin{bmatrix} -t^2 + t^2 \ln t \\ -t + 2t \ln t \end{bmatrix}$

(b) $\begin{bmatrix} t^3/2 \\ 3t^2/2 \end{bmatrix}$

(c) $\begin{bmatrix} 2t^2 - t^2 \ln t \\ 2tt - 2t \ln t \end{bmatrix}$

14. $\begin{bmatrix} e^t \tan t \\ 2e^t \tan t \end{bmatrix}$

16. $\begin{bmatrix} t\mathrm{Tan}^{-1}t + t^2 \\ t^3 \\ 0 \end{bmatrix}$

18. $\mathbf{x} = \begin{bmatrix} 1 \\ 2 \end{bmatrix} e^{-t} - \begin{bmatrix} 1 \\ 1 \end{bmatrix} e^{-2t}$

20. $\mathbf{x} = 7\begin{bmatrix} \cos 2t + \sin 2t \\ -\cos 2t \end{bmatrix} e^{-t}$

22. $\mathbf{x} = \frac{1}{25}\begin{bmatrix} -9 \\ 4 \end{bmatrix}\cos t + \frac{1}{25}\begin{bmatrix} -13 \\ 3 \end{bmatrix}\sin t$

24. $\mathbf{x} = \begin{bmatrix} 3 \\ 3 \end{bmatrix} e^{-t} + \begin{bmatrix} 2 \\ 6 \end{bmatrix} e^t + \begin{bmatrix} 2 - \sin t \\ 3 - \cos t - 2\sin t \end{bmatrix}$

26. $\mathbf{x} = \begin{bmatrix} 3t\cos 3t - (\sin 3t)\ln|\cos 3t| \\ 3t\sin t + (\cos 3t)\ln|\cos 3t| \end{bmatrix} e^t$

28. $\mathbf{x} = \begin{bmatrix} 0 \\ 0 \\ 2 \end{bmatrix} e^{-t} + \begin{bmatrix} 1 \\ 2 \\ 1 \end{bmatrix} e^t$

30. $\mathbf{x} = \begin{bmatrix} 2 \\ 1 \\ -1 \end{bmatrix} e^{-t}$

32. $\mathbf{x} = \begin{bmatrix} 1 \\ 2 \\ 1 \end{bmatrix}(6 + \ln t)e^{3t}$

Section 4.5

2. $\mathbf{x} = c_1\begin{bmatrix} -\cos 2t - \sin 2t \\ \cos 2t \end{bmatrix} e^{-t} + c_2\begin{bmatrix} \cos 2t - \sin 2t \\ \sin 2t \end{bmatrix} e^{-t}$

4. $\mathbf{x} = c_1\begin{bmatrix} 1 \\ -1 \end{bmatrix} e^t + c_2\begin{bmatrix} 1 + 2t \\ -2t \end{bmatrix} e^t$

6. $\mathbf{x} = c_1\begin{bmatrix} \cos 2t - \sin 2t \\ -\cos 2t \end{bmatrix} e^t + c_2\begin{bmatrix} \cos 2t + \sin 2t \\ -\sin 2t \end{bmatrix} e^t$

8. $\mathbf{x} = c_1 \begin{bmatrix} 1 \\ -1 \end{bmatrix} e^{2t} + c_2 \begin{bmatrix} 1-t \\ t \end{bmatrix} e^{2t}$

10. $\mathbf{x} = c_1 \begin{bmatrix} 1 \\ 1 \end{bmatrix} e^{-t} + c_2 \begin{bmatrix} 1 \\ 3 \end{bmatrix} e^t + \begin{bmatrix} -\sin t \\ -\cos t - 2\sin t \end{bmatrix}; \quad \mathbf{x} = \begin{bmatrix} 2 \\ 2 \end{bmatrix} e^{-t} + \begin{bmatrix} 1 \\ 3 \end{bmatrix} e^t + \begin{bmatrix} -\sin t \\ -\cos t - 2\sin t \end{bmatrix}$

12. $\mathbf{x} = c_1 \begin{bmatrix} \cos 2t \\ \sin 2t \end{bmatrix} + c_2 \begin{bmatrix} \sin 2t \\ -\cos 2t \end{bmatrix} + \begin{bmatrix} \sin 2t \\ -\cos 2t \end{bmatrix} \ln|\cot 2t|$

14. $\mathbf{x} = -\begin{bmatrix} 5 \\ 0 \\ 2 \end{bmatrix} + \begin{bmatrix} 2 \\ -2 \\ 1 \end{bmatrix} e^t$

16. $\mathbf{x} = c_1 \begin{bmatrix} 1 \\ 0 \\ 1 \end{bmatrix} e^{-t} + c_2 \begin{bmatrix} 1 \\ 1 \\ -1 \end{bmatrix} e^t + \begin{bmatrix} 1 \\ -1 \\ 1 \end{bmatrix} \left\{ c_3 + \ln(1+t^2) \right\}; \quad \mathbf{x} = \begin{bmatrix} 1 \\ -1 \\ 1 \end{bmatrix} \left\{ 1 + \ln(1+t^2) \right\}$

20. $(x, y) = c_1(-2, 1) + c_2(2, -5) e^{-8t} + (1, -1) e^t$

22. $(x, y) = c_1(4, -3) e^t + c_2(5, -3) e^{-2t} + (7, -5) e^{2t}$

24. $(x, y) = a(-2, 1) e^{-t} + b(2, -3) e^{-5t} + (-2\cos t - \sin t, \cos t + 2\sin t)$

26. $(x, y) = a(-4, 1) e^{-t} + b(8, -3) e^t + c(-4, 1) e^{3t} + (34, -10) e^{2t}$

28. $(x, y) = a(\cos t - \sin t, -\cos t + 2\sin t) + b(\cos t + \sin t, -2\cos t - \sin t)$

30. $(x, y) = c_1(1, 0) + c_2(1, 1) e^t - (1 + t + \ln|t|, 1)$

32. $\begin{bmatrix} x \\ y \end{bmatrix} = c_1 \begin{bmatrix} 1 \\ -2 \end{bmatrix} e^t + c_2 \begin{bmatrix} 1 \\ 1 \end{bmatrix} e^{-2t} + \frac{4}{3} \begin{bmatrix} 1 \\ -2 \end{bmatrix} t e^t + \begin{bmatrix} 1 \\ 3 \end{bmatrix} e^{-t} + \frac{5}{3} \begin{bmatrix} 0 \\ 1 \end{bmatrix} e^t$

34. $\begin{bmatrix} x \\ y \end{bmatrix} = a e^{-t} \left(\begin{bmatrix} 2 \\ -1 \end{bmatrix} \cos 3t - \begin{bmatrix} 3 \\ -3 \end{bmatrix} \sin 3t \right) + b e^{-t} \left(\begin{bmatrix} 3 \\ -3 \end{bmatrix} \cos 3t - \begin{bmatrix} 2 \\ -1 \end{bmatrix} \sin 3t \right) + \begin{bmatrix} 1 \\ -2 \end{bmatrix}$

36. $\begin{bmatrix} x \\ y \end{bmatrix} = c_1 \begin{bmatrix} 3 \\ -2 \end{bmatrix} e^t + c_2 \left(\begin{bmatrix} 3 \\ -2 \end{bmatrix} t e^t + \begin{bmatrix} 1 \\ 0 \end{bmatrix} e^t \right) + \begin{bmatrix} -1 \\ 0 \end{bmatrix} + \begin{bmatrix} 1 \\ -1 \end{bmatrix} t$

38. $\begin{bmatrix} x \\ y \end{bmatrix} = c_1 \begin{bmatrix} 1 \\ 1 \end{bmatrix} e^{-t} + c_2 \left(\begin{bmatrix} 1 \\ 1 \end{bmatrix} t e^{-t} + \begin{bmatrix} 0 \\ -3 \end{bmatrix} e^{-t} \right) + \begin{bmatrix} -1 \\ 1/2 \end{bmatrix} \cos t + \frac{1}{3} \begin{bmatrix} 1/2 \\ -1 \end{bmatrix} \sin t$

40. $\ddot{y}_1 = -\lambda^2 (2y_1 - y_2); \quad \lambda^2 = \frac{4Tg}{wl} \quad \ddot{y}_2 = -\lambda^2 (-y_1 + 2y_2 - y_3) \quad \ddot{y}_3 = -\lambda^2 (-y_2 + 2y_3)$

$\omega_1 = \sqrt{2 - \sqrt{2}}\,\lambda, \quad 1:\sqrt{2}:1 \qquad \omega_2 = \sqrt{2}\,\lambda, \quad 1:0:-1 \qquad \omega_3 = \sqrt{2 + \sqrt{2}}\,\lambda, \quad 1:-\sqrt{2}:1$

42. $\begin{bmatrix} x \\ y \end{bmatrix} = c_1 \begin{bmatrix} 2 \\ -3 \end{bmatrix} e^t + c_2 \begin{bmatrix} 3 \\ -5 \end{bmatrix} e^{2t} + \begin{bmatrix} 0 \\ 1/4 \end{bmatrix} e^t + \begin{bmatrix} 1 \\ -3/2 \end{bmatrix} t e^t$

48. $D^m(t^3 e^{\lambda t}) = \lambda^m t^3 e^{\lambda t} + 3m\lambda^{m-1} t^2 e^{\lambda t} + 3m(m-1)\lambda^{m-2} t e^{\lambda t} + m(m-1)(m-2)\lambda^{m-3} e^{\lambda t}$

$p(D)(t^3 e^{\lambda t}) = p(\lambda) t^3 e^{\lambda t} + 3p'(\lambda) t^2 e^{\lambda t} + 3p''(\lambda) t e^{\lambda t} + p'''(\lambda) e^{\lambda t}$

$P(D)(t^3 e^{\lambda t}) = P(\lambda) t^3 e^{\lambda t} + 3P'(\lambda) t^2 e^{\lambda t} + 3P''(\lambda) t e^{\lambda t} + P'''(\lambda) e^{\lambda t}$

54. $\lambda_1 = 1, \quad \mathbf{x}_1 = \begin{bmatrix} 1 \\ 0 \\ 1 \end{bmatrix} e^t; \quad \lambda_2 = 3, \quad \mathbf{x}_2 = \begin{bmatrix} 1 \\ -1 \\ 2 \end{bmatrix} e^{3t}; \quad \lambda_3 = 15, \quad \mathbf{x}_3 = \begin{bmatrix} 0 \\ 1 \\ 1 \end{bmatrix} e^{-5t}$

56. (b) If A is singular, $(AX)^{-1}$ does not exist.

(c) $\begin{bmatrix} e^{4t} \\ e^{4t} \end{bmatrix}$

58. To do so, the nonhomogenous term $\mathbf{f}(t)$ must have only a finite number of linearly independent derivatives. This being the case, write the differential system in the compact matrix form (20) with each operator element of the matrix $\mathbf{P}(D)$ displayed explicitly. Express $\mathbf{f}(t)$ in the form (31) and find a constant coefficient linear differential operator that annihilates $\mathbf{f}(t)$, say $\mathbf{L}(D)$. Then, find a complete solution of the homogeneous system $\mathbf{L}(D)\mathbf{P}(D)\mathbf{x} = \mathbf{0}$. The remaining steps parallel those of the four-step method of undetermined coefficients [Section 2.7]. Should the expanded form (31) of $\mathbf{f}(t)$ contain several terms, Theorem 8, Section 4.4, may be used to expedite the process.

60. (a) $\begin{bmatrix} x \\ y \end{bmatrix} = c_1 \begin{bmatrix} 1 \\ 0 \end{bmatrix} e^{-t} + c_2 \begin{bmatrix} 0 \\ 1 \end{bmatrix} e^t + \begin{bmatrix} 4 \\ 3t \end{bmatrix} e^t$

(b) $\begin{bmatrix} x \\ y \end{bmatrix} = c_1 \begin{bmatrix} 1 \\ -2 \end{bmatrix} e^t + c_2 \begin{bmatrix} 1 \\ 2 \end{bmatrix} e^{5t} + \begin{bmatrix} -3 - t \\ 4 + t \end{bmatrix}$

Chapter 5

Section 5.2

2. (a)

x	$x^3 - 2x^2 + 3$			
0.0	3.000			
		−1.000		
1.0	2.000		0.500	
		−0.250		1.000
1.5	1.875		3.000	
		4.250		1.000
2.5	6.125		5.000	
		11.750		1.000
3.0	12.000		7.000	
		18.750		
3.5	21.375			

(b)

x	$2x^3 - x + 3$			
1.0	4.000			
		8.500		
1.5	8.250		10.000	
		23.500		2.000
2.5	31.750		14.000	
		44.500		2.000
3.0	54.000		19.000	
		73.000		2.000
4.0	127.000		26.000	
		151.000		
6.0	429.000			

4. (a)

x	$x^4 - 3x^2 + 1$			
0	1			
		−2		
1	−1		8	
		6		36
2	5		44	24
		50		60
3	55		104	24
		154		84
4	209		188	24
		342		108
5	551		296	
		638		
6	1189			

(b)

x	$2x^4 - 3x^3 + x - 5$			
0.0	−5.0000			
		0.1792		
0.2	−4.8208		−0.0992	
		0.0800		−0.0288
0.4	−4.7408		−0.1280	0.0768
		−0.0480		0.0480
0.6	−4.7888		−0.0800	0.0768
		−0.1280		0.1248
0.8	−4.9168		0.0448	0.0768
		−0.0832		0.2016
1.0	−5.0000		0.2464	0.0768
		0.1632		0.2784
1.2	−4.8368		0.5248	0.0768
		0.6880		0.3552
1.4	−4.1488		0.8800	0.0768
		1.5680		0.4320
1.6	−2.5808		1.3120	0.0768
		2.8800		0.5088
1.8	0.2992		1.8208	
		4.7008		
2.0	5,.0000			

6. $-\dfrac{\cos(ax - a/2)}{2^{\sin(a/2)}}, \dfrac{\sin(ax - a/2)}{2^{\sin(a/2)}}$

8. (b) The nth divided differences are all divided by c^n.

14. $\triangle^k x^{(n)} = n(n-1) \cdots (n-k+1) x^{(n-k)}$

16. $x^{(n)} = \dfrac{\Delta x^{(n+1)}}{n+1}, \dfrac{\Delta^2 x^{(n+2)}}{(n+1)(n+2)}$

18. (a) $-1 - x^{(1)} + 3x^{(2)} + x^{(3)} = -1 - 2x + x^3$

(b) $6 - 5x^{(1)} + x^{(2)} - x^{(3)} + x^{(4)} = 6 - 14x + 15x^2 - 7x^3 + x^4$

20. (a) $x^{(2)} + 2x^{(1)} + 1$

(b) $2x^{(4)} + 13x^{(3)} + 13x^{(2)} - 2x^{(1)} + 1$

(c) $x^{(5)} + 10x^{(4)} + 25x^{(3)} + 15x^{(2)} + x^{(1)} + 1$

22. $\triangle^k x_h^{(-n)} = (-h)^k n(n+1)\cdots(n+k-1)$
$\quad\quad\bullet\, x_h^{(-n-k)}$

24. $x^{(-3)} - x^{(-4)}$

26. **(a)** $x^{(-2)} - 3x^{(-3)}$

  (b) $x^{(-2)} - 7x^{(-3)} + 16x^{(-4)}$

  (c) $x^{(-2)} - 3x^{(-3)} + 6x^{(-4)} - 6x^{(-5)}$

28. **(a)** $\dfrac{n(n+1)(2n+1)}{6}$

  (b) $\dfrac{n^2(n+1)^2}{4}$

  (c) $\dfrac{n(n+1)(2n+1)(3n^2+3n-1)}{30}$

32. **(a)** $\dfrac{1}{2} - \dfrac{1}{n+2}$

  (b) $\dfrac{1}{2(n+2)(n+3)} - \dfrac{1}{n+2} + \dfrac{5}{12}$

  (c) $\dfrac{1}{12} - \dfrac{1}{2(n+2)(n+3)}$

  (d) $\dfrac{1}{4} - (n+1)^{(-1)} + \dfrac{3}{2}(n+1)^{(-2)}$

  (e) $\dfrac{2}{9} - (n+1)^{(-1)} + 2(n+1)^{(-2)} - \dfrac{4}{3}(n+1)^{(-3)}$

34. **(a)** $S = (n-1)2^{n+1} + 2$

  (b) $S = \dfrac{1}{2}3^{k+1}(k^2 - k + 1) - \dfrac{3}{2}$

  (c) $\dfrac{(n+1)\sin(an+a/2)-\sin(a/2)}{2\sin(a/2)}$

   $+\dfrac{\cos(an+a)-\cos a}{4\sin^2(a/2)}$

  (d) $-\dfrac{(n+1)\cos(an+a/2)-\cos(a/2)}{2\sin(a/2)}$

   $-\dfrac{\sin(an+a)-\sin a}{2\sin^2(a/2)}$

Section 5.3

2. **(a)** 1.338

  (b) 2.818

4. $0.78435 + 0.30051x - 0.03418x^2 + 0.00267x^3$
$- 0.00009x^4$

20. **(b)** Sufficient conditions for the inequality are that the second derivative of the spline function vanish at $x = a$ and at $x = b$.

22. No, because at least one polynomial must be a linear function and thus have non zero slope.

24. $S(x) = \begin{cases} 5.5 - x \\ 18.46 - 6.76x + 0.64x^2 \\ -91.3 + 24.6x - 1.6x^2 \end{cases}$

  (1) $3.0 \leqq x \leqq 4.5$
  (2) $4.5 \leqq x \leqq 7.0$
  (3) $7.0 \leqq x \leqq 9$

Section 5.4

2. At $x = 200.5$: $(\ln x)' = 0.00498753$
$\quad\quad\quad\quad\quad (\ln x)'' = -0.00002487$
$\quad\quad\quad\quad\quad (\ln x)''' = 0.00000024$
 At $x = 204.5$: $(\ln x)' = 0.00488998$
$\quad\quad\quad\quad\quad (\ln x)'' = -0.00002390$
$\quad\quad\quad\quad\quad (\ln x)''' = 0.00000025$
The first four answers are accurate to eight places. The fifth and sixth are high by 1 and 2 in the eighth place.

4. Write $\displaystyle\int_x^{x_o} f(t)\,dt = -\int_{x_0}^x f(t)\,dt$ and proceed as in the text.

6.

x	$\int_x^1 \frac{\sin t}{t}\, dt$
0.0	0.946
0.1	0.846
0.2	0.746
0.3	0.647
0.4	0.549
0.5	0.543
0.6	0.358
0.7	0.265
0.8	0.174
0.9	0.086
1.0	0.000

10. $y'_0 = \frac{1}{12h}(-25y_0 + 48y_1 - 36y_2 + 16y_3 - 3y_4)$

$y'_1 = \frac{1}{12h}(-3f_0 - 10f_1 + 18f_2 - 6f_3 + f_4)$

$y'_2 = \frac{1}{12h}(f_0 - 8f_1 + 8f_3 - f_4)$

$y'_3 = \frac{1}{12h}(-f_0 + 6f_1 - 18f_2 + 10f_3 + 3f_4)$

$y'_4 = \frac{1}{12h}(3f_0 - 16f_1 + 36f_2 - 48f_3 + 25f_4)$

Section 5.5

2. (a) $y = 2.24 + 2.54x$

(b) $E^2/5 = 0.85$

4. (a) $y = 2.32 + 4.60x - 0.74x^2$

(b) Yes

(c) $E^2/5 = 0.862$

6. (a) $y = 0.0196 + 1.3039x$

(b) $y = 0.511 + 1.406x$
Minimizing the squares of the vertical distance is preferable to minimizing the squares of the horizontal distances because the x's are known more accurately than the y's.

8. (a) $-0.89x + 0.94y - 1 = 0$, or
$y = 1.06 + 0.95x$

(b) $-0.95x + y - 1.05 = 0$, or
$y = 1.05 + 0.95x$

(c) $x - 1.05y - 1.10 = 0$, or
$y = 1.05 + 0.96x$
The answers are almost identical. In general, however, the answers may differ, because the different locations of the coefficients produce different weightings of the data.

10. $A = 1.000$, $a = 0.499$

12. $y = a + bx$, where $a = \frac{8(\pi-3)}{\pi^2} \doteq 0.115$,
$b = \frac{24(8-2\pi)}{\pi^3} \doteq 0.664$

14. $y = 1 - \frac{35}{83}x^2$

16. $y = 1 - 0.4707x^2 + 0.0248x^4$

18. After a has been found, A can be determined by applying the method of least squares to the equations
$y_1 = Ae^{ax_1}$, $y_2 = Ae^{ax_2}$, ..., $y^n = Ae^{ax_n}$
in which A is the only unknown. This method is generally to be preferred to linearizing by taking logarithms because it does not introduce any unwarranted weighting of the data. It is clearly preferable to linearizing by taking logarithms and then using Taylor's series.

20. The second method involves no radicals, and therefore appears to be algebraically simpler than the first method.

Section 5.6

2. $y(0.1) = -1.100$, $y(0.2) = -1.209$,
$y(0.3) = -1.326$

4. $y(0.1) = -1.1048$, $y(0.2) = -1.2184$,
$y(0.3) = -1.3399$

6. $y(0.1) = 1.1103$, $y(0.2) = -1.2428$,
$y(0.3) = 1.3997$. These answers are correct to
four places.

8.

x	$\int_0^x e^{-t^2} dt$
0.0	0.00000
0.2	0.19736
0.4	0.37965
0.6	0.53515
0.8	0.65766
1.0	0.74681

10. $\triangle y_1 \equiv k_1 = f(x_0, y_0)h$

$\triangle y_2 \equiv k_2 = f(x_0 + h/2, y_0 + \frac{1}{2}k_1)h$

$\triangle y_3 \equiv k_3 = f(x_0 + h, y_0 + 2k_2 - k_1)h$

$\triangle y = \frac{1}{6}k_1 + \frac{4}{6}k_2 + \frac{1}{6}k_3$

12. $y(0.4) = 0.0193$, $y(0.5) = 0.0369$,
$y(0.6) = 0.0624$

16. $y(0.4) = 0.4085$, $y(0.5) = 0.5155$,
$y(0.6) = 0.6248$

18.

x	y	z
0.0	0.0000	1.0000
0.1	0.0050	1.0005
0.2	0.0200	1.0040
0.3	0.0542	1.0135
0.4	0.0815	1.0322
0.5	0.1296	1.0635
0.6	0.1921	1.1112
0.7	0.2717	1.1799
0.8	0.3742	1.2756
0.9	0.5072	1.4066
1.0	0.6844	1.5855

20. $-h^5 y_{n-3}^{(5)} / 90$

22. **(a)** $\frac{1}{6}h^4 y^{iv}$

(b) No, because $5y_0 - 4y_1 + 2hy_0' + 4hy_1'$
is the only polynomial of the given form
which agrees with y_2 through terms in h^3.

24. **(a)** $\frac{7}{12}h^4 y^{iv}$

(b) No, because $-y_0 + 2y_1 + h^2 y_1''$ is the only
polynomial of the given form which agrees
with y_2 through terms in h^3.

Section 5.7

2. $(E^3 - 9E^2 + 26E - 24)y = x^2$

4. $(E^2 - E - 1)y = 0$

10. $y_0 = 1$, $y_1 = 0$, $y_2 = 2$, $y_3 = 3$, $y_4 = 1$, $y_5 = 0$

12. $y_0 = 0$, $y_1 = 1$, $y_2 = 2$, $y_3 = 2$, $y_4 = -4$,
$y_5 = -20$

14. $y_0 = 0$, $y_1 = 0$, $y_2 = 0$, $y_3 = 4$, $y_5 = 9$

(b) $S_n = \dfrac{\sin r + \sin rn - \sin r(n+1)}{2(1-\cos r)}, r \neq 2j\pi,$

$\quad j = 1, 2, 3, \ldots$

(c) $S_n = \dfrac{-1 + \cos r + \cos rn - \cos r(n+1)}{2(1-\cos r)}, r \neq 2j\pi$

$\quad j = 1, 2, 3, \ldots$

16.

y_{-2}	y_{-1}	y_0	y_1	y_2	y_3	y_4	y_5
$\frac{23}{2}$	$\frac{11}{2}$	1	2	$\frac{1}{4}$	$\frac{31}{12}$	$-\frac{3}{4}$	$\frac{65}{4}$

18. $y = c_1 3^n + c_2 n 3^n + \frac{3}{2}$

40. $V_n = \dfrac{V_0}{1+2^{2N+1}} \left[\dfrac{2^{2N+1}}{2^n} + 2^n \right]$

20. $y = c_1 2^n + c_2 (-2)^n + c_3 n(-2)^n + \frac{3^n}{25}$

42. $V_n = V_0 \dfrac{\sinh(N-n)\mu}{\sinh N\mu}, \cosh\mu = 1 + \frac{1}{2k}$

22. $y = c_1 + c_2(-3)^n + \frac{1}{2}$

44. $x_n = \dfrac{\sinh n\mu}{2k\cosh\left(N+\frac{1}{2}\right)\mu \sinh(\mu/2)},$

$\quad \cosh\mu = 1 + \frac{\lambda}{2}$

24. $y = c_1 2^n + 2^{n/2}\left(c_2 \cos\frac{n\pi}{4} + c_3 \sin\frac{n\pi}{4}\right) - n + 2$

26. $y = c_1 + c_2 2^n + n2^{n-1} + \frac{4}{3} 2^{-n}$

48. The form of y shows that it should (but probably does not) satisfy the difference equation $y_{n+2} - (a+b)y_{n+1} + aby_n = 0$. Evaluating this equation for each of the n pairs (x_i, y_i), $i = 1, \ldots n$, gives n equations from which $a+b$ and ab can be found by standard least-square methods.

Subsequently, with a and b, and therefore e^a and e^b, known, A and B can be found similarly from the n equations

$y_i = A(e^a)^{x_i} + B(e^b)^{x_i}.$

When y is the sum of more than two exponentials, the only difference is that it satisfies a difference equation of higher order.

28. $y = c_1 2^n + c_2 n 2^n + n^2 2^{n-3}$

30. $y = c_1 \cos\frac{n\pi}{2} + c_2 \sin\frac{n\pi}{2}$

$\quad + 3^n\left(c_3 \cos\frac{n\pi}{2} + c_4 \sin\frac{n\pi}{2}\right)$

$\quad + \frac{1}{82}\left(8\cos\frac{n\pi}{4} + 5\sin\frac{n\pi}{4}\right)$

36. (a) $D_n = -2^{n+2} + 3^{n+2}$

(b) $D_n = -2^{n+1} + 3^{n+1}$

(c) $D_n = 2^n + n2^n$

(d) $D_n = 2^n\left(\cos\frac{n\pi}{3} + \frac{1}{\sqrt{3}}\sin\frac{n\pi}{3}\right)$

50. (a) $b_n = \dfrac{1}{2^{(n+2)/2}}\left(\cos\frac{n\pi}{4} + \sin\frac{n\pi}{4}\right)$

(b) $b_n = \dfrac{\sin(n+1)\theta}{\sin\theta}$

52. $y_n = -4n3^n + 2^n$, $z_n = 4n3^n + 4(3^n) - 2^{n+1}$

38. (a) $S_n = \dfrac{r + [n(r-1)-1]r^{n+1}}{(r-1)^2}, r \neq 1;$

$\quad S_n = \dfrac{n(n+1)}{2}, r = 1$

56. $y_k = c_1 + c_2 6^k - \frac{1}{5}\sum\limits_{i=1}^{k-1} i + \frac{1}{30}\sum\limits_{i=1}^{k-1} i/6^i$

58. $c_1 \begin{bmatrix} 1 \\ -3 \end{bmatrix} 2^k + c_2 \begin{bmatrix} k \\ -2-3k \end{bmatrix} 2^k$

60. $y_k = \frac{1}{3} \begin{bmatrix} 5 \\ -3 \end{bmatrix} \sum\limits_{n=1}^{k} \ln nc + \frac{(-2)^k}{3}$

$\cdot \begin{bmatrix} 4 \\ -3 \end{bmatrix} \sum\limits_{n=1}^{k} (-2)^{-n} \ln nc$

Section 5.8

2. The solution obtained by Euler's method is
$y = c(1+ah)^{(x_n - x_0)/h}$ which approaches the true solution $y = ce^{Ax}$ for all values of A as $h \to 0$.

Section 5.9

2. $y_n = 3 \times 2^{n-2} + \frac{7}{3}(-2)^{n-2} - \frac{1}{3}$

4. $y_n = \frac{4}{\sqrt{3}} \left[3^n \sin \frac{2(n+1)\pi}{3} \right] + \frac{14}{\sqrt{3}} \left[3^{n-1} \sin \frac{2n\pi}{3} \right]$

6. $y_n = -\frac{1}{7}(-4)^n + \frac{1}{7} 3^n$

8. $y_n = 3^n \frac{\sin(n+1)\phi}{\sin \phi} + 7 \times 3^{n-1} \frac{\sin n\phi}{\sin \phi}$

$z_n = -3^{n+1} \frac{\sin(n+1)\phi}{\sin \phi} - 16 \times 3^{n-1} \frac{\sin n\phi}{\sin \phi}$

10. $y_n = 4(n+1)(-3)^n + 24n(-3)^{n-1}$

$z_n = -(n+1)(-3)^n + 3n(-3)^{n-1}$

12. (a) $f_n = 0, 1, 1, 1, \ldots$

(b) $f_n = 0, 0, 1, 1, \ldots$

20. $G(\cos na) = \frac{1}{1+a^2 n^2 s^2}$

22. $G[\cos(n+1)a] = \frac{\cos a}{1+a^2 n^2 s^2} - \frac{\sin^2 a}{1-2s\cos a + s^2}$

24. $G[\cos(na+b)] = \frac{\cos b}{1+a^2 n^2 s^2} - \frac{\sin a \sin b}{1-2s\cos a + s^2}$

26. $G^{-1}\left[\frac{F(s)}{1-s} \right] = \sum\limits_{j=0}^{n} y_{n-j}$

28. $y_n(t) = \int_0^t \frac{a^n (t-u)^n}{n!} f'(u)\,du + \sum\limits_{j=0}^{n} \frac{a^j t^j g_{n-j}}{j!}$

30. $G(e^{aTn}) = \frac{1}{1-e^{aT}s}, \quad z\left(e^{aTn}\right) = \frac{z}{z-e^{aT}}$

32. $G\left(e^{at} \sin bt\right) = \frac{\left(e^a \sin b\right)s}{1-2\left(e^a \cos b\right)s + e^{2a}s}$

34. $G[(n+r)f_n] = \frac{1}{s^{r-1}} \frac{d}{ds}\left[s^r G(f_n) \right]$

Chapter 6

Section 6.2

2. $(0, 2), (1, 5)$

4. $(0, 0), (1, 1), (2, 2)$

6. $x = c_1 e^{-t} + c_2^{-2t}$,
$y = -c_1 e^{-t} - 2 c_2^{-2t}$;
$x + y = k(2x + y)^2$

8. $x = c_1 \cos 2t + c_2 \sin 2t$,
$y = 2 c_2 \cos 2t - 2 c_1 \sin 2t$;
$4x^2 + y^2 = 4$

10. $x = c_1 \cos t - c_2 \sin t$,
$y = c_2 \cos t + c_1 \sin t$;
$x^2 + y^2 = k^2$

12. $x = c_1 e^{2t} + c_2 e^{-2t}$,
$y = 3 c_1 e^{2t} - c_2 e^{-2t}$; $(x + y)(3x - y) = k$

14. Just one, by the Fundamental Existence and Uniqueness Theorem.

16. $A = 4$, $B = 1$. The trajectory is the positive half of the line $y = x/4$.

Section 6.3

2. Spiral point, unstable

4. Spiral point, unstable

6. Spiral point, stable

8. $\triangle > 0$, asymptotically stable node; $\triangle = 0$, asymptotically stable node; $\triangle < 0$, asymptotically stable sprial point if $c \neq 0$, stable (but not asymptotically stable) center if $c = 0$.

Section 6.4

2. Either a center or a spiral point; stability cannot be determined by Theorem 2.

4. Spiral point, asymptotically stable

6. Node, asymptotically stable

8. Node, asymptotically stable

10. $x = c/(y + \sin y)$

12. $(1, -1)$, node, asymptotically stable; $(\frac{3}{2}, 0)$, saddle point, necessarily unstable.

14. $(1, 1)$, node, asymptotically stable; $(-1, -1)$, saddle point; necessarily unstable.

20. $\frac{dx}{dt} = y$, $\frac{dx}{dt} = \frac{1}{m} F(x)$

26. Let $h_1 = V(x_1)$ be an arbitrary value of h in the domain of V. Then the trajectory correspond-ing to h_1 is a hyperbola-like arc, passing through the point (x_1, h_1) and convex toward the direction in which V is increasing.

28. $V(x) = -x^2 - x^4$ has a maximum at the critical point $(0, 0)$. Hence by Exercise 24, $(0, 0)$ is a saddle point, and necessarily unstable.

30. The system has three critical points: $(0, 0)$, $(-\sqrt{2}/2, 0)$, and $(\sqrt{2}/2, 0)$. Since $V(x) = -x^2 + x^4$ has a maximum at $(0, 0)$, this is a saddle point. Since V has neither a maximum nor a minimum at either of the other critical points, the results of Exercises 23 and 24 cannot be applied. However, after translating the origin to each of the other critical points in turn, Part 6, Theorem 1 can be applied, and it follows that each of these points is either a center or a spiral point. From the graphs of the required trajectories shown in the figure below, it appears that each is a center.

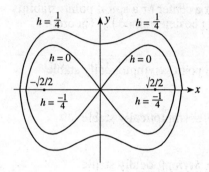

Section 6.6

2. $r = 1$, $\theta = -t - t_0$; semistable.

4. $r = 2$, $\theta = t + t_0$; unstable.

6. $r = 2m + 1$, $\theta = -t + t_0$, stable;

$r = 2m$, $\theta = -t + t_0$, unstable.

12. Each limit cycle is traversed in the counter-clockwise direction.

20. $\lambda > 1$

Section 6.5

2. Use $x^2 + y^2$

4. Use $x^2 + y^2$

6. $A = 1, B = -4$; $(0, 0)$ is unstable.

8. $A = B = 1$; $(0, 0)$ is at least stable.

10. $A = 2, B = 3$; $(0, 0)$ is asymptotically stable.

14. (a) Positive definite

(b) Positive definite

(c) Indefinite

(d) Positive semidefinite

(e) Indefinite

(f) Indefinite

(g) Positive semidefinite

(h) Indefinite

Chapter 7

Section 7.2

2. (a) $k = k_1 + k_2$

   (b) $k = k_1 + k_2$

4. In equilibrium the distance of the weight from the left-hand support is $\frac{k_1 l_1 + k_2(l - l_2)}{k_1 + k_2}$.
   The required differential equation is
   $\frac{w}{g}\ddot{x} + (k_1 + k_2)x = 0$ where x is the displacement from equilibrium.

6. $LC\frac{d^2 e_i}{dt^2} + RC\frac{de_i}{dt} + e_i = -\omega^2 LCE_0 \cos \omega t$

8. (b) $I\ddot{\theta} = -k\theta$

10. $\ddot{\theta} + \frac{2g}{\ell}\theta = 0$

12. $\ddot{\theta} + \frac{5g}{9(R-r)}\theta = 0$

Section 7.3

2. $b < 3$ for oscillatory motion; $b = 4(1 - \pi^2)$ for frequency of 1 Hz.

4. $y = \frac{1}{4}\left(5e^{-16t/5} - e^{-16t}\right)$ ft; y is never zero.

6. $y = e^{-6t}(-\cos 8t - \frac{1}{2}\sin 8t)$ in

8. $y = \frac{27}{4}e^{-8t} - \frac{19}{4}e^{-12t}$ inches

10. The resonant frequency is $\omega_r = \frac{8}{5}\sqrt{82}$.
    $Y = M\delta_{st}\cos(20t - \alpha)$ in where $M = \frac{16}{15}$,
    $\alpha = \tan^{-1}(-4/3)$, and $\delta_{st} = \frac{1}{8}$.

12. The resonant frequency is $\omega_r \doteq 24$
    $Y = M\delta_{st}\cos(24t - \alpha)$ in where $M = 50$,
    $\delta_{st} = \frac{1}{6}$, and $\alpha = \frac{\pi}{2}$.

14. $c_c = \frac{15}{4}$, $y = \frac{1}{106}e^{-48t/5}(25 + 240t)$

16. c/c_c must be increased to 0.256

18. $x = -\frac{5\sqrt{15}}{12}\sin\frac{4\sqrt{15}}{5}t$

20. The weight falls to a point $2w/k$ below its initial position. $y = -\frac{w}{k}(1 - \cos\sqrt{\frac{kg}{w}}t)$

26. $y = -e^{-6t}(\cos 8t + \frac{1}{2}\sin 8t)$

28. $y = -e^{-4.2t}(2\cos 14.4t + \frac{7}{12}\sin 14.4t)$

40. In the critically damped case, $t_{max} = 1/\omega_n$ and $y_{max} = v_0/\omega_n e$.

44. $y = \frac{25}{36}\sqrt{6/41}\sin(\frac{48}{5}t - \alpha)$, where
    $\alpha = \tan^{-1}\frac{4\sqrt{2}}{3}$

46. The magnification ratio is
    $$M = \frac{(\omega/\omega_n)2}{\sqrt{\left[1 - (\omega/\omega_n)^2\right]^2 + \left[2(\omega/\omega_n)(c/c_c)\right]^2}}$$
    and is to be applied to the static deflection produced in the system by a force equal to the amplitude of the disturbing force at the frequency ω_n. The phase angle is the same

[Eq. (13)] whether the amplitude of the excitation is constant or proportional to ω^2.

48. Period $= \tau = 2\pi\sqrt{a/\mu g}$. Hence $\mu = 4\pi^2 a/g\tau^2$.

50. $x = (x_0 - \frac{\mu w}{k})\cos \omega_n t + \frac{\mu w}{k} \quad 0 \leq t \leq \frac{2\pi}{\omega_n}$

$= -(x_0 - \frac{3\mu w}{k})\cos \omega_n(t - \frac{\pi}{\omega_n}) - \frac{\mu w}{k}$

$\frac{\pi}{\omega_n} \leq t \leq \frac{2\pi}{\omega_n}$

$= (x_0 - \frac{5\mu w}{k})\cos \omega_n(t - \frac{2\pi}{\omega_n}) + \frac{\mu w}{k}$

$\frac{2\pi}{\omega_n} \leq t \leq \frac{3\pi}{\omega_n} \cdots$

During each cycle the amplitude decreases by the constant amount $4\mu\omega/k$. The body will come to rest when the maximum amplitude is such that the spring force in that position is, for the first time equal to or less than the static frictional force, μw. Incidentally, the period of the motion with Coulomb damping is exactly the same as the period without any damping.

52. $y = \frac{1}{2}\delta_{st}(\sin \omega_n t - \omega_n t \cos \omega_n t)$,

$y_0 = -\frac{1}{2}\delta_{st}\omega_n t \cos \omega_n t$,

$y - y_0 = \frac{1}{2}\delta_{st}\sin \omega_n t$.

The limiting function y_0 gives the part of y that comes from just its second term.

54. $y_a = -\frac{\omega_n \delta_{st}}{2\varepsilon}\sin \omega_n t \sin \varepsilon t$

$y_0 = \lim_{\varepsilon \to 0} y_a = -\frac{1}{2}\omega_n\delta_{st}t \sin \omega_n t$

56. $M = \frac{3\sqrt{2}}{4}$, $k = 9$ lb/ft, $w = 18$ lb,

$y = \frac{1}{2}\cos(4t/\sqrt{3} - \pi/4)$ ft.

58. The amplitude of the steady-state response varies between the values

$\frac{F_1}{\omega^2 - \omega_1^2} - \frac{F_2}{\omega^2 - \omega_2^2}$ and $\frac{F_1}{\omega^2 - \omega_1^2} + \frac{F_2}{\omega^2 - \omega_2^2}$

60. Work/cycle $= M\delta_{st}\pi F_0\sin \alpha$

64. $0 \leq \omega \leq \sqrt{2}\omega_r$, $0 \leq c/c_c \leq 1/\sqrt{2}$

Section 7.4

2. 0.116 watt-sec

4. $i = -\frac{10^5}{64}t\exp(-10^5 t/8)$

6. $i = \frac{1}{28}\left[-e^{-5,000t} + e^{-1,000t/3}\right]$

8. $i = \frac{5}{6400}e^{-2,500t} + \frac{125}{16}te^{-2,500t} - \frac{5}{6400}e^{-500t}$

10. $i = \dfrac{e^{-400t}(-1,728\cos 300t + 1,754\sin 300t)}{12,125}$

$+ \dfrac{1,728\cos 600t + 396\sin 600t)}{12,125}$

12. $e = 2,500 te^{-500t}$

14. The electrical analog of δ_{st} is the quantity Q_{st} defined to be the charge on the condenser produced by a constant voltage equal to the amplitude E_0; i.e., $Q_s = E_0 C$.

16. The required particular integral is

$Q = \dfrac{-E_0 \cos(\omega t + \beta)}{\left(1/C - \omega^2 L\right)^2 + (\omega R)^2}$

18. (a) $Z = Z_1 + \dfrac{Z_2 Z_3}{Z_2 + Z_3}$

(b) $Z = \dfrac{Z_1 Z_2}{Z_1 + Z_2} + \dfrac{Z_3 Z_4}{Z_3 + Z_4}$

(c) $Z = \dfrac{Z_3(Z_1 + Z_2)}{Z_1 + Z_2 + Z_3}$

(d) Zero, since there is a zero-impedance path through the network.

22. $|Z| = R\sqrt{1 + Q^2\left(\frac{\Omega}{\Omega_n} - \frac{\Omega_n}{\Omega}\right)^2}$

$\delta = \text{Tan}^{-1}Q\left(\frac{\Omega}{\Omega_n} - \frac{\Omega_n}{\Omega}\right)$

24. $i_\infty = E/R$, when $t = L/R$

Section 7.5

2. $\omega_1^2 = 1$, $A_1:A_2 = 1:1$; $\omega_2^2 = 5$, $A_1:A_2 = 3:-1$

4. (a) $\omega_1^2 = \frac{1}{2}$, $A_1:A_2:A_3 = 1:2:2$

$\omega_2^2 = 1$, $A_1:A_2:A_3 = 1:0:-2$

$\omega_3^2 = 2$, $A_1:A_2:A_3 = 1:-4:2$

(b) $\omega_1^2 = 1$, $A_1:A_2:A_3 = 2:2:1$

$\omega_2^2 = 2$, $A_1:A_2:A_3 = -2:1:2$

$\omega_3^2 = 7$, $A_1:A_2:A_3 = 1:-2:2$

6. $x_1 = \frac{1}{3}\cos t + \frac{2}{3}\cos 2t$, $x_2 = \frac{1}{3}\cos t - \cos 2t$

8. $x_1 = \frac{5}{2}\sin t - 2\sin 2t + \frac{1}{2}\sin 3t$
$x_2 = 5\sin t + 2\sin 2t - 3\sin 3t$

10. At $\omega_1 = 6\sqrt{6}$,

$\begin{bmatrix} y \\ \theta \end{bmatrix} = \begin{bmatrix} 32 \\ 1 \end{bmatrix}(c_1\cos 6\sqrt{6}t + c_2\sin 6\sqrt{6}\ t)$

At $\omega_2 = 12\sqrt{5}$,

$\begin{bmatrix} y \\ \theta \end{bmatrix} = \begin{bmatrix} 8 \\ -3 \end{bmatrix}(c_3\cos 12\sqrt{5}t + c_4\sin 12\sqrt{5}t$

12. $x_1 = \frac{F_0}{4\sqrt{37}}\sin(3t + \alpha)$, where $\alpha = \text{Tan}^{-1}6$.

$x_2 = -\frac{F_0}{2\sqrt{74}}\sin(3t + \beta)$, where $\beta = \text{Tan}^{-1}\frac{5}{7}$.

M_1 leads F by $\alpha/3$ units of time. M_2 lags F by $(\pi - \beta)/3$ units of time.

16. $k_2 = \omega^2 M_2$, $a_2 = -F_0/k_2$. Friction introduced to reduce the amplitude of a_2 makes it impossible to keep M_1 strictly at rest, although its motion will be within acceptable limits.

18. $x_1 = \cos 9t + \cos 11t$, $x_2 = \cos 9t - \cos 11t$. Since these can be written in the form $x_1 = 2\cos 10t \cos t$ and $x_2 = 2\sin 10t \sin t$, it is clear that both x_1 and x_2 appear to vary with frequency $(\omega_1 + \omega_2)/2 = 10$ with slowly varying amplitudes $2\cos t$ and $2\sin t$ respectively. Thus the system exhibits the phenomenon of beats.

20. $y_1 = -F_0\dfrac{\omega^2 - 2}{4(\omega^2 - 1)(\omega^2 - 4)}\sin \omega t$

$y_2 = F_0\dfrac{2}{4(\omega^2 - 1)(\omega^2 - 4)}\sin \omega t$

The amplitudes of these expressions are functions of ω which become infinite as the impressed frequency ω approaches either of the natural frequencies $\omega = 1$ and $\omega = 2$. (These expressions are roughly analogous to the magnification ratio which we developed in Sec. 7.3.)

22. (a), (b) Since $\omega = 2$ is one of the natural frequencies of the system, the system is being driven at resonance, and the amplitudes of M_1 and M_2 become infinite, as expected.

(c) The expression for y_1 and y_2 assume the indeterminate form 0/0.
If the force $F = \sin \omega t$ is applied simultaneously to M_1 and M_2, the solution is

$y_1 = \dfrac{-(\omega^2 - 4)\sin \omega t}{4(\omega^2 - 1)(\omega^2 - 4)}$, $y_2 = \dfrac{-(\omega^2 - 4)\sin \omega t}{2(\omega^2 - 1)(\omega^2 - 4)}$,

$\omega \neq 1, 2$
As $\omega \to 2$, the limits of y_1 and y_2 exist and are $y_1 = \dfrac{-\sin 2t}{4(\omega^2 - 1)}$ and $y_2 = \dfrac{-\sin 2t}{2(\omega^2 - 1)}$ $\omega \neq 1$
Thus, under special circumstances, a system may be driven at resonance without infinite amplitudes building up.

24. $i_1 = \dfrac{Q_0}{60\sqrt{LC}}\left(16\sin\dfrac{t}{3\sqrt{LC}} + \sin\dfrac{t}{12\sqrt{LC}}\right)$

$i_2 = \dfrac{Q_0}{20\sqrt{LC}}\left(4\sin\dfrac{t}{3\sqrt{LC}} - \sin\dfrac{t}{12\sqrt{LC}}\right)$

26. (a) $\begin{bmatrix} i_1 \\ i_2 \end{bmatrix} = \begin{bmatrix} 17 \\ 0 \end{bmatrix} - \begin{bmatrix} 8 \\ 6 \end{bmatrix}e^{-20t} + \begin{bmatrix} -9 \\ 6 \end{bmatrix}e^{-3t}, A$

As $t \to \infty, i_1 \to 17A$ and $i_2 \to 0$.

(b) $\begin{bmatrix} i_1 \\ i_2 \end{bmatrix} = E_0\sqrt{\dfrac{C}{L}}\left(\dfrac{1}{80}\begin{bmatrix} 243 \\ 216 \end{bmatrix}\sin\dfrac{3t}{\sqrt{LC}} + \dfrac{1}{240}\right.$

$\left. \bullet \begin{bmatrix} -1 \\ 8 \end{bmatrix}\sin\dfrac{t}{3\sqrt{LC}} - \begin{bmatrix} 1 \\ 1 \end{bmatrix}\sin\dfrac{t}{\sqrt{LC}}\right)$

28. The respective currents are

$i_1 = \dfrac{1}{Z}E_0 e^{j\omega t}, \quad i_2 = \dfrac{Z^*}{ZZ_4}E_0 e^{j\omega t},$

$i_3 = \dfrac{Z^*}{ZZ_3}E_0 e^{j\omega t}, \quad i_4 = \dfrac{Z^*}{ZZ_4}E_0 e^{j\omega t},$ where

$Z = \dfrac{Z_1 Z_2 Z_3 + Z_1 Z_2 Z_4 + Z_1 Z_3 Z_4 + Z_2 Z_3 Z_4}{Z_2 Z_3 + Z_3 Z_1 + Z_1 Z_2}$ is the

impedance of the entire system, and

$Z^* = \dfrac{Z_2 Z_3 Z_4}{Z_2 Z_3 + Z_3 Z_4 + Z_4 Z_2}$ is the impedance of

the three parallel branches.

30. (a) $i = \dfrac{E_0\left(1-\omega^2 LC\right)\left[R\left(1-\omega^2 LC\right)\cos\omega t + \omega L\sin\omega t\right]}{R^2\left(1-\omega^2 LC\right)^2 + \omega^2 L^2}$

(b) $i = \dfrac{E_0\left(1-\omega^2 LC\right)\left[-\omega L\cos\omega t + R\left(1-\omega^2 LC\right)\sin\omega t\right]}{R^2\left(1-\omega^2 LC\right)^2 + \omega^2 L^2}$

32. $\omega_1^2 = 1/4LC, \quad \omega_2^2 = 9/LC$

34. $\omega_1^2 = 5/9LC, \quad \omega_2^2 = 4/LC$

Section 7.6

2. In the definition of μ, $\cos\mu$ had to be between -1 and 1, exclusive, in order for periodic solutions to exist. If $N = n$, $\mu_N = \pi$, which contradicts this requirement.

4.

n	5	10	15
θ_n / θ_0	-1.25	3.60	1.18

8. $\omega_n = 2\sqrt{\dfrac{k}{m}}\sin\dfrac{(2N+1)\pi}{(2n+1)2}, \quad N = 0, 1, \ldots, n-1$

$\left(a_{n-j}\right)_N = \sin\left(\dfrac{2N+1}{2n+1}\pi j\right) - \sin\left[\dfrac{2N+1}{2n+1}\pi(j-1)\right]$

10. $\omega_N = 2\sqrt{\dfrac{c}{I}}\sin\dfrac{2N\pi}{2n+1}; \; \left(A_k\right)_N$ is proportional

to $\cos\dfrac{2Nk\pi}{2n+1}$ for $N = 1, 2, \ldots, n$

12. For a wave of frequency ω to pass through the system, ω must satisfy the inequality

$\sqrt{\dfrac{K}{I}} < \omega < \sqrt{\dfrac{K}{I}\left(1 + \dfrac{4c}{k}\right)}$.

14. As μ, and hence ω, approaches zero, the velocity of the wave approaches $\ell\sqrt{\dfrac{c}{I}}$, where ℓ is the distance between consecutive disks. In this case, the length of the wave becomes infinite. The maximum value of μ is π, when $\omega = 2\sqrt{\dfrac{c}{I}}$, and in this case there is a standing wave of length 2ℓ.

16. There is a wave of length $2\pi\,\ell/\mu$ and velocity $\ell\,\omega/\mu$, where ℓ is the distance between the "rungs" of the ladder and $\cos\mu = 1 + \dfrac{L}{2C}$.

20. All values are given by $\left|\sin\dfrac{N\pi}{2n}\right|$

$N = 0, 1, 2, \ldots, n$

Section 7.7

4. $\dfrac{d^2X}{dT^2} + \dfrac{c}{Iv^2}\dfrac{dX}{dT} + \dfrac{k}{Iv^2}X = \dfrac{T_0}{I\alpha v^2}\cos\dfrac{\omega}{v}T$ where v is an arbitrary frequency, α is an arbitrary angle, and $X = \theta/\alpha$ and $T = vt$ are dimensionless variables.

6.
$$\frac{d^2 X_1}{dT^2} + \frac{R}{L_1 v}\frac{dX_1}{dT} + \frac{C_1 + C_2}{C_1 C_2 L_1 v^2} X_1$$

$$-\frac{q_2}{C_1 L_1 q_1 v^2} X_2 = 0$$

$$-\frac{q_1}{C_2 L_2 q_2 v^2} X_1 + \frac{d^2 X_2}{dT^2} + \frac{1}{C_2 L_2 v^2} X_2$$

$$= \frac{E_0}{L_2 q_2 v^2}\cos\frac{\omega}{v} T$$

where v is an arbitrary frequency, q_1 and q_2 are arbitrary charges, $X_i = Q/q_i$ and $T = vt$.

8. (a)

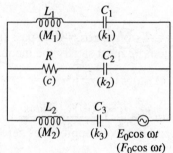

(b)

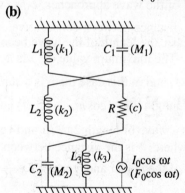

10. (a)

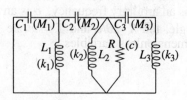

(b)

12. (a)

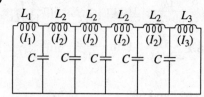

(b)

Chapter 8

Section 8.1

2. **(a)** $62°$ and $68°$

   (b) 6 hr

   (c) $t = \frac{3}{2} + 6n$ hr

4. $k = b/p$

6. No; consider $f(x) = \sin\frac{\pi x}{p} + \cos\frac{2\pi x}{p}$ and

   $g(x) = -\sin\frac{\pi x}{p} + \sin\frac{2\pi x}{p}$.

   No; consider $f(x) = \sin\frac{\pi x}{p}$ and $g(x) = \cos\frac{\pi x}{p}$.

8. $2p$

12. $1/500$

14. **(a)** The set of positive integers.

    (b) -1

    (c) 2

Section 8.2

2. $f(t) = \frac{4}{\pi}[\sin t + \frac{\sin 3t}{3} + \frac{\sin 5t}{5} + \ldots]$

4. $a_0 = \frac{5}{4}$, $a_n = -\frac{1}{n\pi}\sin\frac{3n\pi}{4}$

   $b_n = -\frac{1}{n\pi}[1 - \cos\frac{3n\pi}{4}]$

6. $a_0 = 2$; $a_n = 0$, $n \neq 0$,

   $b_n = -\frac{1}{n\pi}[1 - 2\cos\frac{2n\pi}{3}]$

8. $f(t) = 1 - \frac{8}{\pi^2}\sum_{n=1}^{\infty}\frac{1}{(2n+1)^2}\cos\frac{(2n+1)\pi t}{2}$

10. $f(t) = 1 - \frac{8}{\pi^2}\sum_{n=1}^{\infty}\frac{1}{(2n+1)^2}\cos\frac{(2n+1)\pi t}{2}$

12. $f(t) = \frac{2}{\pi} + \frac{4}{\pi}\sum_{n=1}^{\infty}\frac{(-1)^{n+1}}{4n^2-1}\cos 2nt$

16. $f(t) = \frac{a^2}{6} - \frac{a^2}{\pi^2}\sum_{n=1}^{\infty}\frac{1}{n^2}\cos\frac{2n\pi t}{a}$

18. $f(t) = \frac{1}{2}\sin\frac{\pi t}{2} + \frac{4}{\pi}\sum_{n=1}^{\infty}\frac{(-1)^{n+1}n\sin n\pi t}{4n^2-1}$

20. $\frac{1}{16}(10\sin t - 5\sin 3t + \sin 5t)$

24. $\frac{2\sinh\pi}{\pi}\left[\frac{1}{2} + \sum_{n=1}^{\infty}\frac{(-1)^n}{n^2+1}(\cos nt - n\sin nt)\right]$;

    $\frac{\pi}{2\sinh\pi}$

Section 8.3

2. $a_0 = \frac{1}{p}$, $a_n = \frac{1}{n\pi}\sin\frac{n\pi}{p}$, $b_n = \frac{1}{n\pi}\left(1 - \cos\frac{n\pi}{p}\right)$

4. $a_n \equiv 0$, $b_{2n} = -\frac{1}{n\pi}$, $b_{2n-1} = \frac{6}{(2n-1)\pi}$

6. $a_0 = -2/3$ $a_n =$

   $\frac{4}{n^2\pi^2}(-1)^{n+1}$, $b_n = \frac{2}{n\pi}(-1)^{n+1}$

8. $\frac{5}{3} + \frac{16}{\pi^2} \sum_{n=1}^{\infty} \frac{(-1)^{n+1}}{n^2} \cos \frac{n\pi t}{2}$

10. $a_0 = \frac{4}{3}$, $a_n = \frac{2}{n^2\pi^2}(-1)^n$, $b_{2n} = -\frac{1}{2n\pi}$,

$b_{2n-1} = \frac{3(2n-1)^2\pi^2 - 4}{(2n-1)^3\pi^3}$

12. $a_0 = -\frac{1}{3}$, $a_{2n} = -\frac{2}{n^2\pi^2}$, $a_{2n-1} = \frac{-4}{(2n-1)^2\pi^2}$,

$b_{2n} = -\frac{1}{n\pi}$, $b_{2n-1} = -\frac{2[8+(2n-1)^2\pi^2]}{(2n-1)^3\pi^3}$

14. $\frac{\pi^4}{5} + 8\sum_{n=1}^{\infty}(-1)^n\left[\frac{n^2\pi^2 - 6}{n^4}\right]\cos nt$

16. $a_0 = \frac{4}{\pi}$, $a_n = -\frac{4}{(4n^2-1)\pi}$, $b_n \equiv 0$.

18. $b_n = \frac{2n\pi(-1)^{n+1}\sinh a}{n^2\pi^2 + a^2}$

20. $a_1 = \frac{1}{2}$, $a_n = 0$, $n \neq 1$;

$b_{2n} = \frac{4n}{(4n^2-1)\pi}$, $b_{2n-1} = 0$

22. $a_0 = \frac{4+\pi}{2\pi}$, $a_1 = -\frac{2+\pi}{4\pi}$, $b_1 = \frac{2+\pi}{4\pi}$,

and for $n > 1$,

$a_{4n} = \frac{-2}{\pi(4n-1)(4n+1)}$

$a_{4n-1} = \frac{-1}{2\pi(2n-1)(4n-1)}$, $a_{4n-2} = 0$

$a_{4n-3} = \frac{-1}{2\pi(2n-1)(4n-3)}$

$b_{4n} = 0$, $b_{4n-1} = \frac{-1}{2\pi(4n-1)(2n-1)}$

$b_{4n-2} = \frac{1}{\pi(2n-1)(4n-1)(4n-3)}$

$b_{4n-3} = \frac{1}{2\pi(2n-1)(4n-3)}$

24. The coefficients will decrease as fast as c/n^2, but no faster.

26. The coefficients will decrease as fast as c/n^3, but no faster.

28. The coefficients decrease as fast as c/n^4, but no faster.

30. $a = 1$, $b = -2$. Since the expansion is

$t^2(1-t)^2 = \frac{1}{30} - \frac{3}{\pi^4} \sum_{n=1}^{\infty} \frac{1}{n^4} \cos 2n\pi t$ we have

on evaluating this for $t = 0$, $\frac{\pi^4}{90} = \sum \frac{1}{n^4}$

32. The function is continuous but its derivative has at least one discontinuity.

34. Since $f(t) = \frac{\pi}{2} - \frac{4}{\pi} \sum_{n=1}^{\infty} \frac{\cos(2n-1)t}{(2n-1)^2}$, and since the natural circular frequency of the system is 15 rad/s, $f(t)$ will produce a condition of pure resonance because of the presence of the term containing $\cos 15t$.

36. Since $f(t) = \frac{4}{\pi} \sum_{n=1}^{\infty} \frac{\sin(2n-1)t}{(2n-1)}$, the term containing $\sin 15t$ will produce a condition of pure resonance.

38. Yes, because $\omega_2 = 2$, the Fourier expansion of f contains a term involving $\cos 2t$, and friction is negligible.

Section 8.4

2. For the half-range cosine series, $a_0 = \frac{1}{2}$,

$a_n = \frac{2}{n\pi} \sin \frac{n\pi}{4}$

For the half-range sine series,

$b_n = \frac{2}{n\pi}(1 - \cos\frac{n\pi}{4})$

4. $a_0 = \frac{2-p}{3}$, $a_n = \frac{6p}{n^2\pi^2}(1 - \cos\frac{n\pi}{3})$;

$b_n = \frac{2}{n^2\pi^2}\left\{n\pi\left[1 + (p-1)\cos\frac{n\pi}{3}\right] - 3p\sin\frac{n\pi}{3}\right\}$

6. A suitable translation of the horizontal axis will result in odd symmetry.

8. $\frac{4a}{\pi}\sum_{n=1}^{\infty}\frac{1}{2n-1}\sin(2n-1)\frac{\pi t}{p}$

10. $a_0 = 2(e-1)$, $a_n = \frac{2\left[(-1)^n e - 1\right]}{n^2\pi^2 + 1}$, $b_n \equiv 0$

12. $\frac{1}{3} + \frac{4}{\pi^2}\sum_{n=1}^{\infty}\frac{(-1)^n}{n^2}\cos n\pi t + \frac{2}{\pi}\sum_{n=1}^{\infty}\frac{(-1)^{n+1}}{n}\sin n\pi t$

14. $\frac{3}{8} + \frac{1}{2}\cos 2\pi t + \frac{1}{8}\cos 4\pi t$

$+ \frac{2}{\pi}\sum_{n=1}^{\infty}\frac{(-1)^{n+1}}{n}\sin n\pi t$

16. $a_0 = 2$, $a_n = 0$, $n \neq 0$;

$b_{2n} = 0$, $b_{2n-1} = \frac{4}{(2n-1)\pi}$

18. $\frac{4}{\pi}\sum_{n=0}^{\infty}\frac{2n+1}{(2n+1)^2-4}\sin\frac{(2n+1)t}{2}$; $\cos t$

20. $a_0 = 2$, $a_n = \begin{cases} -2/n\pi & n = 1,5,9,\ldots \\ 0 & n = 2,4,6,\ldots \\ 2/n\pi & n = 3,7,11,\ldots \end{cases}$

$b_n = \begin{cases} -2/n\pi & n = 1,3,5,\ldots \\ -4/n\pi & n = 2,6,10,\ldots \\ 0 & n = 4,8,12,\ldots \end{cases}$

22. $a_0 = \frac{2}{p}(1 - e^{-p})$, $a_n = \frac{2p\left[1 - (-1)^n e^{-p}\right]}{n^2\pi^2 + p^2}$

$b_n = \frac{2n\pi\left[1 - (-1)^n e^{-p}\right]}{n^2\pi^2 + p^2}$

24. $a_n = (-1)^{n+1}\frac{2a\sin a\pi}{\pi(n^2 - a^2)}$

$b_n = \frac{2n\left[1 - (-1)^2\cos a\pi\right]}{\pi(n^2 - a^2)}$

28. $b_{2n+1} = \frac{8p}{4p^2 + (2n+1)^2\pi^2}\left[\frac{(2n+1)\pi}{2p}\right.$

$\left. - \frac{e^{-p}\sin(2n+1)\pi}{2}\right]$

30. a_n decreases as c/n^2, b_n decreases as c/n^3.

32. a_n decreases as c/n^2, b_n decreases as c/n^3.

34. $f(t) = \frac{1}{2} - \frac{11}{4}\left(x - \frac{3}{2}\right) + 10\left(x - \frac{3}{2}\right)^3 - 12\left(x - \frac{3}{2}\right)^5$,

$1 \leqq t \leqq 2$

38. $\frac{32}{\pi^3}\sum_{n=0}^{\infty}\frac{\sin\left(n+\frac{1}{2}\right)\pi t}{(2n+1)^3}$

40. $\sin a\left(\frac{\pi}{2} - x\right) = \frac{4a}{\pi}\sum_{n=0}^{\infty}\frac{\cos(2n-1)}{(2n-1)^2 - a^2}$

Section 8.5

2. $A_0 = \frac{p}{4}$, $A_{2n-1} = \frac{p}{(2n-1)^2\pi^2}\sqrt{(2n-1)^2 + 4}$,

$A_{2n} = \frac{p}{n\pi}$, $\gamma_{2n-1} = \tan^{-1}(p/n\pi)$,

$\delta_{2n-1} = \tan^{-1}(-n\pi/p)$, $\gamma_{2n} = \frac{\pi}{2}$, $\delta_{2n} = 0$

4. $A_0 = \frac{p}{12}$, $A_{2n-1} = \frac{4p^2}{n^3\pi^3}$, $A_{2n} = \frac{2p^2}{n^2\pi^2}$

$\gamma_{2n-1} = \frac{\pi}{2}$, $\delta_{2n-1} = 0$; $\gamma_{2n} = \pi$, $\delta_{2n} = -\frac{\pi}{2}$

6. $A_0 = \frac{1}{3}$, $A_n = \frac{2}{n^2\pi^2}\sqrt{n^2\pi^2+4}$;

$\gamma_n = \tan^{-1}(-n\pi/2)$, $\delta_n = \tan^{-1}(-2/n\pi)$

8. $f(t) = \frac{1}{2} + \sum_{n=-\infty}^{n=\infty} \frac{1-e^{-ni\pi}}{2ni\pi}e^{ni\pi t}$

10. $f(t) = \frac{1}{2} + \sum_{n=-\infty}^{n=\infty} \frac{i}{2n\pi}e^{2ni\pi t}$

12. $f(t) = \sum_{n=-\infty}^{n=\infty} \frac{2(-1)^n}{\pi(1-4n^2)}e^{2nit}$, $c_0 = 0$

14. $f(t) = \sum_{n=-\infty}^{n=\infty} \frac{ni\pi(-1)^n\sinh(1)}{1+n^2\pi^2}e^{ni\pi t}$, $c_0 = 0$

16. $f(t) = \frac{3}{2} - \sum_{n=-\infty}^{n=\infty} \frac{i}{(2n-1)\pi}e^{(2n-1)\pi it/2}$

18. $\sum_{n=1}^{\infty} \frac{8}{\pi^3(2n-1)^3}\sin(2n-1)\pi t$

20. $c_{2n-1} = \frac{4}{[(2n-1)\pi]^3}e^{-i\pi/2}$,

$c_{-(2n-1)} = \frac{4}{[(2n-1)\pi]^3}e^{i\pi/2}$

Section 8.6

2. $y_{ss} \doteq 0.36\sin(2\pi t - 0.040)$
$+ 0.74\sin(6\pi t - 2.316)$

$+ 0.031\sin(10\pi t - 3.056)$
$+ 0.01\sin(14\pi t - 3.056) + \ldots$

4. $y_{ss} = F_0[\frac{1}{64} + 0.0103\sin(\pi t - 0.020)$
$+ 0.0051\sin(3\pi t - 0.090)$
$+ 0.0193\sin(5\pi t - 1.217)$
$+ 0.0016\sin(7\pi t - 2.988)\ \ldots]$

6. $y_{ss} = F_0\left[\frac{1}{6} + 0.227\sin(\pi t - 0.056)\right.$
$+ 0.171\sin(3\pi t - 0.389)$
$+ 0.056\sin(5\pi t - 2.790)$
$+ 0.013\sin(7\pi t - 2.987) + \ \ldots]$

8. $y_{ss} = F_0[0.011\sin(2\pi t - 0.136)$
$- 0.019\sin(4\pi t - 1.708)$
$+ 0.002\sin(6\pi t - 2.197) + \ \ldots]$

10. The complete solution will originally appear in the form $y = c_1y_1 + c_2y_2 + Y$ where Y is the Fourier series obtained as the answer to Example 1. Imposing initial conditions of displacement and velocity will thus lead to a pair of simultaneous linear equations in c_1 and c_2 in which the constant terms will involve the infinite series which result from the evaluation of Y and Y' when $t = 0$. Although there is no theoretical problem in determining c_1 and c_2 from these equations, the arithmetic complications are obvious.

12. The result is simply $I(t) = \frac{E(t)}{R}$, that is,

$$I(t) = E_0\left[\frac{1}{2R} - \frac{1}{\pi R}\sum_{n=-\infty}^{n=\infty} \frac{i}{2n-1}e^{200(2n-1)i\pi t}\right]$$

where now, since the capacitor is no longer in the circuit, the constant voltage component appears in the solution.

14. $i_{ss} = 2E_0 \sum_{n=-\infty}^{n=\infty} \frac{ie^{200ni\pi t}}{250n\pi + i(4n^2\pi^2 - 2{,}500)}$, $n \neq 0$

16. (a) $i_{ss} = \dfrac{E_0}{2,000} \displaystyle\sum_{n=-\infty}^{n=\infty} \dfrac{ie^{100ni\pi t}}{5n\pi + 2i(n^2\pi^2 - 25)}$, $n \neq 0$

(b) $i_{ss} = \displaystyle\sum_{n=-\infty}^{n=\infty} \dfrac{200ne^{100ni\pi t}}{(1-4n^2)\left[100n\pi + i(40n^2\pi^2 - 1,000)\right]}$, $n \neq 0$

18. (a) $y(t) = \left[\dfrac{\pi}{2} - \dfrac{4}{\pi} \displaystyle\sum_{n=1}^{\infty} \overline{(2n-1)^4 + (2n-1)^2} \right]$

$\bullet \cosh t - \dfrac{\pi}{2} + \dfrac{4}{\pi} \displaystyle\sum_{n=1}^{\infty} \dfrac{\cos(2n-1)t}{(2n-1)^4 + (2n-1)^2}$

(b) $y(t) = \sinh t + \left[-\dfrac{\pi}{2} + \dfrac{4}{\pi} \displaystyle\sum_{n=1}^{\infty} \dfrac{1}{(2n-1)^3 + (2n-1)^2} \right]$

$\bullet \cosh t + \dfrac{\pi}{2} - \dfrac{4}{\pi} \displaystyle\sum_{n=1}^{\infty} \dfrac{\cos(2n-1)t}{(2n-1)^3 + (2n-1)^2}$

(c) $y(t) = \left[-\dfrac{\pi}{8} - \dfrac{4}{\pi} \displaystyle\sum_{n=1}^{\infty} \dfrac{1}{(2n-1)^4 - 4(2n-1)^2} \right]$

$\bullet \cos 2t + \dfrac{\pi}{8} + \dfrac{4}{\pi} \displaystyle\sum_{n=1}^{\infty} \dfrac{\cos(2n-1)t}{(2n-1)^4 - 4(2n-1)^2}$

(d) $y(t) = \left[-\dfrac{\pi}{18} + \dfrac{1}{2\pi} - \dfrac{4}{\pi} \displaystyle\sum_{n=1}^{\infty} \dfrac{1}{(2n-1)^4 - 9(2n-1)^2} \right]$

$\bullet \cos 3t + \dfrac{\pi}{18}$

$- \dfrac{4}{\pi}\left[\dfrac{\cos t}{8} + \dfrac{t\sin t}{54} - \displaystyle\sum_{n=1}^{\infty} \dfrac{\cos(2n-1)t}{(2n-1)^4 - 9(2n-1)^2} \right]$

20. $a = 4e - 10 \doteq 0.873$,
$b = -6e + 18 \doteq 1.690$

22. (a) $b = \dfrac{5}{13} \doteq 0.385$; approximation to first intercept of cos x: 1.612.

(b) $b = 20/(3\pi^2 + 40) \doteq 0.287$, approximation to first intercept of cos x: 1.866

(c) $b = \dfrac{40}{176} \doteq 0.227$, approximation to first intercept of cos x: 2.098.

24. $y(x) = -\dfrac{4P_0\ell^4}{EI\pi^5} \displaystyle\sum_{n=1}^{\infty} \dfrac{\sin(2n-1)\pi x/\ell}{(2n-1)^5}$

26. $y(x) = \dfrac{8P_0\ell^4}{EI\pi^6} \displaystyle\sum_{n=1}^{\infty} (-1)^{n+1} \dfrac{1}{(2n+1)^6} \sin\dfrac{(2n-1)\pi x}{\ell}$

28. $y(x) = -\dfrac{\ell^4}{EI\pi^5}\left[(\pi + 4)\sin\dfrac{\pi x}{\ell} \right.$

$\left. + 4 \displaystyle\sum_{n=2}^{\infty} (-1)\dfrac{\sin(2n-1)\pi x/\ell}{(2n-1)^5} \right]$, $0 \leqq x \leqq \ell$

30. $y(x) = \dfrac{P_0\ell^3}{EI\pi^4} \displaystyle\sum_{n=1}^{\infty} \dfrac{1}{n^4} \sin\dfrac{n\pi}{2} \sin\dfrac{n\pi x}{\ell}$

32. They would encounter frequency ranges in which the points they plotted fell approximately on lines of slope –3, –4, . . .

34. $a_n = \dfrac{2}{\pi} \sin\dfrac{n\pi}{2} \cos\dfrac{n\pi}{4a} \dfrac{8a^2}{n(4a^2 - n^2)}$,

$n \neq 2a$; $a_{2a} = 0$. If $n \gg a$, then $a_n \sim c/n^3$, as it should, since $f'(t)$ is everywhere continuous. If $a \gg n$, then $a_n \sim ca^2/n(4a^2 - n^2) \sim c*/n$, which is to be expected, since for large a the function appears to have an abrupt jump at $t = 1$.

36. $y(x) = -\dfrac{2P_0\ell^2}{aT\pi^3} \displaystyle\sum_{n=1}^{\infty} \dfrac{1}{3} \sin\dfrac{n\pi}{2} \sin\dfrac{n\pi a}{\ell} \sin\dfrac{n\pi x}{\ell}$

At $a \to 0$, this becomes

$-\dfrac{2P_0\ell}{T\pi^2}\displaystyle\sum_{n=1}^{\infty}\dfrac{1}{n^2}\sin\dfrac{n\pi}{2}\sin\dfrac{n\pi x}{\ell}$ which gives the deflection of the string when a force of magnitude P_0 acts on the string at its midpoint.

38. $y(x)=\dfrac{4P_0\ell^3}{\pi^4 T}\displaystyle\sum_{n=0}^{\infty}\dfrac{(-1)^n}{(2n+1)^2}\sin\dfrac{(2n+1)\pi}{\ell}$

Chapter 9

Section 9.1

2. (a) $A(\omega) = \frac{2}{\pi} \frac{1+e^{-1}(\omega \sin \omega - \cos \omega)}{1+\omega^2}$,

$$f(t) = \frac{2}{\pi e} \int_0^\infty \frac{e+\omega \sin \omega - \cos \omega}{1+\omega^2} \cos \omega t \, d\omega$$

(b) $A_p(\omega) = \frac{2}{\pi} \frac{1-e^{-p}\cos p\omega}{1+\omega^2}$,

$$f(t) = \frac{2}{\pi} \int_0^\infty \frac{\cos \omega t}{1+\omega^2} d\omega$$

The amplitude function in Part **(a)** is independent of p, but not in Part **(b)**. As $\omega \to \infty$, the coefficient of $\cos \omega t$ in the integrand of $f(t) = \lim_{p \to \infty} f_p(t)$ tends to zero as $1/\omega$ in Part **a**, while in Part **(b)** it tends to zero as $1/\omega^2$; thus, the Fourier integral of f represents a discontinuous function in Part **(a)**, but a continuous function in Part **(b)**.

4.

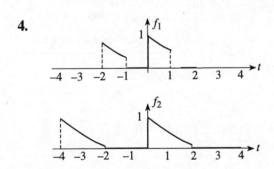

6.

8. $f(t) = \frac{1}{2\pi i} \int_{-\infty}^\infty \frac{1-e^{-i\omega}}{\omega} e^{i\omega t} d\omega$,

$$f(t) = \frac{1}{\pi} \int_0^\infty \frac{\sin \omega(1-t) + \sin \omega t}{\omega} d\omega$$

10. $f(t) = \frac{1}{2\pi i} \int_{-\infty}^\infty \frac{i(1-e^{-i\omega}) - \omega e^{-i\omega}}{\omega^2} e^{i\omega t} d\omega$

$$f(t) = \frac{1}{\pi} \int_0^\infty \frac{\cos \omega t + \omega \sin \omega(1-t) - \cos \omega(1+t)}{\omega^2} d\omega$$

12. $f(t) = \frac{1}{2\pi} \int_{-\infty}^\infty$

$$\frac{(1+i\omega)\sinh(1-i\omega)p + (1-i\omega)\sinh(1+i\omega)p}{1+\omega^2} e^{i\omega t} d\omega$$

$$f(t) = \frac{2}{\pi} \int_0^\infty \frac{\sinh p \cos \omega p + \omega \cosh p \sin \omega p}{1+\omega^2} \cos \omega t \, d\omega$$

14. $f(t) = 2 \int_0^\infty (\cos \omega - 1) \frac{\sin \omega t}{\omega} d\omega$

16. $f(t) = \frac{2}{\pi} \int_0^\infty \frac{\pi \omega \cos \pi \omega - \sin \pi \omega}{\omega^2} \sin \omega t \, d\omega$

18. $f(t) = \frac{2}{\pi} \int_0^\infty \frac{\sin \omega \pi \sin \omega t}{1-\omega^2} d\omega$

20. $f(t) = \frac{2}{\pi} \int_0^\infty \frac{[(b-a)+2a\cos \omega]\sin \omega}{\omega} \cos \omega t \, d\omega$

22. $f(t) = \frac{2}{\pi} \int_0^\infty \frac{2\omega \cos \omega + (\omega^2-2)\sin \omega}{\omega^3} \cos \omega t \, d\omega$

24. $f(t) = 2 \int_0^\infty \frac{1+\cos \omega}{\pi^2 - \omega^2} \cos \omega t \, d\omega$

26. $f(t) = \frac{e^{-ab}}{\pi} \int_0^\infty \frac{a \cos \omega(t-b) + \omega \sin \omega(t-b)}{a^2 + \omega^2} d\omega$

28. $\begin{cases} f(t) = \frac{2}{\pi} \int_0^\infty \frac{\sin \omega - \sin 2\omega}{\omega} \cos \omega t \, d\omega \\ f(t) = \frac{2}{\pi} \int_0^\infty \frac{\cos 2\omega - \cos \omega}{\omega} \sin \omega t \, d\omega \end{cases}$

30. $\begin{cases} f(t) = \frac{2}{\pi} \int_0^\infty \frac{2\sin\omega - \omega(1+\cos\omega)}{\omega^3} \cos\omega t\, d\omega \\ f(t) = \frac{2}{\pi} \int_0^\infty \frac{2(1-\cos\omega) - \omega\sin\omega}{\omega^3} \sin\omega t\, d\omega \end{cases}$

32. $\begin{cases} f(t) = \frac{2}{\pi} \int_0^\infty \left[\frac{1+\cos\pi\omega}{1-\omega^2} + \frac{\cos\pi\omega - \cos 2\pi\omega}{\pi\omega^2} \right] \\ \qquad \cdot \cos\omega t\, d\omega \\ f(t) = \frac{2}{\pi} \int_0^\infty \left[\frac{1}{\omega} + \frac{\sin\pi\omega}{1-\omega^2} + \frac{\sin\pi\omega - \sin 2\pi\omega}{\pi\omega^2} \right] \\ \qquad \cdot \sin\omega t\, d\omega \end{cases}$

34. f is discontinuous; $C(\omega) \to 0$ as c/ω.

36. f and f' are continuous, f'' is discontinuous; $C(\omega) \to 0$ as c/ω^3.

50. $B(\omega) = \sqrt{\frac{2}{\pi}} \omega e^{-\omega^2/2}$;

$f(t) = \sqrt{\frac{2}{\pi}} \int_0^\infty \omega e^{-\omega^2/2} \sin\omega t\, d\omega$;

$\int_0^\infty \omega e^{-\omega^2/2} \sin\omega\, d\omega = \sqrt{\frac{\pi}{2e}}$

52. $C(\omega) = \frac{1}{2\pi\sqrt{a^2+\omega^2}} e^{-i(\omega b + \phi)}$,

where $\phi = \tan^{-1}\frac{\omega}{\alpha}$

54. $C(\omega) = \frac{\sqrt{2(1-\cos\omega)}}{2\pi\omega} e^{-i\phi}$,

where $\phi = \tan^{-1}\frac{\sin\omega}{1-\cos\omega}$

58. $A'(\omega) = -\frac{1}{\omega} B''(\omega) - \frac{1}{\pi\omega} \sum_k J'_k \sin\omega t'_k$

$B'(\omega) = \frac{1}{\omega} A''(\omega) + \frac{1}{\pi\omega} \sum_k J'_k \cos\omega t'_k$

60. $f(t) = \frac{k}{\pi} \int_0^\infty \frac{(\sin\omega + \sin b\omega)\cos\omega t}{\omega}$

$\qquad + \frac{(\cos\omega - \cos b\omega)\sin\omega t}{\omega}\, d\omega$

62. $f(t) = \frac{1}{\pi} \int_0^\infty \frac{\cos\omega t + \cos(\pi - t)\omega}{1 - \omega^2}\, d\omega$

64. $f(t) = \frac{4}{\pi} \int_0^\infty \frac{\omega\cos\omega - \sin\omega}{\omega^3} \cos\omega t\, d\omega$

66. $f(t) = \frac{2k}{\pi} \int_0^\infty \frac{\cos\omega t}{1 + \omega^2}\, d\omega$

68. $f(t) = \frac{2}{\pi} \int_0^\infty \frac{\sin b\omega - \sin\omega}{\omega} \cos\omega t\, d\omega$

$f(t) = \frac{2}{\pi} \int_0^\infty \frac{\cos\omega - \cos b\omega}{\omega} \sin\omega t\, d\omega$

70. $f(t) = \frac{2}{\pi} \int_0^\infty \frac{e(\cos\omega + \omega\sin\omega) - 1}{1 + \omega^2} \cos\omega t\, d\omega$

$f(t) = \frac{2}{\pi} \int_0^\infty \frac{e(\sin\omega - \omega\cos\omega) + \omega}{1 + \omega^2} \sin\omega t\, d\omega$

72. $f(t) = \frac{1}{\pi} \int_0^\infty \frac{2\omega(2\cos\omega - 1) + (5\omega^2 - 2)\sin\omega}{\omega^3}$

$\qquad \cdot \cos\omega t\, d\omega$

$f(t) = \frac{1}{\pi} \int_0^\infty \frac{(2 - 5\omega^2)\cos\omega + 4\omega\sin\omega + 2(\omega^2 - 1)}{\omega^3}$

$\qquad \cdot \sin\omega t\, d\omega$

74. $\frac{1}{\lambda} \left[Si(e^{\lambda b}) - Si(e^{\lambda a}) \right]$

76. $3\, Si\, 3$

78. $\frac{1}{2} \left[\frac{\sin a}{a^2} - \frac{\sin b}{b^2} + \frac{\cos a}{a} - \frac{\cos b}{b} - Si\ b + Si\ a \right]$

80. $Ci(2^n) - Ci(1)$

82. $\frac{1}{2} \left[Ci(b) - Ci(a) + Ci(3b) - Ci(3a) \right]$

84. $Ei(6)$

86. $\frac{1}{2}e^{-2} - Ei\,(2)$

Section 9.2

2. $P(\omega_0,t) = \frac{1}{\pi}\left[Si\;\omega_0(t-p) - 2Si\;\omega_0 t\right.$
$\left. + Si\;\omega_0(t+p)\right]$

4. $P(\omega_0,t) = \frac{1}{\pi}\left[Si\;\omega_0(t+2) - Si\;\omega_0(t-2)\right.$
$\left. - Si\;\omega_0(t+1) + Si\;\omega_0(t-1)\right]$

6. $P(\omega_0,t) = \frac{1}{\pi}\left[\frac{2(1-\cos\omega_0)\cos\omega_0 t}{\omega_0}\right.$
$\left. + t\{2Si\;\omega_0 t - Si\;\omega_0(t+1) - Si\;\omega_0(t+1)\}\right]$

8. See the answer to Exercise 4.

10. See the answer to Exercise 6.

Section 9.3

2. (a) $f(t) = \begin{cases} 0 & t<2 \\ \frac{1}{3}e^{-(t-2)} & t>2 \end{cases}$

(b) $f(t) = \begin{cases} 0 & t<-3 \\ \frac{1}{\pi}e^{-2(t+3)} & t>-3 \end{cases}$

(c) $f(t) = \begin{cases} 0 & t<0 \\ e^{-2t} & 0<t<3 \\ e^{-2t}-e^{-2(t-3)} & 3<t \end{cases}$

(d) $f(t) = \begin{cases} 0 & t<1 \\ \frac{1}{2\pi}\left[e^{-(t-1)}-e^{-2(t-1)}\right] & 1<t \end{cases}$

(e) $f(t) = \begin{cases} 0 & t<1 \\ e^{-2t} & 1<t \end{cases}$

(f) $f(t) = \begin{cases} 0 & t<3 \\ \frac{1}{2}e^{-3(t-3)/2} & 3<t \end{cases}$

(g) $f(t) = \begin{cases} 0 & t<-1 \\ \frac{1}{2}e^{-a(t+1)} & -1<t<1 \\ \frac{1}{2}\left[e^{-a(t+1)}-e^{-a(t-1)}\right] & 1<t \end{cases}$

$f(t) = \begin{cases} 0 & t<2 \\ \frac{1}{2}\left[e^{-(t-2)}-e^{-3(t-2)}\right] & 2<t \end{cases}$

4. (a) $f(t) = \begin{cases} 0 & t<-1 \\ \frac{1}{2}e^{-2t} & -1<t<1 \\ 0 & 1<t \end{cases}$

(b) $f(t) = \begin{cases} 0 & t<-1/2 \\ \frac{1}{2} & -1/2<t<1/2 \\ 0 & 1/2<t \end{cases}$

(c) $f(t) = \begin{cases} 0 & t<0 \\ \frac{1}{2}t^2 e^{-t} & 0<t \end{cases}$

(d) $f(t) = \begin{cases} \frac{1}{2}e^{t-1} & -\infty<t\le 0 \\ \frac{1}{2}e^{-(t-1)} & 1\le t<\infty \end{cases}$

6. (b) $\dfrac{1+\cos\pi\omega}{\pi(1-\omega^2)};\quad -\dfrac{\sin\pi\omega}{\pi(1-\omega^2)}$

12. (a) $f(t) = \begin{cases} 0 & t<0 \\ te^{-at} & 0<t \end{cases}$

(b) $f(t) = \begin{cases} 0 & t<0 \\ \frac{1}{2}t^2 e^{-at} & 0<t \end{cases}$

14. (a) $f(t) = \begin{cases} 0 & t<0 \\ e^{-t}+e^{-2t}+te^{-2t} & 0<t \end{cases}$

(b) $f(t) = \begin{cases} 0 & t<0 \\ te^{-t}-te^{-3t} & 0<t \end{cases}$

20. Let the Fourier series of the function from which the pulse is "cut" be $\sum\limits_{-\infty}^{\infty} a_n e^{ni\pi t}$. The series defining the

pulse is then $\sum\limits_{-\infty}^{\infty} a_n e^{ni\pi t} p(t)$. Since the transform of each term in the last series has just been determined, the transform of the pulse is now determined. If the function from which the pulse is cut is given by a real trigonometric series, the trigonometric functions can be replaced by their exponential equivalents and the preceding method can then be applied to each term.

22. No; $f(t)$ and $g(t)$ are not identical functions. In fact, since $f(t)$ is an even function, its Fourier cosine integral, according to Theorem 2, Sec. 9.1, is equal to twice the real part of the Fourier integral of $g(t)$. In terms of transforms $\mathscr{F}[f(t)] = \sqrt{2\pi}\,\mathscr{F}_c[g(t)]$.

Section 9.4

2. $Y = \dfrac{2}{\pi}\displaystyle\int_0^\infty \dfrac{\left(b-\omega^2\right)\cos \omega t + a\omega \sin \omega t}{\left(b-\omega^2\right)^2 + (a\omega)^2}\cdot\dfrac{1-\cos\omega}{\omega^2}\,d\omega$

4. $Y = \dfrac{8}{\pi}\displaystyle\int_0^\infty \dfrac{-a\omega\cos \omega t + \left(b-\omega^2\right)\sin \omega t}{\left(b-\omega^2\right)^2 + (a\omega)^2}\cdot\dfrac{\omega\cos\omega}{\pi^2-(2\omega)^2}\,d\omega$

6. $y(x) = \dfrac{-P_0}{2\pi\ell}\displaystyle\int_0^\infty \left\{\dfrac{\left[\sin\omega(b+\ell)-\sin\omega(b-\ell)\right]\cos\omega x}{\omega\left(EI\omega^4+k\right)} + \dfrac{\left[\cos\omega(b-\ell)-\cos\omega(b+\ell)\right]\sin\omega x}{\omega\left(EI\omega^4+k\right)}\right\}d\omega$

$\lim\limits_{\ell\to 0} y(x) = -\dfrac{P_0}{\pi}\displaystyle\int_0^\infty \dfrac{\cos\omega b\cos\omega x + \sin\omega b\sin\omega x}{EI\omega^4+k}\,d\omega$

8. $y(x) = -\dfrac{2c}{\pi}\displaystyle\int_0^\infty \dfrac{\cos\omega x}{\left(c^2+\omega^2\right)\left(EI\omega^4+k\right)}\,d\omega$

10. $y(x) = \begin{cases} -\dfrac{P_0}{4k\ell}\left[e^{a(x-b+\ell)}\cos a(x-b+\ell) - e^{a(x-b+\ell)}\cos a(x-b-\ell)\right], & -\infty < x \le b-\ell \\[2ex] -\dfrac{P_0}{4k\ell}\left[2 - e^{a(x-b-\ell)}\cos a(x-b-\ell) - e^{-a(x-b+\ell)}\cos a(x-b+\ell)\right], & b-\ell \le x \le b+\ell \\[2ex] -\dfrac{P_0}{4k\ell}\left[e^{-a(x-b-\ell)}\cos a(x-b-\ell) - e^{-a(x-b+\ell)}\cos a(x-b+\ell)\right], & b+\ell \le x < \infty \end{cases}$

where $a = (k/4EI)^{1/4}$

12. $y(x) = \begin{cases} -b\left\{4a^3 e^{cx} + ce^{ax}\left[\left(c^2 - 2a^2\right)\cos ax - \left(c^2 + 2a^2\right)\sin ax\right]\right\}, & -\infty < x \le 0 \\ -b\left\{4a^3 e^{-cx} + ce^{-ax}\left[\left(c^2 - 2a^2\right)\cos ax + \left(c^2 + 2a^2\right)\sin ax\right]\right\}, & 0 \le x < \infty \end{cases}$

where $a = (k/4EI)^{1/4}$ and

$b = \left\{4EIa^3\left[(a+c)^2 + a^2\right]\left[(a-c)^2 + a^2\right]\right\}^{-1}$

16. $Y(t) = \begin{cases} c_1 e^{-t} + c_2 e^{-2t}, & -\infty < t < -1 \\ c_3 e^{-t} + c_4 e^{-2t} + \frac{1}{2}, & -1 < t < 1 \\ c_5 e^{-t} + c_6 e^{-2t}, & 1 < t < \infty \end{cases}$

18. $Y = \frac{1}{2}\left(e^{-t} - 2e^{-2t} + e^{-3t}\right)$

20. $Y = \begin{cases} 0 & -\infty < t \le 0 \\ 1 - e^{-t} & 0 \le t \le 1 \\ (e-1)e^{-t} & 1 \le t < \infty \end{cases}$

provides a particular solution on $(-\infty, 0)$, $(0, 1)$ and $(1, \infty)$

22. $Y = e^t$

24. $Y = \frac{1}{2}(\sin t - \cos t)$

26. $Y = te^{-t}$

28. $Y = \begin{cases} 0 & -\infty < t \le 0 \\ \frac{1}{2}e^{-2t} - e^{-t} + \frac{1}{2} & 0 \le t \le 1 \\ \frac{1}{2}\left(1 - e^2\right)e^{-2t} + (e-1)e^{-t} & 1 \le t < \infty \end{cases}$

gives a trivial solution on $(-\infty. 0)$ and nontrivial solutions on the normal intervals $(0, 1)$ and $(1, \infty)$.

30. $y(t) = \int_0^{\infty} \frac{e^{-\lambda/3} - e^{-\lambda/2}}{1 + (t-\lambda)^2} d\lambda$

32. $y = (1 + t)e^{-t}$

34. $y = \begin{cases} c\left[kb - \left(k + a^2 + b^2\right)v(t)\right] & 0 \le t \le 1 \\ c\left[kv(t-1) - \left(k + a^2 + b^2\right)v(t)\right], & 1 \le t < \infty \end{cases}$

where $c = 1/[b(a^2 + b^2)]$ and
$v(t) = e^{-at}(a \sin bt + b \cos bt)$.

36. $\mathfrak{F}[y'(t)] = i\omega Y(\omega) + y(0)$. $y = ke^{at}$, $t \le 0$. Yes. Since the differential equation is normal on $(-\infty, \infty)$, on every interval containing $t = 0$, the solution of the initial-value problem is unique.

38.

$Y_{ss} = \frac{1}{2\pi k} \int_{-\infty}^{\infty} M(\omega) \int_{-\infty}^{\infty} f(s)$
$\quad \bullet \cos\left[\omega s - \omega t + \alpha(\omega)\right] ds\, d\omega,$

where $M(\omega)$ and $\alpha(\omega)$ are, respectively, the magnification ratio and the phase shift at the frequency ω, and k is the modulus of the spring.

Section 9.5

4. $F(\omega) = \frac{\sin \omega a}{a\omega}$, $\lim_{a \to 0} F(\omega) = 1$

6. $F(\omega) = \frac{2(1 - \cos \omega a)}{a^2 \omega^2}$, $\lim_{a \to 0} F(\omega) = 1$

8. $I = \frac{2}{3a} \cos\left(\frac{9\pi}{4} + \frac{3a}{2}\right) \sin\frac{3a}{2}$,

$$\lim_{a\to 0} I(a) = \cos\frac{9\pi}{4} = \cos 3t\Big|_{t=\frac{3\pi}{4}}$$

10. **(b)** $I = \dfrac{1 - 2e^{-i\omega} + e^{-2ia\omega}}{a^2 i\omega}$

    (c) $\displaystyle\lim_{a\to 0} I = i\omega$

    (d) $I = \dfrac{1 - 2\cos 2a + \cos 4a}{2a^2}$

    (e) $\displaystyle\lim_{a\to 0} I = -2 = \dfrac{d(\sin 2t)}{dt}\Big|_{t=0}$

    (f) The two appear to have the same effect.

18. $Y(t) = \begin{cases} \dfrac{-1}{4} & t \le 0 \\ \dfrac{1}{4} + \dfrac{1}{2}e^{-2t} - e^{-t} & 0 \le t \end{cases}$

gives nontrivial solutions on the normal intervals $(-\infty, 0)$ and $(0, \infty)$.

20. $Y(t) = \begin{cases} 0 & t \le 0 \\ 4 + 5e^{-t} + 2te^{-t} - 9e^{-t/3} & 0 \le t \end{cases}$

gives a trivial solution $(-\infty, 0)$ and nontrivial solution on the normal interval $(0, \infty)$.

Section 9.6

2. t^2 does not have a unilateral Fourier transform. $t^2 e^{-at}$ does, namely
$G(\omega) = 2/(a + i\omega)^3$

4. No; yes, $G(\omega) = \dfrac{k}{(a + i\omega)^2 + k^2}$

Chapter 10

Section 10.1

2. $y = c_1 e^t + c_2 e^{-2t} - \frac{1}{9} e^t + \frac{t}{3} e^t$

4. $y = c_1 e^{3t} + c_2 e^{-2t} - \frac{1}{25} e^{-2t} - \frac{t}{5} e^{-2t}$

6. $y = c_1 e^{2t} + c_2 t e^{2t} + \frac{1}{2} t^2 e^{2t}$

8. $y = c_1 e^{-2t} + c_2 e^t + c_3 e^{-t} - \frac{1}{12} e^{-t} - \frac{t}{2} e^{-t}$

Section 10.2

2. The abscissa of convergence of e^{-bt} is $-b$.

4. a, b, d, e

Section 10.3

6. No. $G'(s)$ does not converge uniformly.

8. Yes. $G'(s)$ converges uniformly.

10. $G(s) = \frac{\sqrt{\pi}}{2} e^{-s^2/4}$

Section 10.4

8. Transform each differential equation, using the appropriate formulas. This yields a set of linear, algebraic equations from which the Laplace transforms of the dependent variables can be found by familiar steps. In particular, for two simultaneous differential equations in y and z the result is

$$\mathcal{L}\{y\} = \frac{\begin{vmatrix} \mathcal{L}\{f_1\}+a_1 y_0+c_1 z_0 & c_1 s+d_1 \\ \mathcal{L}\{f_2\}+a_2 y_0+c_2 z_0 & c_2 s+d_2 \end{vmatrix}}{\begin{vmatrix} a_1 s+b_1 & c_1 s+d_1 \\ a_2 s+b_2 & c_2 s+d_2 \end{vmatrix}}$$

$$\mathcal{L}\{z\} = \frac{\begin{vmatrix} a_1 s+b_1 & \mathcal{L}\{f_1\}+a_1 y_0+c_1 z_0 \\ a_2 s+b_2 & \mathcal{L}\{f_2\}+a_2 y_0+c_2 z_0 \end{vmatrix}}{\begin{vmatrix} a_1 s+b_1 & c_1 s+d_1 \\ a_2 s+b_2 & c_2 s+d_2 \end{vmatrix}}$$

12. (a) $b_n = -\frac{4}{\pi n^3} + (-1)^n \left(\frac{4}{\pi n^3} - \frac{2\pi}{n} \right)$

  (b) $a_n = \frac{12}{\pi n^4} - (-1)^n \left(\frac{12}{\pi n^4} - \frac{6\pi}{n^2} \right)$

14. If $f(t)$, $f'(t)$, ..,$f^{(k)}(t)$ are all piecewise regular and of exponential order and if $f^{(k)}(t)$ is the first of these quantities which is not everywhere continuous, which requires, of course that

$$f(0^+) = f'(0^+) = .. = f^{(k-1)}(0^+) = 0$$

then $\{f\} \sim \frac{A}{s^{k+1}}$ as $s \to \infty$

Section 10.5

2.

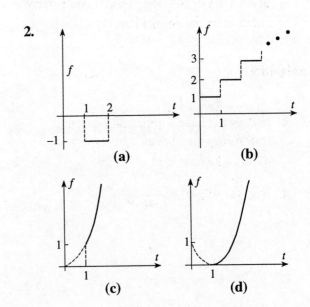

(a)   (b)

(c)   (d)

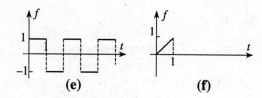

(e) (f)

14. **(a)** $\Gamma\left(\frac{1}{2}\right)=\sqrt{\pi}$

(b) $2\Gamma(2)=2$

(c) $\frac{1}{3}\left[1+2\Gamma\left(\frac{2}{3}\right)+\Gamma\left(\frac{1}{3}\right)\right]$

4. $\dfrac{s\cos b-a\sin b}{s^2+a^2}$

20. $a\sqrt{\dfrac{m\pi}{k}}$ where k is the proportionality constant in the force law.

6. **(a)** e^{-3t}

(b) $\frac{1}{3!}t^3$

(c) $\frac{1}{3}\sin 3t$

(d) $2\cos 3t+\sin 3t$

(e) $\frac{1}{4}e^{-5t/4}$

(f) $\frac{1}{6}\sin\frac{3t}{2}$

(g) e^t+2e^{-3t}

(h) $\cosh 2t+3\sinh 2t$

(i) $2e^{-2t}-e^{-3t}$

22. **(a)** $\sqrt{\pi}\,\Gamma\left(\frac{1}{4}\right)/4\Gamma\left(\frac{3}{4}\right)$

(b) $\dfrac{\Gamma(1+1/k)\Gamma(1/k)}{k\Gamma(1+2/k)}$

(c) $\dfrac{a^{(n+2)/2}\Gamma(1/n)\Gamma\left(\frac{3}{2}\right)}{n\Gamma\left(1/n+\frac{3}{2}\right)}$

24. Yes. Carry y_0 and z_0 as arbitrary constants to be determined by the conditions on y' and z' after the general solutions have been found.

Section 10.6

8. **(a)** $y=\frac{3}{2}e^{-t}-\frac{2}{3}e^{-2t}+\frac{1}{6}e^t$

(b) $y=8e^{-t}-9e^{-2t}+3e^{-3t}$

(c) $y=\frac{1}{3}-\frac{1}{2}e^{-t}+\frac{1}{6}e^{-3t}$

(d) $y=\frac{4}{5}e^{4t}+\frac{1}{5}e^{-t}$

y_0 cannot be assigned, it is determined by the equation.

2. **(a)** $\dfrac{1}{(s-1)^3}+\dfrac{1}{(s+1)^3}$

(b) $\dfrac{s-1}{(s+1)(s-3)}$

(c) e^{-s}/s

4. **(a)** $\dfrac{3\sqrt{\pi}}{4(s-1)^{5/2}}$

(b) $\dfrac{2}{(s+1)\left(s^2+2s+5\right)}$

(c) $\dfrac{e^{-2(s-2)}}{s-2}$

10. $y=\frac{11}{6}e^{-2t}-\frac{25}{12}e^t-\frac{3}{4}e^t$,

$z=-\frac{11}{6}e^{-2t}+\frac{5}{6}e^t+e^{-t}$

12. $y=-\frac{7}{4}e^{-2t}+\frac{7}{4}\cos 2t-\frac{1}{4}\sin 2t$

$z=\frac{3}{4}e^{-2t}-\frac{3}{4}\cos 2t+\frac{1}{2}\sin 2t$

6. **(a)** $\dfrac{e^{-5(s-2)}}{(s-2)^2}$

(b) $\dfrac{120}{(s+3)^6}+\dfrac{s+3}{s^2+6s+10}$

(c) $\dfrac{se^{-s}}{s^2+1}$

8. (a) $\dfrac{1+e^{-\pi s}}{s+1}$

 (b) $e^{-s}\left(\dfrac{2}{s^3}+\dfrac{2}{s^2}+\dfrac{1}{s}\right)-e^{-2s}\left(\dfrac{2}{s^3}+\dfrac{4}{s^2}+\dfrac{3}{s}\right)$

 (c) $\dfrac{e^{4-2s}}{s-2}$

10. $\dfrac{e^{-s}}{s^2}+\dfrac{e^{-s}}{s}$

12. $\dfrac{1-e^{-(s+a)}}{s+a}$

14. (a) $te^{-t}\left(1+\dfrac{t}{2}\right)$

 (b) $1-\cos t$

 (c) $\dfrac{1}{6}t^3e^{-2t}$

16. (a) $2te^{7t}(2+7t)$

 (b) $\dfrac{6e^t t^{1/3}}{\Gamma\left(\frac{1}{3}\right)}$

 (c) $e^{-2t}\cos 3t+e^{-2t}\sin 3t$

18. (a) $2t^{1/2}$

 (b) $\dfrac{1}{4}e^{-t}(1-\cos 2t)$

 (c) $\dfrac{1}{24}(t-1)^4 u(t-1)e^{-2(t-1)}$

20. (a) $y=\left(1-t+\dfrac{t^3}{6}\right)$

 (b) $y=\left(1-\dfrac{3}{2}t\right)\cos t$

 (c) $y=e^{-2t}\cos t$
 $+\dfrac{1}{5}[1-e^{-2(t-2)}\cos(t-2)$
 $-2e^{-2(t-2)}\sin(t-2)]u(t-2)$

22. (a) $y=\dfrac{1}{2}te^{-t}-\dfrac{3}{4}e^{-3t}+\dfrac{7}{4}e^{-t}$

 (b) $y=2e^{-t}(1-t)\cos 2t$

 (c) $y=2e^{-3t}\sin t+\dfrac{1}{10}[1-e^{-3(t-3)}\cos(t-3)$
 $-3e^{-3(t-3)}\sin(t-3)]u(t-3)$

24. (a) $y=t^2+t-1+\dfrac{1}{2}(e^{-t}+\cos t-\sin t)$

 (b) $y=\dfrac{3}{8}e^{-t}-\dfrac{5}{12}e^{-3t}+\dfrac{1}{24}e^{3t}$

 (c) $y=\dfrac{1}{6}\left(2e^{2t}-3e^t+e^{-t}\right)+$
 $\dfrac{1}{6}\left[3+e^{2(t-2)}-3e^{(t-2)}-e^{-(t-2)}\right]u(t-2)$

26. (a) $y=e^t\left(1+\dfrac{1}{24}t^4\right)$

 (b) $y=\dfrac{1}{42}e^{-t}t^6(7-t)$

 (c) $y=1+e^t(t-1)+u(t-\pi)\cosh(t-\pi)$

28. (a) $x=5e^t(\cos 2t+\sin 2t)$,
 $y=5e^t(-\cos 2t+\sin 2t)$

 (b) $x=(1+2t)e^t+\cos t$,
 $y=-2te^t-\dfrac{3}{2}\cos t-\dfrac{1}{2}\sin t$

 (c) $y=e^{-3t}(1+6t)+e^{-3(t-3)}[(t-3)$
 $+3(t-3)^2]u(t-3)$
 $z=-4te^{-3t}-2e^{-3(t-3)}(t-3)^2 u(t-3)$

30. $a=\dfrac{1}{6}$, $k=3$

32. $\pi/2$

34. $\mathcal{L}^{-1}\left\{\sqrt{\pi}/s\right\}=t^{-1/2}$

36. $y(t)=\dfrac{1}{2}bt^2+b\displaystyle\sum_{n=1}^{\infty}\left[\dfrac{1}{(2n+2)!}(t-n)^{2n+2}u(t-n)\right]$

38. $y = -\frac{aw}{24} x(x^3 - 2\ell x^2 + \ell^3)$

24. $\frac{(1-\cos 2t)e^{-t}}{4}$

40. $\theta(\ell, t) = \theta_0 \left[1 - \frac{a}{\ell} H\left(\frac{2\ell}{a}, t\right) \right]$

26. $\frac{\sinh t}{t}$

Section 10.7

28. $-\frac{1}{4} t\cos 2t + \frac{1}{8} \sin 2t$

2. $\frac{1}{(s-2)^2}$

30. $\frac{te^{-2t}\sin t}{2}$

4. $\frac{4(s+3)}{(s^2+6s+13)^2}$

32. $\frac{(-t\cos t + \sin t)e^{-t}}{2}$

6. $\frac{2a(3s^2-a^2)}{(s^2+a^2)^3}$

34. $y = e^{-t} - e^{-2t} + \left[e^{-(t-1)} + \frac{1}{2} e^{-2(t-1)} \right.$
$\left. + \frac{1}{2} \right] u(t-2)$

8. $\frac{2(3s^2+12s+13)}{(s^3+6s^2+13s)^2}$

36. $y = e^{-t} \left[\frac{7}{8} \cos 3t - \frac{4}{3} \sin 3t + \frac{1}{8} \cos t \right]$

10. $\frac{4(s+3)}{s(s^2+6s+13)^2}$

38. It should be possible to obtain a number of linear equations in the unknown coefficients from which they could be approximated by least square methods.

12. $\frac{2}{s^3(s+2)}$

40. $y = c_1 e^{-2t} + c_2 t^3 e^{-2t}$

14. $\ln \frac{s}{s-2}$

42. $y = c_1(e^{-4t} + 2te^{-4t}) + c_2(2t-1)$

16. $\frac{1}{s} \ln \frac{s^2+4}{s-1}$

44. $y = \frac{1}{3} t(1-t)(1+t+t^2)$

18. $\frac{1}{s} \cot^{-1} \frac{s+a}{b}$

Section 10.8

20. $1 - e^{-t} - te^{-t}$

2. $f(0^+) = 0$; $\lim_{t\to\infty} f(t)$ does not exist, since one zero of the denominator of the transform is $s = 2$, which has nonnegative real part.

22. $\frac{e^{-bt} - e^{-at}}{t}$

4. $f(0^+) = 1;\ \lim\limits_{t\to\infty} = 0$

6. $\cot^{-1}\frac{1}{2}$

8. $\frac{1}{2}\ln\frac{13}{10}$

10. $\tan^{-1}\frac{p}{q} - \tan^{-1}\frac{a}{b}$

12. $1 - \tanh^{-1} 2$

16. $\lim\limits_{t\to\infty} f^{(n)}(t) = \lim\limits_{s\to 0} s[s^n \mathcal{L}\{f\}$
$$-\sum_{j=1}^{n-1} s^{n-j-1} f^{(j)}(0)]$$
provided $f, f', f'' \ldots, f^{(n+1)}$ are all piecewise regular and of exponential order, and the abscissa of convergence of $f^{(n+1)}$ is negative.

20. **(a)** $Y(s) = \dfrac{1}{s(s-1)(s^2+1)}$ has no limit as $s \to 0$.

(b) No, since $Y(s)$ is not bounded as $s \to 1$ or $s \to \pm i$.

(c) $y(t) = \frac{1}{2}e^t - 1 + \frac{1}{2}(\cos t - \sin t)$ has no limit as $t \to \infty$

Section 10.9

2. $\frac{5}{6}e^t - \frac{5}{2}e^{-t} + \frac{8}{3}e^{-2t}$

4. $(t-2)e^{-3t} + (t+2)e^{-3t}$

6. $\frac{t}{4}(e^t - e^{-t})$

8. $\frac{1}{3}(\cos t + 2\sin t - \cos 2t - \sin 2t)$

10. $\frac{3}{20}e^t - \frac{1}{4}e^{-t} + \frac{1}{10}(\cos t - 2\sin t)e^{-2t}$

12. $\frac{1}{125}\left[\left(50t^2 - 20t - 1\right)e^{-2t} + 11\cos t - 2\sin t\right]$

14. $y = \frac{1}{16}e^t + \frac{1}{48}e^{-t}\left(4t^3 - 6t^2 - 6t - 3\right)$

16. $y = \frac{1}{2}(-e^{2t} + 5e^{-4t})$
$z = \frac{1}{3}\left(e^{-t} + 3e^{-2t} - 10e^{-4t}\right)$

18. $y = -\frac{5}{4}(1 - \cos 2t)e^{-3t}$
$z = \frac{1}{2}e^{-3t}(3 - 3\cos 2t + \sin 2t)$

20. The method of this exercise can be used to handle irreducible quadratic factors in general.

22. When $q(s)$ contains only unrepeated real linear factors and unrepeated irreducible quadratic factors, the coefficient of s^{n-1} in $p(s)$ is equal to the sum of the numerators of all the fractions arising from the unrepeated zeros of $q(s)$, plus the sum of the coefficients of s in the numerators of the fractions arising from the irreducible quadratic factors of $q(s)$.

Section 10.10

4. $\dfrac{1}{(1+s^2)(1-e^{-\pi s})}$

6. $\dfrac{1-e^{-as}}{s(1+e^{-2as})}$

8. $2[\phi_5(\tau,2,2)-\phi_5(t,2,2)]$

$-[\phi_5(\tau,1,2)-\phi_5(t,1,2)]$

10. $\frac{1}{5}[1-e^{-t}(\cos t + \frac{1}{2}\sin t)]-\frac{1}{5}[\,\phi_2(t,1)$

$-\{(-1)^n\phi_8(\tau,1,2,1)+\phi_8(t,1,2,1)\}$

$-\frac{1}{2}\{(-1)^n\phi_{10}(\tau,1,2,1)+\phi_{10}(t,1,2,1)\}]$

12. $[\phi_9(\tau,0,1,2)-\phi_9(t,0,1,2)]$

$-[\phi_9(\tau,0,2,2)-\phi_9(t,0,2,2)]$

14. $y=\frac{1}{4}\Big[\phi_2(t,1)-\{(-1)^n\phi_6(\tau,2,1)+\phi_6(t,2,1)\}$

$-2\{(-1)^n\phi_{12}(\tau,2,1)+\phi_{12}(t,2,1)\}\Big]$

16. $f(t)=\phi_2(t,1)+\phi_2(t-1,2)u(t-1);$

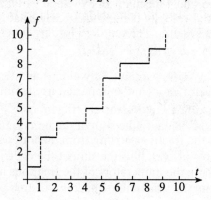

18. When $a=0$, $b=2$, and $k=\pi/2$, the inverse is the periodic function

$$f(t)=\begin{cases}\sin 2t & 0<t\le\pi/2 \\ 0 & \pi/2\le t<\pi\end{cases}$$

20. To find $\mathcal{L}\{f\}$ for $\mathcal{L}\{F\}$, divide $\mathcal{L}\{F\}$

by $1-e^{-ks}$.

22. No, because $k>0$ since it is the period of $f(t)$ and s can always be supposed positive since it is restricted only to be greater than the abscissa of convergence of $f(t)$.

26. $\dfrac{1}{(s^2+1)(1+e^{-\pi s})}$

28. $\displaystyle\sum_{j=1}^{\infty}(2j-1)u(t-j)$, a staircase function.

30. $-2\phi_2(t,1)+2\phi_1(t,2)$

32. $f(t)=\displaystyle\sum_{n=0}^{\infty}f_n(t),\ 0\le t$

34. $\mathcal{L}\{f(t)\}=\dfrac{\mathcal{L}\{f_0(t)\}}{1-e^{-ks}}$

36. $\phi(s)\equiv\mathcal{L}\{f(t)\}=\dfrac{\coth(\pi s/2)}{s^2+1}$

38. $\phi(s)\equiv\mathcal{L}\{f(t)\}=\dfrac{1}{s}\tanh s$

Section 10.11

2. $t-\sin t$

4. $\frac{1}{3}(\cos t - \cos 2t)$

6. $\frac{1}{6}(3t\cos 3t+\sin 3t)e^{-2t}$

8. $\delta(t)-2e^{-2t}$

10. $\delta(t-1)e^{-(t-1)}u(t-1)$

12. $Y = \int_0^t (t-\lambda)e^{-a(t-\lambda)}f(\lambda)d\lambda$

$= \int_0^t \lambda e^{-a\lambda}f(t-\lambda)d\lambda$

18. $\dfrac{3}{4}\dfrac{(2as-2)+(2as+2)e^{-2as}}{(as)^3}; \; 1$

20. (a) $y = t + \dfrac{1}{2}t^2$

(b) $y = \dfrac{1}{4}[u(t) + 2t - e^{-2t}]$

(c) $y = 2e^{-t} - 2u(t) - t$

22. (a) $y = \dfrac{1}{12}(5e^{2t} - 5e^{-2t} - 4e^{-t} + 4e^t)$

(b) $y = \dfrac{1}{10}(3\cos 2t + 4\sinh t)$

24. (a) $y = u(t) - \dfrac{5}{3}(e^t - e^{4t})$

(b) $y = u(t) + 4te^{2t}$

(c) $y = u(t) + 10te^{5t}$

(d) $y = \dfrac{1}{5}u(t) - \dfrac{8}{5}e^{-4t}\sin 5t$

26. (a) $y = e^{-t} - e^{-2t}$. The system cannot be reduced to a passive state by the subsequent application of an impulse $kI(t-t_0)$. It can be reduced to a passive state by the simultaneous application of an impulse $kI(t-t_0)$ and a doublet $\ell D(t-t_0)$ provided

$k = e^{-2t_0} - 2e^{-t_0}$ and $\ell = e^{-2t_0} - e^{-t_0}$.

(b) $y = e^{-t}\sin t$; The system cannot be reduced to a passive state by the subsequent application of a $kI(t-t_0)$. It can be reduced to a passive state by the simultaneous application of an impulse $kI(t-t_0)$ and a doublet $\ell D(t-t_0)$

provided $k = -e^{t_0}\left(\sin t_0 + \cos t_0\right)$

and $\ell = -e^{-t_0}\sin t_0$.

28. $\mathcal{L}\{f(t)\} = \dfrac{1}{1+e^{-t_0 s}}$

30. (a) $A(t) = \dfrac{1}{4} - \dfrac{\cos t}{3} + \dfrac{\cos 2t}{12}$,

$h(t) = \dfrac{\sin t}{3} - \dfrac{\sin 2t}{6}$

$x_2(t) = \int_0^t \dfrac{2\sin\lambda - \sin 2\lambda}{6}f(t-\lambda)d\lambda$

(b) $A(t) = \dfrac{1}{4} - \dfrac{\cos t}{3} + \dfrac{\cos 2t}{12}$,

$h(t) = \dfrac{\sin t}{3} - \dfrac{\sin 2t}{6}$

$x_1(t) = \int_0^t \dfrac{2\sin\lambda - \sin 2\lambda}{6}f(t-\lambda)d\lambda$

The equality of the results in Part **a** and Part **b** illustrates the <u>law of reciprocity</u> The displacement at x_i due to a unit force applied at x_j is equal to the displacement at x_j due to a unit force applied at x_i''.

32. The unit impulse can be thought of as a theoretical mechanism by which a non zero initial velocity is instantaneously established in a system. The required forcing function is $(by_0 + ay_0')\delta(t) + ay_0 D(t)$

34. $e^t - \dfrac{2e^t}{\sqrt{\pi}}\int_0^{\sqrt{t}} e^{-t^2}dt$

40. $t^n/n!$

44. $\dfrac{m!n!}{(m+n+1)!}t^{m+n+1}$

46. $y = 7t - 32\sqrt{t}$

48. $y = t\left(3 + \dfrac{1}{2}t^2\right)$

Section 10.12

4. $\dfrac{Tz}{(z-1)^2}$

6. $0, 1, 4, 4^2, 4^3, \ldots$

8. (a) (b) Spectrum $= \dfrac{2-i\omega}{4+\omega^2}$

$= \dfrac{1}{\sqrt{4+\omega^2}} e^{-i\tan^{-1}(\omega/2)}$

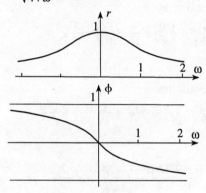

10. (a) Yes; spectrum $= \dfrac{3-i\omega}{9+\omega^2}$

$= \dfrac{1}{\sqrt{9+\omega^2}} e^{-i\tan^{-1}(\omega/3)}$

(b) No; the abscissa of convergence of the solution is positive.

Chapter 11

Section 11.2

2. (a) $u(x) = 100x$, Yes

(b) $u(x) = 100 - 50x$, Yes

4. (a) All values of a, b

(b) $a + b + c = 0$

(c) $3a + 2b + c = 0$ and $b + 2c + 3d = 0$

(d) $a = b = c = 0$

6. (a) $u = -\frac{1}{5}\cos(x + 2y)$

(b) $u = 2e^{2x+3y}$

(c) $u = \frac{5}{6}x^3 - \frac{1}{2}x^2y$

(d) $u = [-24 + 6(x^2 + y^2)]\sin t$

8. (a) $A = 0$, B arbitrary, $\lambda = \left(n + \frac{1}{2}\right)\pi / \ell$

(b) There are no nontrivial solutions meeting the prescribed conditions.

10. (b) It is not.

12. $k\dfrac{\partial[A(x)\frac{\partial u}{\partial y}]}{\partial x} = \dfrac{c\rho}{g}A(x)\dfrac{\partial u}{\partial t}$

14. The graph of the temperature is everywhere convex up if $A'(x)$ is positive, and convex down if $A'(x)$ is negative.

18. $\dfrac{\partial}{\partial r}\left[r\dfrac{\partial u}{\partial r}\right] = a^2 r\dfrac{\partial u}{\partial t}$, $a^2 = \dfrac{c\rho}{kg}$

20. $\dfrac{\partial}{\partial}\left[r^2\dfrac{\partial u}{\partial r}\right] = a^2 r^2\dfrac{\partial u}{\partial t}$, $a^2 = \dfrac{c\rho}{kg}$

24. $u = \dfrac{100[\sinh bx + \sinh b(1-x)]}{\sinh b}$

32. (a) $u(x,t) = \dfrac{x\sin\ell - \ell\sin x}{\sin\ell}\sin t$, $\ell \ne n\pi$

(b) $u(x,t) = x\left[1 + (-1)^{n+1}\cos x\right]\sin t$
$+(-1)^{n+1}\sin x(t\cos t)$
$+(\beta\sin t + \gamma\cos t)\sin x$;

β, γ parameters, $\ell = n\pi$

34. The equation is

$a^2\left(\dfrac{\partial^2 z}{\partial r^2} + \dfrac{1}{r}\dfrac{\partial z}{\partial r} + \dfrac{1}{r^2}\dfrac{\partial^2 z}{\partial\theta^2}\right) = \dfrac{\partial^2 z}{\partial t^2}$

36. The equation is

$a^2\dfrac{\partial u}{\partial t} = \dfrac{\partial^2 u}{\partial r^2} + \dfrac{1}{r}\dfrac{\partial u}{\partial r} + \dfrac{1}{r^2}\dfrac{\partial^2 u}{\partial\theta^2} + \dfrac{\partial^2 u}{\partial z^2}$

40. $\dfrac{\partial^2[EI(x)\partial^2 y/\partial x^2]}{\partial x^2} = -\dfrac{\rho}{g}A(x)\dfrac{\partial^2 y}{\partial t^2}$

$-f(x, y, \dot{y}, t) + \dfrac{\rho}{g}\dfrac{\partial}{\partial x}[I(x)\dfrac{\partial^3 y}{\partial^2 t\partial x}]$

Section 11.3

2. (a) $y(x, t) = \dfrac{1}{a}(\sin x \sin at)$

(b) $y(x,t) = \dfrac{1}{2a}(\sin 2x \sin 2at)$
Since the velocity is defined by the same analytic expression over the entire length of the string, there is no need to use step functions.

4. (a) $y(x, t) = \displaystyle\sum_{n=1}^{\infty} B_n \sin\dfrac{n\pi x}{\ell}\cos\dfrac{n\pi at}{\ell}$

$\omega_n \dfrac{n\pi a}{\ell}$ rad/unit time

(b) $y(x, t) = \dfrac{\ell}{n\pi a}\displaystyle\sum_{n=1}^{\infty}\sin\dfrac{n\pi x}{\ell}\sin\dfrac{n\pi at}{\ell}$

6.

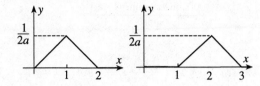

10. For $0 < at \leq 1$:

$$x < -at - 1 \quad y = 0$$
$$-at - 1 < x < at - 1 \quad y = \frac{1}{a\pi}\left[1 + \sin\frac{\pi}{2}(x + at)\right]$$
$$at - 1 < x < -at + 1 \quad y = \frac{2}{a\pi}\cos\frac{\pi x}{2}\sin\frac{\pi at}{2}$$
$$-at + 1 < x < at + 1 \quad y = \frac{1}{a\pi}\left[1 + \sin\frac{\pi}{2}(x - at)\right]$$
$$at + 1 < x \quad y = 0$$

For $1 < at$:

$$x < -at \quad y = 0$$
$$-at - 1 < x < -at + 1 \quad y = \frac{1}{a\pi}\left[1 + \sin\frac{\pi}{2}(x + at)\right]$$
$$-at + 1 < x < at - 1 \quad y = \frac{2}{a\pi}$$
$$at - 1 < x < at + 1 \quad y = \frac{1}{a\pi}\left[1 + \sin\frac{\pi}{2}(x - at)\right]$$
$$at + 1 < x \quad y = 0$$

In this problem the displacement curve is smooth; in Exercise 7 the deflection curve has corner points.

12. $0 < x < at \quad y(x, at) = \frac{1}{2a}\ln\frac{1 + x + at}{1 - x + at}$

$\quad at < x \quad y(x, at) = \frac{1}{2a}\ln\frac{1 + x + at}{1 + x - at}$

14. $K.E. = \frac{\rho}{8}(1 + e^{-2at})$

16.

$$x < -at \quad y = -\frac{1}{a}e^x \sinh at$$
$$-at < x < at \quad y = \frac{1}{a}e^{-at}\sinh x$$
$$at < x \quad y = \frac{1}{a}e^{-x}\sinh at$$

18. $\phi(x) = -(1 + \cos x) \quad x < 0$

20. No wave traveling to the left:
$\quad \theta(x) = 2ax\exp(-x^2)$.
No wave traveling to the right:
$\quad \theta(x) = -2ax\exp(-x^2)$.

24. (a) The two-dimensional wave equation has solutions of the form
$u(x, y, t) = f(\lambda x + \mu y \pm t)$ for all values of λ and μ which satisfy the equation
$\lambda^2 + \mu^2 = 1$.

(b) The given equation has solutions of the form $u(x, y) = e^{\lambda x + \mu y}$ for all values of λ and μ which satisfy the equation
$A\lambda^2 + B\lambda\mu + C\mu^2 + D\lambda + E\mu + F = 0$

26. $y(x, t) = \frac{1}{2a}[(x + at + 1)u(x + at + 1)$
$\quad - (x + at + 4)u(x + at + 4)$
$\quad + (x + at - 1)u(x + at - 1)$
$\quad - (x + at - 4)u(x + at - 4)$
$\quad - (x - at + 1)u(x - at + 1)$
$\quad + (x - at + 4)u(x - at + 4)$
$\quad - (x - at - 1)u(x - at - 1)$
$\quad + (x - at - 4)u(x - at - 4)]$

28. $y(1, t) = \frac{1}{2a}[(at + 2) - (at + 5) + at - (-at + 2) + (-at + 5)] = \frac{t}{2}, \quad 0 < at < 2$

$\quad = \frac{1}{2a}[(at + 2) - (at + 5) + at + (-at + 5)] = \frac{1}{a}, \quad 2 < at < 3$

$\quad = \frac{1}{2a}[(at + 2) - (at + 5) + at - (at - 3) + (-at + 5)] = \frac{-at + 5}{2a} \quad 3 < at < 5$

$\quad = \frac{1}{2a}[(at + 2) - (at + 5) + at - (at - 3)] = 0 \quad 5 < at$

30. $y(3, at) = 0$, $\dot{y}(3, at) = 0$ $\qquad\qquad 0 < at < 2$

$y(3, at) = \frac{1}{2}at - 1$, $\dot{y}(3, at) = \frac{a}{2}$ $\qquad 2 < at < 3$

$y(3, at) = 2 - \frac{1}{2}at$, $\dot{y}(3, at) = -\frac{a}{2}$ $\qquad 3 < at < 4$

$y(3, at) = 0$, $\dot{y}(3, at) = 0$ $\qquad\qquad 4 < at$

32. $y(x,t) = \frac{1+\cos(x-at)}{2a}\left[u(x-at+\pi)-u(x-at-\pi)\right]-\frac{1+\cos(x+at)}{2a}\left[u(x+at+\pi)-u(x+at-\pi)\right]$

34. $y(x, 0) = \phi(x) = -(x-2)(x-3)[u(x-2)-u(x-3)]$

36. $y(\pi, at) = \sin^2 at$, $\dot{y}(\pi, at) - a\sin 2at$ $\qquad 0 \leqq at \leqq \pi$

$y(\pi, at) = -\sin^2 at$, $\dot{y}(\pi, at) = -a\sin 2at$ $\qquad \pi \leqq at \leqq 2\pi$

$y(\pi, at) = 0$, $\dot{y}(\pi, at) = 0$ $\qquad\qquad 2\pi \leqq at$

38. $y(1, at) = \frac{1}{2}at(1-at)$, $\dot{y}(1, at) = \frac{a}{2}(1-2at)$ $\qquad 0 < at \leqq 1$

$y(1, at) = \frac{1}{2}(1-at)(2-at)$, $\dot{y}(1, at) = a\left(\frac{3}{2}-at\right)$ $\qquad 1 \leqq at \leqq 2$

$y(1, at) = 0$, $\dot{y}(1, at) = 0$ $\qquad\qquad 2 < at$

40. **(a)** $y(x, t) = [u(x-at-2\pi)-u(x-at-3\pi)]\sin(x-at)+[u(x+at-2\pi)-u(x+at-3\pi)]\sin(x+at)$

(b)

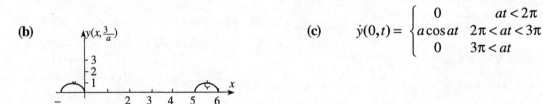

(c) $\dot{y}(0,t) = \begin{cases} 0 & at < 2\pi \\ a\cos at & 2\pi < at < 3\pi \\ 0 & 3\pi < at \end{cases}$

(d) $\dot{y}(0, t) < 0$ when $\frac{5\pi}{2} < at < 3\pi$

Section 11.4

4. **(a)** $u = f(x + y) + g(x + 3y)$

(b) $u = f(x + 2y) + g(2x + y)$

(c) $u = f(x - 3y) + xg(x - 3y)$

(d) $u = f(x - 2y) + xg(x - 2y) - \frac{1}{16}\sin(x + 2y)$

(e) $u = f(x + y) + g(3x - y) - \frac{1}{7}e^{x + 2y}$

(f) $u = f(x + 5y) + xg(x + 5y) + \frac{1}{300}x^4 + \frac{1}{6}y^3$

10. (a) $u = f(y - x^2) + g(y + x^2)$

    (b) $u = f(x) + xg(y/x)$

    (c) $u = xf(y/x) + g(y/x)$

    (d) $u = xf(xy) + g(xy)$

Section 11.5

2. As expected, the frequency equations are the same. Under the substitution $x \to \ell - x$ the amplitude distribution functions are the same.

4. $y(x, t) = \sum_{n=1}^{\infty} (A_n \cos \frac{n\pi at}{\ell} + B_n \sin \frac{n\pi at}{\ell}) \sin \frac{n\pi x}{\ell}$, $A_n = \frac{2}{\ell} \int_0^{\ell} f(x) \sin \frac{n\pi x}{\ell} dx$ and $B_n = \frac{2}{n\pi a} \int_0^{\ell} g(x) \sin \frac{n\pi x}{\ell} dx$

8. $\theta(x, t) = \frac{8k\ell}{\pi^2} \sum_{n=1}^{\infty} \frac{(-1)^{n-1}}{(2n-1)^2} \cos \frac{(2n-1)\pi at}{2\ell} \sin \frac{(2n-1)\pi x}{2\ell}$

10. $\theta(x, t) = -\frac{4k\ell}{\pi^2} \sum_{n=1}^{\infty} \frac{1}{(2n-1)^2} \cos \frac{(2n-1)\pi x}{\ell} \cos \frac{(2n-1)\pi at}{\ell}$

12. $u(x, y) = \frac{400}{\pi} \sum_{n=1}^{\infty} \frac{1}{2n-1} \sin(2n-1)\pi x e^{-(2n-1)\pi y}$

14. $y(x, t) = \sin \frac{\pi x}{\ell} \cos \frac{\pi at}{\ell} + \frac{4\ell}{\pi^2} \sum_{n=1}^{\infty} \frac{1}{n^2} \sin \frac{n\pi}{2} \sin \frac{n\pi}{4} \sin \frac{n\pi x}{\ell} \sin \frac{n\pi at}{\ell}$

20. $C(x, t) = \frac{8\ell^2}{\pi^3} C_0 \sum_{\substack{n=1 \\ n \text{ odd}}}^{\infty} \frac{1}{n^3} \sin \frac{n\pi x}{\ell} \exp\left(-n^2 \pi^2 t / a^2 \ell^2\right)$

22. A free-free shaft of length ℓ, vibrating at its nth natural frequency, has n nodes: $x_n = \frac{(2m-1)\ell}{2n}$, $m = 1, 2, \ldots, n$. A fixed-free shaft, vibrating at its nth natural frequency, has $n - 1$ nodes: $x_n = \frac{2m\ell}{2n-1}$, $m = 1, 2, \ldots, \quad n - 1$.

24. The normal modes of a uniform shaft of length ℓ vibrating torsionally with its left end fixed and its right end free are given by the formula $\sin\frac{(2n-1)\pi x}{2\ell}$, $n = 1, 2, 3, \ldots$, and the corresponding natural frequencies are $4\ell/(2n-1)a$. For a similar shaft of length 2ℓ vibrating torsionally with both ends fixed, the normal modes and the natural frequencies are, respectively, $\sin(m\pi x/\ell)$ and $4\ell/ma$, $m = 1, 2, 3, \ldots$ Clearly, for every value of n, the nth natural frequency of the shaft is the same as the natural frequency of order $m = 2n - 1$ of the second shaft. Moreover, the nth normal mode of the first shaft is clearly congruent to the portion of the $(2n-1)$st normal mode of the second shaft which lies between 0 and ℓ. The converse is not true, however, for neither the normal modes not the natural frequencies of even order of the shaft of length 2ℓ correspond to possible motions of the shaft of length ℓ.

26. (a) $u(x,t) = \displaystyle\sum_{n=0}^{\infty} A_n \cos\frac{(2n+1)\pi x}{2\ell} \exp\left[-(2n+1)^2 \pi^2 t/4a^2\ell^2\right]$ where $A_n = (-1)^n \dfrac{400}{(2n+1)\pi}$

(b) $u(x,t) = 100 - \displaystyle\sum_{n=0}^{\infty} A_n \cos\frac{(2n+1)\pi x}{2\ell} \exp\left[-(2n+1)^2 \pi^2 t/4a^2\ell^2\right]$ where $A_n = (-1)^n \dfrac{400}{(2n+1)\pi}$

28. (a) $u(x,t) = \dfrac{2}{\pi}u_0 + \displaystyle\sum_{n=1}^{\infty} \frac{(-1)^n}{n}\sin\frac{n\pi x}{\ell}\exp\left(-n^2\pi^2 t/a^2\ell^2\right)$

(b) $u(x,t) = \dfrac{1}{2}u_0 + \displaystyle\sum_{n=1}^{\infty} A_n \cos\frac{n\pi x}{\ell}\exp\left(-n^2\pi^2 t/a^2\ell^2\right)$ where $A_n = \begin{cases} 0 & n \text{ even} \\ -4u_0/n^2\pi^2 & n \text{ odd} \end{cases}$

30. (a) $\dfrac{800c\rho A\ell}{g\pi^2}\displaystyle\sum_{n=1}^{\infty}\frac{1}{n^2}\exp(-n^2\pi^2\alpha)$, n odd where A is the cross-sectional area of the rod.

(b) $\dfrac{800c\rho A\ell}{g\pi^2}\displaystyle\sum_{n=0}^{\infty}\frac{1}{(2n+1)^2}\exp[-(2n+1)^2\pi^2\alpha]$ where A is the cross-sectional area of the rod.

32. $u(x,t) = 100 - \dfrac{400}{\pi}\displaystyle\sum_{n=0}^{\infty}\frac{1}{2n+1}e^{-\pi^2(2n+1)^2 t/a^2}\sin(2n+1)\pi x$

34. $u(x,y) = \dfrac{8}{\pi}\displaystyle\sum_{n=1}^{\infty}\frac{\sin(2n-1)x\sinh[(2n-1)(1-y)]}{(2n-1)^3\sinh(2n-1)}$

Section 11.6

2. $a = 0$, $b = -\dfrac{5}{3}$, $h(x) = 1 - \dfrac{5}{3}x^2$

4. $f(n) = \dfrac{2}{2n+1}$

6. $\lambda_n = n/6$, $y_n = \sin\dfrac{n\pi(x+1)}{2}$

8. $u(x, y) = 100h \displaystyle\sum_{n=1}^{\infty} \dfrac{\sin\lambda_n \cos\lambda_n x \sinh\lambda_n y}{\lambda_n[h+\sin^2\lambda_n]\sinh\lambda_n}$, $0 \leq x, y \leq 1$, where the λ_n satisfy the characteristic equation
$h\cos\lambda - \lambda\sin\lambda = 0$

10. $u(x, t) = \displaystyle\sum_{n=1}^{\infty} A_n \cos\lambda_n x \exp(-\lambda_n^2 t / a^2)$ where $A_n = \dfrac{2}{\ell}\displaystyle\int_0^{\ell} f(x)\cos\lambda_n x \, dx$, $\lambda_n = z_n/\ell$, the z's are determined
from the characteristic equation $\alpha z = \cot z$ and $\alpha = 1/h\ell$.

12. $u(x, t) = 100 - \dfrac{100xh}{1+h\ell} + \displaystyle\sum_{n=1}^{\infty} B_n \sin\lambda_n x \exp(-\lambda_n^2 t / a^2)$ where $B_n = \dfrac{2}{\ell(1+\alpha\cos^2 z_n)}\displaystyle\int_0^{\ell}\phi(x)\sin\lambda_n x \, dx$, $\alpha = \dfrac{1}{h\ell}$,

$\phi(x) = f(x) - 100 + \dfrac{100hx}{1+h\ell}$, $\lambda_n = z_n\ell$, and $\tan z = -\alpha z$.

14. (a) $u(x, y) = \displaystyle\sum_{n=1}^{\infty} B_n \sin n\pi x(n\pi\cosh n\pi y + h\sinh n\pi y)$, $B_n = \dfrac{2\int_0^1 f(x)\sin n\pi x \, dx}{n\pi\cosh n\pi + h\sinh n\pi}$

(b) $u(x, y) = \displaystyle\sum_{n=1}^{\infty} B_n \sinh\lambda_n x \sin\lambda_n y$, $B_n = \dfrac{2\lambda_n\int_0^1 f(y)\sin\lambda_n y \, dy}{\sinh\lambda_n(\lambda_n - \cos\lambda_n \sin\lambda_n)}$

16. (a) $u(x, y) = \displaystyle\sum_{n=1}^{\infty} B_n \sin\lambda_n x \exp(-\lambda_n y)$, $\tan\lambda = -\lambda/h$, $B_n = \dfrac{2\lambda_n\int_0^1 f(x)\sin\lambda_n x \, dx}{\lambda_n - \sin\lambda_n \cos\lambda_n}$

(b) $u(x, y) = \displaystyle\sum_{n=1}^{\infty} A_n \cos\lambda_n x \exp(-\lambda_n y)$, $\tan\lambda = h/\lambda$, $A_n = \dfrac{2\lambda_n\int_0^1 f(x)\cos\lambda_n x \, dx}{\lambda_n + \sin\lambda_n \cos\lambda_n}$

18. (a) $u(x, t) = \displaystyle\sum_{n=1}^{\infty} B_n \sin\lambda_n x \exp\left[-(\lambda_n^2 + b^2)t/a^2\right]$, $\tan\lambda\ell = -\lambda/h$, $B_n = \dfrac{2\lambda_n\int_0^{\ell} f(x)\sin\lambda_n x \, dx}{\ell(\lambda_n - \sin\lambda_n\ell\cos\lambda_n\ell)}$

(b) $u(x, t) = \displaystyle\sum_{n=1}^{\infty} A_n \cos\lambda_n x \exp\left[-(\lambda_n^2 + b^2)t/a^2\right]$, $\cot\lambda\ell = -\lambda/h$, $B_n = \dfrac{2\lambda_n\int_0^{\ell} f(x)\cos\lambda_n x \, dx}{\ell(\lambda_n + \sin\lambda_n\ell\cos\lambda_n\ell)}$

20. $u(x, y) = \dfrac{400}{\pi} \displaystyle\sum_{\substack{n=1 \\ n \text{ odd}}}^{\infty} \dfrac{\sin n\pi x \cosh \sqrt{b^2+n^2\pi^2}\, y}{n \cosh \sqrt{b^2+n^2\pi^2}}$

22. $u_1 = 100 k_2 k_3 x/D$, $u_2 = [100 k_1 k_3 (x - a_1) + 100 a_1 k_2 k_3]/D$, $u_3 = 100 + 100 k_1 k_2 (x - a_1 - a_2 - a_3)/D$
where $D = a_1 k_2 k_3 + a_2 k_1 k_3 + a_3 k_1 k_2$

24. $\cot z = \alpha z$, where $z = \lambda\, \ell/a$ and $\alpha = E_s J/k\,\ell$

28. $k = 444{,}000$ (in-lb)/rad

30. $\cot z = \alpha z$, where $z = \lambda\, \ell/a$ and $\alpha = I_p/I_s$, I_s being the polar moment of inertia of the shaft.

32. **(a)** $\sin z = 0$; $X_n = \sin(z_n x/\ell)$

(b) $\cos z \cosh z = 1$, $X_n = (\sin z_n - \sinh z_n)[\cos(z_n x/\ell) - \cosh(z_n x/\ell] - (\cos z_n - \cosh z_n)$
$\quad\quad\quad\quad \bullet [\sin(z_n x/\ell) - \sinh(z_n x/\ell)]$

(c) $\cos z \cosh z = 1$, $X_n = (\sin z_n\, z - \sinh z_n)[\cos(z_n x/\ell) + \cosh(z_n x/\ell)] - (\cos z_n - \cosh z_n)$
$\quad\quad\quad\quad \bullet [\sin(z_n x/\ell) + \sinh(z_n x/\ell)]$

(d) $\tan z = \tanh z$, $X_n = (\sin z_n - \sinh z_n)[\cos(z_n x/\ell) - \cosh z_n x/\ell)] - (\cos z_n - \cosh z_n)$
$\quad\quad\quad\quad \bullet [\sin(z_n x/\ell) - \sinh(z_n x/\ell)]$

(e) $\tan z = \tanh z$, $x_n = (\sin z_n + \sinh z_n)[\cos(z_n x/\ell) + \cosh(z_n x/\ell)] - (\cos z_n + \cosh z_n)$
$\quad\quad\quad\quad \bullet [\sin(z_n x/\ell) - \sinh(z_n x/\ell)]$

34. $(1 + \cos z \cosh z) + rz(\cos z \sinh z - \sin z \cosh z) = 0$ where $z = \ell\sqrt{\lambda/a}$ and r is the ratio of the end mass to the mass of the shaft. If the end mass is zero the configuration is a simple cantilever; if the end mass is infinite the configuration is a simple fixed-fixed beam. In each case, the frequency equation reduces to what we expect.

42. **(a)** $y_n = \sin(n\pi \ln x)/\sqrt{x}$

(b) $y_n = \sin(\lambda_n \ln x)/x$ where the λ's are the roots of the characteristic equation
$\tan(\lambda/2) = \lambda$ and $\mu = 1 + \lambda^2$.

52. $X(x) = \dfrac{\lambda^2 \rho}{E_s g} \displaystyle\int_0^x \dfrac{1}{J(s)} \int_s^\ell J(r) X(r)\, dr\, ds + \dfrac{IX(\ell)g}{\rho} \int_0^x \dfrac{ds}{J(s)}$

54. $X(x) = \dfrac{\lambda^2 \rho}{E_s g} \displaystyle\int_0^x \int_0^v \dfrac{1}{I(u)} \int_u^\ell \int_s^\ell A(r) X(r)\, dr\, ds\, du\, dv$

56. The problem reduces to the solution of the corresponding problem for a uniform sheet of length $a_1 + a_2$.

64. If $a\ell + b < 1$, the solution set consists exclusively of trigonometric functions. If $a\ell + b = 1$, then in addition to the trigonometric functions, the solution set contains the algebraic function x. If $a\ell + b > 1$, then in addition to the trigonometric functions, the solution set contains one hyperbolic function.

68. $W[f(x), g(x)] > 0$, so the zeros of f and g separate each other on $(0, \infty)$.

70. $u = X_0(x) + \sum_{n=1}^{\infty} C_n X_n(x) \exp(-\lambda_n^2 t)$ where $X_0 = \begin{cases} \frac{100k}{k_1 + k_2}(x+1) & -1 < x < 0 \\ 100 - \frac{100k_1}{k_1 + k_2}(1-x) & 0 < x < 1 \end{cases}$

$X_n = \begin{cases} \sin \lambda_n a_2 \sin \lambda_n a_1 (1+x) & -1 < x < 0 \\ \sin \lambda_n a_1 \sin \lambda_n a_2 (1-x) & 0 < x < 1 \end{cases}$, $C_n = \frac{-200 k_2 a_2 \sin \lambda_n a_1}{\lambda_n \left[k_1 a_1^2 \sin^2 \lambda_n a_2 + k_2 a_2^2 \sin^2 \lambda_n a_1 \right]}$

and the λ_n's are the roots of the characteristic equation $k_1 a_1 \tan \lambda a_2 + k_2 a_2 \tan \lambda a_1 = 0$

74. $F(z) \equiv f_1(z) f_4(z) - f_2(z) f_3(z) = 0$ where $f_1(z) = b \cos cz$, $f_2(z) = c \sin cz$, $f_3(z) = \sin hz$, $f_4(z) = \cos hz$,
$b = E_2 r_2^4 / E_1 r_1^4$, $h = \frac{1}{\beta} - 1$, $c = a_2 / a_1$, $z = \lambda \beta / a_2$.

76. **(a)** $\begin{cases} \text{I. } (\theta_1)_{tt} = a_1^2 (\theta_1)_{xx}, \ -2 < x < 0; \ (\theta_2)_{tt} = a_2^2 (\theta_2)_{xx}, \ 0 < x < 3; \ 0 < t \\ \text{II. } (\theta_1)_x(-2, t) = 0, \ a_i^2 = (E_s)_i g / \rho_i, \ i = 1, 2 \\ \text{III. } \theta_1(0^-, t) - \theta_2(0^+, t) = 0 \\ \text{IV. } (E_s)_1 J_1 (\theta_1)_x(0^-, t) - (E_s)_2 J_2 (\theta_2)_x(0^+, t) = 0 \\ \text{V. } \theta_2(3, t) = 0 \end{cases}$

(b) $\begin{cases} 1. \ X_1'' + \frac{\lambda^2}{a_1^2} X_1 = 0, \ -2 < x < 0; \ X_2'' + \frac{\lambda^2}{a_2^2} X_2 = 0, \ 0 < x < 3; \ \lambda > 0 \\ 0;1. \ X_1''(-2) = 0 \\ 1,1. \ X_1(0^-) - X_2(0^+) = 0 \\ 1,2. \ b_1 X_1'(0^-) - b_2 X_2'(0^+) = 0; \\ \quad b_i = (E_s)_i J_i, \ i = 1, 2 \\ 1;2. \ X_2(3) = 0 \end{cases}$

(c) $P(x) = \begin{cases} \frac{1}{a_1^2} = \rho_1 / (E_s)_1 g & -2 < x < 0 \\ \frac{b_2}{b_1} \frac{1}{a_2^2} = \frac{J_2 \rho_2}{(E_s)_1 J_1 g} & 0 < x < 3 \end{cases}$

78. (a)
$$\begin{cases} \text{I. } (\theta_1)_{tt} = a_1^2 (\theta_1)_{xx}, \ -1 < x < 0; \ (\theta_2)_{tt} = a_2^2 (\theta_2)_{xx}, \ 0 < x < 1; \ 0 < t \\ \text{II. } \theta_1(-1, t) = 0, \quad 0 < t \\ \text{III. } \theta_1(0^-, t) - \theta_2(0^+, t) = 0, \quad 0 < t \\ \text{IV. } (\theta_1)_x(0^-, t) - 4(\theta_2)_x(0^+, t) = 0, \ 0 < t; \ \text{since } \frac{(E_s)_2 J_2}{(E_s)_1 J_1} = 4 \\ \text{V. } (\theta_2)_x(1, t) = 0, \quad 0 < t \\ \text{VI. } \theta_t(x, 0) = 0, \quad -1 \leqq x \leqq 1 \\ \text{VII. } \theta(x, 0) = f(x), \quad -1 \leqq x \leqq 1 \end{cases}$$

(b)
$$\begin{cases} \text{1. } X_1'' + 16\pi^2 \lambda^2 X_1 = 0, \ -1 < x < 0; \ X_2'' + \pi^2 \lambda^2 X_2 = 0, \quad 0 < x < 1 \\ \text{0;1. } X_1(-1) = 0 \\ \text{1, 1. } X_1(0^-) - X_2(0^+) = 0 \\ \text{1, 2. } X_1'(0^-) - 4X_2'(0^+) = 0 \\ \text{1; 2. } X_2'(1) = 0 \end{cases}$$

(c) $F(\lambda) = \cos 5\pi\lambda = 0; \ \lambda_n = \frac{2n-1}{10}, \ n = 1, 2, 3, \ldots$

(d) $X_n(x) = \begin{cases} \cos \pi\lambda_n \sin 4\pi\lambda_n(x+1) & -1 \leqq x \leqq 0 \\ \sin 4\pi\lambda_n \cos \pi\lambda_n(x-1) & 0 \leqq x \leqq 1 \end{cases}$

$\quad P(x) = \begin{cases} 16\pi^2 & -1 < x < 0 \\ 4\pi^2 & 0 < x < 1 \end{cases}$

(e) $\theta(x, t) = \sum_{n=1}^{\infty} c_n X_n(x) \cos \lambda_n t, \ \text{where} \ c_n = \frac{2(1 - \cos \pi\lambda_n) \sin 4\pi\lambda_n}{\pi^2 \lambda^2 (4\cos^2 \pi\lambda_n + \sin^2 4\pi\lambda_n)}$

Section 11.7

2. (a) $u(x, y, t) = 100x + \sum_{n=0}^{\infty} \sum_{m=1}^{\infty} E_{mn} \sin m\pi x \cos n\pi y \exp\left[-(m^2 + n^2)\pi^2 t / a^2\right], \ E_{mn} = \begin{cases} 0 & n \neq 0 \\ 200(-1)^m & n = 0 \end{cases}$

(b) $u(x, y, t) = 100x + \sum_{n=0}^{\infty} \sum_{m=1}^{\infty} E_{mn} \sin m\pi x \cos n\pi y \exp\left[-(m^2 + n^2)\pi^2 t / a^2\right]$

$\quad E_{mn} = \begin{cases} 0 & n = 0, \ m \ \text{odd} \\ \frac{200}{m\pi} & n = 0, \ m \ \text{even} \\ 0 & n \neq 0, \ m \ \text{or} \ n \ \text{even} \\ -\frac{1600}{mn^2\pi^3} & m \ \text{and} \ n \ \text{odd} \end{cases}$

4. (a) $u(x, y, t) = \sum\limits_{n=0}^{\infty} \sum\limits_{m=0}^{\infty} E_{mn} \cos n\pi y \cos \frac{2m+1}{2}\pi x \exp\left[-\left(\frac{2m+1}{2}\right)^2 + n^2]\pi^2 t / a^2\right]$, $E_{mn} = \begin{cases} 0 & n \neq 0 \\ \dfrac{400(-1)^m}{(2m+1)\pi} & n = 0 \end{cases}$

(b) $u(x, y, t) = \sum\limits_{n=0}^{\infty} \sum\limits_{m=0}^{\infty} E_{mn} \cos n\pi y \cos \frac{2m+1}{2}\pi x \exp\left[-\left(\frac{2m+1}{2}\right)^2 + n^2]\pi^2 t / a^2\right]$,

$$E_{mn} = \begin{cases} -\dfrac{1600}{(2m+1)\pi^3 n^2} & n \text{ odd} \\ 0 & n \text{ even}, n \neq 0 \\ \dfrac{200(-1)^m}{(2m+1)\pi} & n = 0 \end{cases}$$

6. (a) $u(x, y, t) = \sum\limits_{n=0}^{\infty} \sum\limits_{m=0}^{\infty} E_{mn} \cos m\pi x \cos n\pi y \exp\left[-(m^2 + n^2)\pi^2 t / a^2\right]$, $E_{mn} = \begin{cases} \dfrac{1}{4} & m, n = 0 \\ 0 & m \text{ even}, m \neq 0 \\ -\dfrac{4}{m^2\pi^2} & m \text{ odd} \\ 0 & n \text{ odd}, n \neq 0 \\ -\dfrac{4}{n^2\pi^2} & n \text{ odd} \\ \dfrac{16}{m^2 n^2 \pi^2} & m, n \text{ odd} \end{cases}$

(b) $u(x, y, t) = \sum\limits_{n=1}^{\infty} \sum\limits_{m=1}^{\infty} E_{mn} \cos m\pi x \cos n\pi y \exp\left[-(m^2 + n^2)\pi^2 t / a^2\right]$, $E_{mn} = \begin{cases} 1 & m, n = 0 \\ 0 & mn = 0 \\ 0 & m \text{ even}, mn \neq 0 \\ -\dfrac{8}{m^2\pi^2} & m \text{ odd}, n \neq 0 \\ 0 & n \text{ even}, mn \neq 0 \\ -\dfrac{8}{n^2\pi^2} & n \text{ odd}, m \neq 0 \end{cases}$

8. (a) $y_{ss} = \left[\dfrac{\ell \sin(\omega x/a)}{\omega^2 \sin(\omega\ell/a)} - \dfrac{x}{\omega^2}\right]\sin \omega t, \quad \omega \neq \dfrac{n\pi a}{\ell}$

(b) $y_{ss} = \left[\dfrac{2a^2 \cos[(\omega(\ell-2x)/2a]}{\omega^4 \cos(\omega\ell/2a)} + \dfrac{x^2}{\omega^2} \dfrac{x\ell}{\omega^2} - \dfrac{2a^2}{\omega^4}\right]\cos \omega t, \quad \omega \neq \dfrac{n\pi a}{\ell}$

10. $Y(x, t) = \sum\limits_{n=1}^{\infty} C_n \sin \dfrac{n\pi x}{\ell} \sin \omega t$, where, $C_n = \begin{cases} (-1)^{n+1} \dfrac{4}{n\pi} \sin \dfrac{n\pi k}{2\ell} \Big/ \left[\dfrac{a^2 n^2 \pi^2}{\ell^2} - \omega^2\right] & n \text{ odd} \\ 0 & n \text{ even} \end{cases}$

The natural frequencies of the string are $\omega_n = \dfrac{n\pi a}{\ell}$, but resonance cannot occur in the present case when n is even since all even harmonics are missing from the expansion of $\phi(x)$. Moreover, even when n is odd resonance will not occur if k is such that $\dfrac{n\pi k}{2\ell} = m\pi$ or $k = \dfrac{2m\ell}{n}$.

14. Method **(a)** is usually preferable because it is more straightforward, leads directly to the steady-state solution, and gives more information about the possibility of resonance.

16. $y(x, t) = \sum\limits_{n=1}^{\infty} \sin\frac{n\pi x}{\ell}\left[A_n \cos\sqrt{\frac{n^2\pi^2 a^2}{\ell^2}+c^2}\,t + B_n \sin\sqrt{\frac{n^2\pi^2 a^2}{\ell^2}+c^2}\,t\right]$ where $A_n = \frac{2}{\ell}\int_0^{\ell} g(x)\sin\frac{n\pi x}{\ell}dx$ and

$B_n = \frac{2}{\sqrt{n^2\pi^2 a^2 + c^2\ell^2}}\int_0^{\ell} h(x)\sin\frac{n\pi x}{\ell}dx$. The natural frequencies, $\omega_n = \sqrt{\frac{n^2\pi^2 a^2}{\ell^2}+c^2}$ are not in arithmetic progression.

18. $Y(x, t) = \frac{2}{a^2\pi^2(1-n^2)-c^2\ell^2}\sin\frac{\pi x}{\ell}\sin\frac{n\pi a t}{\ell} \quad \frac{n^2 a^2\pi^2}{\ell^2} \neq \frac{n^2\pi^2 a^2}{\ell^2}-c^2 = \omega_n^2$ (See Ex. 16)

20. $u(x, y, t) = \sum\limits_{m=1}^{\infty}\sum\limits_{n=1}^{\infty} E_{mn}\sin m\pi x\sin n\pi x\exp\left[-(b^2+m^2\pi^2+n^2\pi^2)t/a\right]$

$E_{mn} = 4\int_0^1\int_0^1 g(x,y)\sin m\pi x\sin n\pi x\,dx\,dy$

22. (a) The problem can be solved by super-imposing the solutions to the problems defined by the following sets of boundary conditions:

$u(x, 0) = f_1(x), \; u(x, 1) = u(0, y) = u(1, y) = 0, \; u(x, 1) = f_2(x), \; u(x, 0) = u(0, y) = u(1, y) = 0$
$u(0, y) = f_3(y), \; u(x, 0) = u(x, 1) = u(1, y) = 0, \; u(1, y) = f_4(y), \; u(x, 0) = u(x, 1) = u(0, y) = 0$

(b) Once the steady-state is known, proceed just as in Example 1.

24. $u(x, t) = \sin\left(\omega t - a\sqrt{\frac{\omega}{2}}x\right)\exp(-a\sqrt{\omega}x/\sqrt{2})$ By applying this formula to each term in the Fourier expansion of an arbitrary periodic end condition, the steady-state temperature distribution produced by such an end condition can be determined by superposition.

26. (a) $B(\lambda) = \frac{2\lambda}{(1+\lambda^2)\pi}$

(b) $B(\lambda) = \frac{2}{\lambda\pi}T_0(1-\cos k\lambda)$

30. $u(x, t) = \sum\limits_{n=1}^{\infty} c_n\exp[-n^2\pi^2 t/a^2\ell^2]\sin\frac{n\pi x}{\ell} + \phi(x)$ where $\phi(x) = \frac{x}{k\ell}\int_0^{\ell}\int_0^s \phi(r)\,dr\,ds - \frac{1}{k}\int_0^x\int_0^s \phi(r)\,dr\,ds$

and $C_n = \frac{2}{\ell}\int_0^{\ell}[g(x)-\phi(x)]\sin\frac{n\pi x}{\ell}dx$

32. $u(x, y, t) = \sum_{n=1}^{\infty} \int_0^\infty E_{n\mu} \sin n\pi x \sin \mu y \exp\left[-(n^2\pi^2 + \mu^2)t/a^2\right]d\mu$ where

$E_{n\mu} = \frac{4}{\pi} \int_0^\infty \int_0^1 g(x, y) \sin n\pi x \sin \mu y\, dx\, dy$

34. $u(x, y, t) = \sum_{n=1}^{\infty} \int_0^\infty E_{n\mu} \cos n\pi x \sin \mu y \exp\left[-(n^2\pi^2 + \mu^2)t/a^2\right]d\mu$, where

$E_{n\mu} = \frac{\alpha}{\pi} \int_0^\infty \int_0^1 g(x, y) \cos n\pi x \sin \mu y\, dx\, dy$ and $\alpha = 2$ if $n = 0$ and 4 if $n \neq 0$

36. $u(x, y, t) = \sum_{m=1}^{\infty} \sum_{n=1}^{\infty} E_{mn} \sinh[\sqrt{m^2 + n^2}\,\pi(1 - z)] \sin m\pi x \sin n\pi y$ where

$E_{mn} = \dfrac{4}{\sinh\sqrt{m^2 + n^2}\,\pi} \int_0^1 \int_0^1 f(x, y) \sin m\pi x \sin n\pi y\, dx\, dy$

38. **(a)** $A(\lambda) = 2T_0 / \pi(1 + \lambda^2)$

   (b) $A(\lambda) = 4T_0(\sin \lambda a - \lambda a \cos \lambda a) / \pi\lambda^3$

   (c) $A(\lambda) = 2T_0(1 - \cos \lambda a) / \pi\lambda^2$

40. **(a)** $u(x, y) = \sum_{n=1}^{\infty} A_n \cos \frac{2n-1}{2}\pi x e^{-(2n-1)\pi y/2} + \int_0^\infty B_\lambda \sinh \lambda x \sinh \lambda y\, d\lambda$ where $A_n = 400/(2n - 1)\pi$ and

   $B_\lambda = 200(1 - \cos \lambda a)/\lambda \pi \sinh \lambda$

   (b) $u(x, y) = \sum_{n=1}^{\infty} A_n \cos \frac{2n-1}{2}\pi x e^{-(2n-1)\pi y/2} + \int_0^\infty B_\lambda \cosh \lambda x \sin \lambda y\, d\lambda$, where $A_n = \frac{400}{(2n-1)\pi} \sin \frac{2n-1}{2}\pi$

   and $B_\lambda = \dfrac{200(1 - \cos \lambda a)}{\lambda \pi \cosh \lambda}$

42. $\omega_n = a\sqrt{m^2 + n^2}/2\ell$, $m, n = 1, 2, 3, \ldots$ and ℓ is the length of the edge of the membrane.

44. **(a)** $Y(x, t) = \dfrac{g/A\rho}{\omega^2 - (a^2\pi^4/\ell^4)} \sin \frac{\pi x}{\ell} \sin \omega t$

   (b) $Y(x, t) = \sum_{n=1}^{\infty} \dfrac{(g/A\rho)^2}{\omega^2 - \omega_n^2} B_n \sin \frac{n\pi x}{\ell} \sin \omega t$ where $B_n = \frac{4}{n\pi} \sin \frac{1}{2}\pi \sin \frac{1}{4}\pi$ and $\omega_n = n^2\pi^2 a/\ell^2$

46. Yes, if the appropriate coefficient in the Fourier expansion of the excitation is equal to zero.

48. $y(x, t) = X(x)\sin \omega t$ where

$$X(x) = \left(\tfrac{\ell}{z}\right)^3 \tfrac{F_0}{EI}\left[(\sin z + \sinh z)\left(\cos \tfrac{zx}{\ell} - \cosh \tfrac{zx}{\ell}\right) + (\cos z + \cosh z)\left(\sinh \tfrac{zx}{\ell} - \sin \tfrac{zx}{\ell}\right)\right]\tfrac{1}{2(\cos z \cosh z + 1)}$$

and $z = \sqrt{\tfrac{\omega}{a}}\,\ell$

50. $(\cos z \cosh z + 1) + \dfrac{k\ell^3}{EIz^3\left(1 - \tfrac{3Mk}{mKz^4}\right)}(\sin z \cosh z - \cos z \sinh z) = 0$ where $z = \sqrt{\omega/a}\,\ell$, $M =$ total mass of the

beam and $K = \ell^3 / 3EI$ is the tip deflection of the beam under a unit load at the free end, i.e., $1/K$ is the modulus of the beam as an end-loaded cantilever spring.

52. $u(x, t) = \dfrac{1}{2\pi} \displaystyle\int_{-\infty}^{\infty}\int_{-\infty}^{\infty} e^{-\omega^2 t/a^2}\, g(s)e^{-i\omega(x-s)}\,ds\,d\omega$

54. $u(x, t) = \dfrac{\alpha x(1-x^2)}{6} - \dfrac{2\alpha}{\pi^3} \displaystyle\sum_{n=1}^{\infty}\dfrac{(-1)^{n+1}}{n^3}e^{-n^2\pi^2 t}\sin n\pi x$ where α is the proportionality constant.

Section 11.8

2. $y(x, t) = \dfrac{\ell}{n\pi a}\sin\dfrac{n\pi a t}{\ell}\sin\dfrac{n\pi x}{\ell}$

4. $y(x, t) = \dfrac{\omega \sin \omega_n t - \omega_n \sin \omega t}{\omega^2 - \omega_n^2}$, $\omega_n = \dfrac{n\pi a}{\ell}$, $\omega \neq \omega_n$

6. $y(x, t) = \dfrac{\sin \omega t}{2\omega^2} - \dfrac{t\cos \omega t}{2\omega}$

8. $\theta(x, t) = \dfrac{2\ell}{(2n+1)\pi a}\sin\dfrac{(2n+1)\pi a t}{2\ell}\sin\dfrac{(2n+1)\pi x}{2\ell}$

10. $\theta(x, t) = \dfrac{\ell}{n\pi a}\sin\dfrac{n\pi a t}{\ell}\cos\dfrac{n\pi x}{\ell}$

12. $e(x, t) = -\displaystyle\int_0^t \dfrac{\partial}{\partial t}\left[\operatorname{erf}\dfrac{ax}{2\sqrt{\tau}}\right]f(t-\tau) - d\tau$

14. $y(x, t) = \begin{cases} \dfrac{v^2 F_0}{a^2 - v^2}\left[\frac{1}{2}\left(t - \frac{x}{v}\right)^2 u\left(t - \frac{x}{v}\right) - \frac{1}{2}\left(t - \frac{x}{a}\right)^2 u\left(t - \frac{x}{a}\right)\right] & v \ne a \\[3mm] -\dfrac{F_0}{2a}\left[x\left(t - \frac{x}{a}\right)u\left(t - \frac{x}{a}\right)\right] & v = a \end{cases}$

16. $e(x, t) = \begin{cases} 1 - \operatorname{erf}\dfrac{ax}{2\sqrt{t}} & 0 \le t \le k \\[3mm] \operatorname{erf}\dfrac{ax}{2\sqrt{t-k}} - \operatorname{erf}\dfrac{ax}{2\sqrt{t}} & t \ge k \end{cases}$

18. $\mathcal{L}\{\theta\} = \dfrac{aT_0 \sinh(sx/a)}{E_s J s \cosh(s\ell/a)}$ when $x = \ell$, this becomes $\dfrac{aT_0}{E_s J}\dfrac{1}{s}\tanh\dfrac{s\ell}{a}$. Hence, in this case θ is the Morse dot function of period $4\ell/a$.

20. $\mathcal{L}(y) = \dfrac{gF_0\omega}{aws(s^2+\omega^2)}\left[e^{-bs/a}\sinh\dfrac{xs}{a} - \sinh\dfrac{(x-b)s}{a}u(x-b)\right]$. If $x = b$, $\mathcal{L}(y) = \dfrac{gF_0\omega}{aws(s^2+\omega^2)}\cdot\dfrac{1-e^{-2bs/a}}{2}$ and

$y(b) = \dfrac{gF_0}{aw}\left[(1 - \cos\omega t)\left\{1 - \cos\omega\left(t - \frac{2b}{a}\right)\right\}u\left(t - \frac{2b}{a}\right)\right]$

Section 11.9

2. Iteration merely reproduces the assumed starting values since the iteration process is equivalent to the solution of the system of mesh equations.

4.

13.4	18.6	13.4
21.6	29.0	21.6
44.0	54.2	44.0

6. (a) $4f_{11} - 2f_{21} = 0$
$\quad 4f_{22} - 2f_{21} - 2f_{32} = 0$
$\quad 4f_{21} - f_{11} - f_{22} - f_{31} = 0$
$\quad 4f_{32} - f_{22} - f_{31} - f_{42} = 100$
$\quad 4f_{31} - f_{21} - f_{32} - f_{41} = 0$
$\quad 4f_{42} - f_{32} - f_{41} = 100$
$\quad 4f_{41} - 2f_{31} - f_{42} = 0$

(b) $4f_{11} - 2f_{21} = 0$
$\quad 4f_{41} - f_{31} = 75$
$\quad 4f_{21} - f_{11} - f_{22} - f_{31} = 0$
$\quad 4f_{22} - 2f_{21} - 2f_{32} = 0$
$\quad 4f_{31} - f_{21} - f_{32} - f_{41} = 0$
$\quad 4f_{32} - f_{22} - f_{31} = 150$

8. $f_{11} \doteq 20.0, \ f_{12} \doteq 38.7, \ f_{13} \doteq 34.7, \ f_{21} \doteq 41.4, \ f_{31} \doteq 45.7$

10. $f_{11} \doteq 8.2, \ f_{21} \doteq 16.4, \ f_{31} \doteq 23.2, \ f_{41} \doteq 24.6, \ f_{22} \doteq 34.1, \ f_{32} \doteq 51.8$

12. $f_{ijk} = (f_{i+1,j,k} + f_{i,j+1,k} + f_{i,j,k+1} + f_{i-1,j,k} + f_{i,j-1,k} + f_{i,j,k-1})/6$

14. (a) After 10 iterations the temperature distribution from left to right is 100, 75.4, 54.9, 34.4, 22.6, 10.8, 6.4, 2.0, 1.1, 0.2, 0.0

(b) Iteration using $m = 1$ leads to absurd values for the temperature.

16. At $x = \ell/10$, u reaches a maximum of 0.66 when $t = 8$.
At $x = 2\,\ell/10$, u reaches a maximum of 0.44 when $t = 10$.
At $x = 3\,\ell/10$, u reaches a maximum of 0.30 when $t = 12$.
At $x = 4\,\ell/10$, u reaches a maximum of 0.20 when $t = 14$.

18. **(a)** $f_{i,j,k+1} = m(f_{i+1,j,k} + f_{i-1,j,k} + f_{i,j+1,k} + f_{i,j-1,k}) + (1 - 4m)f_{i,j,k}$ where $m = k/a^2 h^2$.

(b) $f_{i,j,k+1} = m(f_{i+1,j,k} + f_{i-1,j,k} + f_{i,j+1,k} + f_{i,j-1,k}) + (2 - 4m)f_{i,j,k} - f_{i,j,k-1}$ where $m = k^2/a^2 h^2$.

Chapter 12

Section 12.1

2. (a) $\dfrac{\tau g}{w(x)}\dfrac{X''(x)}{X(x)} = \dfrac{T''(t)}{T(t)} = \mu$, a constant,

   τ = tension in the string

   (b) $\dfrac{E_s g}{J(x)}\dfrac{[J(x)X'(x)]'}{X(x)} = \dfrac{T''(t)}{T(t)} = \mu$, a constant

   (c) $\dfrac{Eg}{\rho}\dfrac{[I(x)X''(x)]''}{A(x)X(x)} = -\dfrac{T''(t)}{T(t)} = \mu$, a constant

Section 12.2

14. $\dfrac{2}{\pi x Y_v(x) J_v(x)}$

20. $y = J_n(t)\displaystyle\int \dfrac{dt}{t J_n^{\,2}(t)}$

22. $y = 3 J_0(x)$

24. (a) $y = A J_1(\lambda x) + B Y_1(\lambda x)$

   (b) $y_n(x) = A_n J_1(\lambda_n x)$. $A_n \neq 0$ an arbitrary constant, $n = 1, 2, 3, \ldots$ where λ_n is the nth positive root of $J_1(\lambda) = 0$.

26. $f_n = \dfrac{1}{2\pi\ell}\sqrt{\dfrac{Eg}{\rho}}\, z_n$, where z_n is the nth positive zero of $J_0(z)$.

Section 12.3

8. $I_v(x)/K_v(x)$

10. $u(r) = 100 I_0(br)/I_0(b\rho)$, where ρ is the radius of the disk.

Section 12.4

2. $y = \sqrt{x}\left[c_1 I_{1/4}\left(x^2/2\right) + c_2 K_{1/4}(x^2/2)\right]$

4. $y = \sqrt{x}[c_1 J_3(2\sqrt{x}) + Y_3(2\sqrt{x})]$

6. $y = c_1 J_0(x) + c_2 Y_0(x)$

8. $y = x^{3/2}\left[c_1 J_{\sqrt{5}}(2\sqrt{x}) + c_2 Y_{\sqrt{5}}(2\sqrt{x})\right]$

10. $y = \sqrt{x}[c_1 J_1(2\sqrt{x}) + c_2 Y_1(2\sqrt{x})]$

12. $y = |x|^{-1/2}\left[c_1 J_{1/2}(2x) + c_2 J_{-1/2}(2x)\right]$

14. $y = x^{3/2}e^{-x/2}[c_1 I_{1/2}(x/2) + c_2 I_{-1/2}(x/2)]$

16. $y = x^{3/2}[c_1 I_{1/2}(x) + c_2 I_{-1/2}(x)]$

18. $y = e^{-x}[c_1 J_2(2^{3/2}\sqrt{x}) + c_2 Y_2(2^{3/2}\sqrt{x})]$

20. $y = |x|^{-1/2}[c_1 J_{(2n-1)/2}(x) + c_2 J_{-(2n-1)/2}(x)]$

22. No.

24. $y = (1+x)^{-1/2}[c_1 J_3\{2\sqrt{3(1+x)}\}$

   $+ c_2 Y_3\{2\sqrt{3(1+x)}\}]$

30. $y = \dfrac{x}{x+3}[c_1 J_{1/6}(x^3/3) + c_2 J_{-1/6}(x^3/3)]$

32. $y = x\cos x[c_1 J_{1/3}(\tfrac{2}{3}x^{3/2}) + c_2 J_{-1/3}(\tfrac{2}{3}x^{3/2})]$

34. $y = c_1 J_0\left(2\sqrt{3|x|}\right) + c_2 Y_0\left(2\sqrt{3|x|}\right)$

$\qquad + c_3 I_0\left(2\sqrt{3|x|}\right) + c_4 K_0\left(2\sqrt{3|x|}\right)$

36. $y = \frac{1}{x}\left[c_1 J_2\left(2\sqrt{3|x|}\right) + c_2 Y_2\left(2\sqrt{3|x|}\right)\right.$

$\qquad \left. + c_3 I_2\left(2\sqrt{3|x|}\right) + c_4 K_2\left(2\sqrt{3|x|}\right)\right]$

38. **(a)** $y = c_1 x + c_2 x(1 - e^{-x})$

$\qquad$ **(b)** $y = x^{3/2} e^{-x/2}[c_1 I_{1/2}(x/2)$

$\qquad\qquad + c_2 I_{-1/2}(x/2)]$

42. $y = 10 I_0(x)$

Section 12.5

4. **(a)** $J_3(x) = \left(\frac{8}{x^2} - 1\right)J_1(x) - \frac{4}{x}J_0(x)$

$\qquad$ **(b)** $J_3(\lambda x^2) = \left(\frac{8}{\lambda^2 x^4} - 1\right)J_1(\lambda x^2)$

$\qquad\qquad - \frac{4}{\lambda x^2}J_0(\lambda x^2)$

6. $\left(\lambda x^4 + \frac{4}{\lambda}x^2\right)J_1(\lambda x) - 2x^3 J_0(\lambda x)$

10. **(a)** $\lambda x^4\left[J_0(\lambda x)J_3(\lambda x) + J_1(\lambda x)J_2(\lambda x)\right]$

$\qquad$ **(b)** $x^3 J_3(\lambda x) + \lambda x^4 J_2(\lambda x)$

$\qquad$ **(c)** $\frac{\lambda[J_2(\lambda x)J_0(\lambda x) - J_1^2(\lambda x)]}{x J_1^2(\lambda x)}$

12. **(a)** $-\frac{1}{2}x^2 J_0(2x) + \frac{x}{2}J_1(2x) + c$

$\qquad$ **(b)** $-\frac{1}{2}J_0^2(x) + c$

16. **(a)** $2\sqrt{x}(x-4)J_1(\sqrt{x}) + 4x J_0(\sqrt{x}) + c$

(b) $2x^{3/2}J_3(\sqrt{x}) + c$

26. $1/x$

32. **(b)** $x J_0(x)\sin x - x J_1(x)\cos x + c$

34. **(a)** $\frac{1}{3}x^2[J_0(x)\cos x + J_1(x)\sin x]$

$\qquad\qquad + \frac{1}{3}x J_1(x)\cos x + c$

$\qquad$ **(b)** $\frac{1}{3}x^2[J_0(x)\cos x + J_1(x)\sin x]$

$\qquad\qquad - \frac{2}{3}x J_1(x)\cos x + c$

40. **(b)** $-J_3(x)$

44. $y_5 = x^2 J_2(\lambda x), \ \ y_6 = x^2 Y_2(\lambda x)$

48. $\lambda\left(a^2 + \lambda^2\right)^{3/2}$

50. $\frac{2}{\sqrt{a^2 + \lambda^2}\left[a + \sqrt{a^2 + \lambda^2}\right]} - \frac{\lambda}{\left(a^2 + \lambda^2\right)^{3/2}}$

54. **(a)** $1/\sqrt{a^2 + \lambda^2}$

$\qquad$ **(b)** $\frac{\lambda}{\sqrt{a^2 - \lambda^2}\left[a + \sqrt{a^2 - \lambda^2}\right]}$

58. **(a)** $\frac{1}{3}J_1(x)(5x\cos x - x^2 \sin x)$

$\qquad\qquad - \frac{1}{3}J_0(x)\left[(x^2 + 6)\cos x + 6x\sin x\right]$

$\qquad$ **(b)** $\frac{1}{3}J_1(x)(5x\sin x + x^2 \cos x)$

$\qquad\qquad - \frac{1}{3}J_0(x)\left[(x^2 + 6)\sin x - 6x\cos x\right]$

Section 12.6

2. $\cos x = J_0(x) - 2 J_2(x) + 2 J_4(x) - \ldots$
$\sin x = 2 J_1(x) - 2 J_3(x) + 2 J_5(x) - \ldots$

4. (b) $\displaystyle\int_0^{2\pi} e^{ix\sin\phi} \cos n\phi \, d\phi = \begin{cases} 0 & n \text{ odd} \\ 2\pi J_n(x) & n \text{ even} \end{cases}$

(c) $\displaystyle\int_0^{2\pi} e^{ix\sin\phi} \sin n\phi \, d\phi = \begin{cases} 2\pi i J_n(x) & n \text{ odd} \\ 0 & n \text{ even} \end{cases}$

8. Simply reverse the steps by which Eqns. (3) and (4) were derived from Theorems 1 and 2.

10. $\displaystyle\int J_1(x)dx = 2[J_2(x) + J_4(x) + J_6(x)$
$\qquad\qquad + \ldots] + c$
$\displaystyle\int J_2(x)dx = 2[J_3(x) + J_5(x) + J_7(x)$
$\qquad\qquad + \ldots] + c$
$\displaystyle\int J_3(x)dx = 2[J_4(x) + J_6(x) + J_8(x)$
$\qquad\qquad + \ldots] + c$

12. (a) $\displaystyle e^x = I_0(x) + 2\sum_{n=1}^{\infty} I_n(x)$

(b) $\displaystyle e^{-x} = I_0(x) + 2\sum_{n=1}^{\infty} (-1)^n I_n(x)$

14. $\displaystyle e^{-x\sin\theta} = I_0(x) + 2\sum_{k=1}^{\infty} (-1)^k I_{2k}(x)\cos 2k\theta$

Section 12.7

2 (a) $b_1 = b_2 = 0$ A spherical shell with $u = 0$ on each spherical boundary.

(b) $b_1 \neq 0$, $b_2 = 0$ A spherical shell with $u = 0$ on the outer surface and either an

insulated or free-escape condition on the inner surface.

(c) $b_1 = 0$, $b_2 \neq 0$ A spherical shell with $u = 0$ on the inner surface and either an insulated or free-escape condition on the outer surface.

(d) $b_1 \neq 0$, $b_2 \neq 0$ A spherical shell with either an insulated or free-escape condition on each spherical boundary.

(e) $x_1 = 0$, $b_2 = 0$ A solid sphere with $u = 0$ on the outer surface.

(f) $x_1 = 0$, $b_2 \neq 0$ A solid sphere with either an insulated or free-escape condition on the outer surface.

6. (a) Under the conditions of the problem, with $x_2 = 1$,

$$\int_0^1 x \cdot 1 \cdot J_0(\lambda_n x)dx = \frac{1}{\lambda_n} J_1(\lambda_n x)\Big|_0^1 = 0$$

for every value of n; that is, $f(x) = 1$ is orthogonal to each of the characteristic functions $\{J_0(\lambda_n x)\}$.

(b) Yes. $f(x) = 1$ is a solution of Bessel's equation of order zero for $\lambda = 0$ and satisfies the given boundary condition.

8. No. Under the given boundary condition,

$$\int_0^x 2 \cdot x \cdot x^\upsilon \cdot J_\upsilon(\lambda_n x)dx \neq 0.$$

14. $\lambda \doteq 2.17$

16. $\lambda \doteq 0.52$

18. Since the characteristic equation $J_1(3\lambda) = 0$ has $\lambda_0 = 0$ as a characteristic value, for $\{J_0(\lambda_n\lambda)\}$ to be a complete orthogonal set on $[0, 3]$ it must contain $J_0(\lambda_0 x) = J_0(0) = 1$. Hence the required expansion is simply

$1 = \sum_{n=0}^{\infty} a_n J_0(\lambda_n x)$ where $a_0 = 1$ and for

$n \geqq 1, a_n = 0$

20. $1 = \sum_{n=1}^{\infty} a_n J_0(\lambda_n x)$, where

$a_n = \dfrac{2}{3\lambda_n(\lambda_n^2 + 1)J_1(3\lambda_n)}$

22. $x = \sum_{n=1}^{\infty} a_n J_1(\lambda_n x)$, where

$a_n = \dfrac{6}{(9\lambda_n^2 - 1)J_1(3\lambda_n)}$

24. The required expansion is x itself, since x is one of the characteristic functions.

26. $4x - x^3 = \sum_{n=1}^{\infty} a_n J_1(\lambda_n x)$, where

$a_n = -\dfrac{32(\lambda_n^2 - 1)}{\lambda_n^2(4\lambda_n^2 - 1)J_1(2\lambda_n)}$

28. $x^2 = \sum_{n=1}^{\infty} a_n J_2(\lambda_n x)$, where

$a_n = -\dfrac{4}{\lambda_n J_1(2\lambda_n)}$

30. The required expansion is x^2 itself, since x^2 is one of the characteristic functions.

32. $f(x) = \sum_{n=1}^{\infty} a_n J_{3/2}(\lambda_n x)$, where

$a_n = \pi^{5/2}\left[\dfrac{1}{\lambda_n \pi} + \dfrac{2}{\lambda_n^3 \pi^3}\left(1 - \dfrac{1}{\cos\lambda_n \pi}\right)\right]$

In the case the series is not a Fourier series.

34. $J_\upsilon(\lambda)J'_{-\upsilon}(2\lambda) - J'_\upsilon(2\lambda)J_{-\upsilon}(\lambda) = 0$ if υ is an integer, $J_{-\upsilon}$ must be replaced by Y_υ.

36. $\sum_{n=1}^{\infty} \dfrac{4x^{1/2}}{\lambda_n J_1(\lambda_n/2)} J_0(\lambda_n x^2/2)$, where

$J_0(\lambda_n/2) = 0$; assuming

$\sqrt{x}\,Y_0(\lambda x^2/2) \to \infty$ which does not appear to be true.

38. 1/16

40. $x^2 = 2 + 4\sum_{n=1}^{\infty} \dfrac{J_0(\lambda_n x)}{\lambda_n^2 J_0(2\lambda_n)}$, where $J_1(2\lambda_n) = 0$

Section 12.8

2. $y(x) = \sum_{n=1}^{\infty} \sqrt{g}\,\lambda_n B_n J_0\left(2\lambda_n \sqrt{x}\right)$, where

$B_n = \dfrac{v}{\lambda_n^2}\sqrt{\dfrac{\alpha}{g\ell}}\,\dfrac{J_1\left(2\lambda_n \sqrt{\alpha\ell}\right)}{J_1^2\left(2\lambda_n \sqrt{\ell}\right)}$ and the λ's are the

roots of the equation $J_0\left(2\lambda\sqrt{\ell}\right) = 0$

4. $f_n = \dfrac{1}{2\pi}\omega_n$ Hz, where ω_n is the nth root of the equation $J_0(b\omega/a) = 0$, a is the parameter in the wave equation, and b is the radius of the membrane.

6. $y = \sum_{n=1}^{\infty} a_n J_0(\lambda_n r)\cos\lambda_n at$, where

$a_n = \dfrac{8}{\lambda_n^3 b J_1(\lambda_n b)}$ and λ_n is the nth root of the equation $J_n(\lambda b) = 0$.

8. $z(r,t) = \dfrac{gF_0}{w\omega^2}\dfrac{J_0(\omega r/a) - 1}{J_0(\omega b/a)}\cos\omega t$

10. $\dfrac{\sqrt{\lambda}I_1(2\alpha\sqrt{\varepsilon a})}{I_1(2\alpha\sqrt{a})}$

14. $u(r,\theta,z)=\sum_{n=1}^{\infty}\sum_{m=1}^{\infty}A_{nm}J_n\left(\frac{m\pi r}{h}\right)\sin\frac{m\pi r}{h}\sin n\theta$

where $A_{nm}=\dfrac{2}{hJ_n(m\pi b/h)}\int_0^h F_n(z)\sin\frac{m\pi z}{h}\,dz$

and $F_n(z)=\frac{2}{\pi}\int_0^{\pi}g(\theta,z)\sin n\theta\,d\theta$

16. $u(r,z)=\sum_{n=1}^{\infty}B_nI_0\left(\frac{n\pi r}{h}\right)\sin\frac{n\pi z}{h}$, where

$B_n=\dfrac{2}{hI_0(n\pi b/h)}\int_0^h f(z)\sin\frac{n\pi z}{h}\,dz$

18. $u(z)=\dfrac{100(h-z)}{h}$

20. $u(r,z)=\sum_{n=1}^{\infty}B_nJ_0(\lambda_n r)\sin\lambda_n z$, where

$B_n=\dfrac{200}{\lambda_n bJ_1(\lambda_n b)\sin\lambda_n h}$ and λ_n is the *n*th root of the equation $J_0(\lambda b)=0$.

22. $u(r,t)=\sum_{n=1}^{\infty}c_nJ_0(\lambda_n r)\exp(-\lambda_n^2 t/a^2)$

where $c_n=\dfrac{200}{\lambda_nJ_n(\lambda_n b)}$ and λ_n is the *n*th root of the equation $J_0(\lambda b)=0$.

24. $u(r,\theta,t)=\sum_{n=1}^{\infty}\sum_{m=1}^{\infty}A_{nm}J_{2n}(\lambda_{nm}r)\sin 2n\theta$

$\times\exp(-\lambda_{nm}^2 t/a^2)$ where

$A_{nm}=\dfrac{800}{n\pi}\int_0^b rJ_{2n}(\lambda_{nm}r)dr\,/\,b^2J_{2n+1}^2(\lambda_{nm}b)$,

and λ_{nm} is the *m*th root of the equation $J_{2n}(\lambda b)=0$.

26. $u(r,t)=100+\sum_{n=1}^{\infty}A_nJ_0(\lambda_n r)\exp(-\lambda_n^2 t/a^2)$

where $A_n=-\dfrac{200(\lambda_n^2b^2-4)}{\lambda_n^3b^3J_1(\lambda_n b)}$ and λ_n is the *n*th root of the equation $J_0(\lambda_{nb})=0$.

28. $u(r,z)=\sum_{n=1}^{\infty}A_nJ_0(\lambda_n r)e^{-\lambda_n z}$, where

$A_n=\dfrac{200}{\lambda_n bJ_1(\lambda_n b)}$ and λ_n is the *n*th root of the equation $J_0(\lambda_n b)=0$.

36. $\dfrac{a^n}{\sqrt{s^2+a^2}\left[s+\sqrt{s^2+a^2}\right]^n}$

38. (a) $1/a$

(b) 0

(c) $1/a^2$

40. (a) $\dfrac{s}{(s^2-a^2)^{3/2}}$

(b) $\dfrac{a}{(s^2-a^2)^{3/2}}$

(c) $\dfrac{2s^2+a^2}{(s^2-a^2)^{5/2}}$

42. $f(t)=\frac{1}{27}e^{-t}t^2J_2(3t)$

46. $\displaystyle\int_0^t J_0(2\lambda)J_0(t-\lambda)d\lambda$

48. $Y(t) = tJ_1(t)$

50. $\sin t - tJ_0(t)$

56. $\dfrac{1}{s}e^{1/s}$

60. $\sigma = \sigma_0 \dfrac{M_0(kr)}{M_0(ka)} \exp[i\{\theta_0(kr) - \theta_0(ka)\}]$

62. $f_1 \doteq 485$ Hz, $f_2 \doteq 1{,}120$ Hz

64. $\displaystyle\theta(x,t) = \sum_{n=1}^{\infty} A_n J_0(\lambda_n x)\cos\lambda_n at$, where

$$A_n = \frac{2(100)^3\,\lambda_n J_1(100\lambda_n) - 2\int_0^{100} J_0(\lambda_n x)dx}{(100)^3\,\lambda_n^2 J_1^2(100\lambda_n)}$$

λ_n is the nth root of the equation

$J_0(100\lambda_n) = 0$, and $a_n^2 = \dfrac{E_s g}{\rho}$

66. The frequency equation is

$$J_0\!\left(\frac{2\lambda}{\alpha}\right)Y_0\!\left(\frac{2\lambda}{\alpha}e^{\alpha\ell/2}\right)$$
$$- J_0\!\left(\frac{2\lambda}{\alpha}e^{\alpha\ell/2}\right)Y_0\!\left(\frac{2\lambda}{\alpha}\right) = 0$$

With $a^2 = Tg/w_0$, the natural frequencies are $f_n = \lambda_n a/2\pi$, $n = 1, 2, 3, \ldots$

68. $x(t) = e^{\alpha t/2}\Big[c_1 I_1(be^{\alpha t/2}) + c_2 K_1(be^{\alpha t/2})\Big]$

where c_1 and c_2 are determined from the equations

$c_1 I_1(b) + c_2 K_1(b) = x_0$

$c_1 I_0(b) + c_2 K_0(b) = 0$, $\quad b = \dfrac{2k}{\alpha\sqrt{m_0}}$

70. $x(t) = (1 + \alpha t)\Big[c_1 I_{2/3}(\lambda\{1+\alpha t\}^{3/2})$
$$+ c_2 I_{-2/3}(\lambda\{1+\alpha t\}^{3/2})\Big]$$

where c_1 and c_2 are determined from the equations

$c_1 I_{2/3}(\lambda) + c_2 I_{-2/3}(\lambda) = x_0$

$c_1 I_{-1/3}(\lambda) + c_2 I_{1/3}(\lambda) = 0$

and $\lambda = 2k/3\alpha\sqrt{m_0}$.

72. $y = \tan\theta\left[x - \dfrac{\sqrt{x}J_1(2a\sqrt{x})}{aJ_0(2a\sqrt{\ell})}\right]$ where

$a^2 = \dfrac{12F\cos\theta}{Ebk^3}$

74. $u(r,z) = \displaystyle\int_0^{\infty} \frac{\lambda^2}{(1+\lambda^2)^{3/2}}e^{-\lambda z}J_0(\lambda r)d\lambda$

76. $u(r,z) = au_0\displaystyle\int_0^{\infty}\frac{\sinh\lambda z + \sinh(1-z)}{\sinh\lambda}J_1(\lambda a)$
$$\times J_0(\lambda r)d\lambda$$

80. $u(x) = u_0 + (u_w - u_0)\dfrac{\alpha\cosh\alpha x + \sinh\alpha x}{\alpha\cosh\alpha a + \sinh\alpha a}$ where

$\alpha^2 = \dfrac{2h}{kw}$ and w = thickness of the fin.

82. (a) $f_1 = 2{,}430$ Hz; $f_2 = 5{,}590$ Hz

(b) $f_1 = 3{,}180$ Hz; $f_2 = 6{,}360$ Hz

(c) $f_1 = 3{,}880$ Hz; $f_2 = 7{,}100$ Hz

(d) $f_1 = 4{,}550$ Hz; $f_2 = 7{,}820$ Hz

84. $u(x) = u_0$

$$+ \frac{(u_c - u_0)[K_1(\alpha B)I_0(\alpha x) + I_1(\alpha B)K_0(\alpha x)]}{I_0(\alpha b)K_1(\alpha B) + I_1(\alpha B)K_0(\alpha b)},$$

$\alpha^2 = \dfrac{2h}{kw}$

86. $J_1(2\lambda\sqrt{\ell})I_2(2\lambda\sqrt{\ell})$
$$+ I_1(2\lambda\sqrt{\ell})J_2(2\lambda\sqrt{\ell}) = 0$$

where $\lambda^4 = 12\rho\omega^2 / Egk^2$ and k is the proportionality constant in the expression for the depth of the beam.

88. $J_{5/2}(\lambda R)J_{-5/2}(\lambda r) - J_{5/2}(\lambda r)J_{-5/2}(\lambda R) = 0$

where $\lambda = \dfrac{\omega\ell}{a(R-r)}$

90. $u(r,\theta) = \dfrac{2}{\pi}\displaystyle\sum_{n=1}^{\infty}\left(\dfrac{r}{b}\right)^n \left\{ \displaystyle\int_0^{\pi}[f(\theta) - u_0]\sin n\theta \, d\theta \right\}$

$\cdot \sin n\theta$

92. $u(r,\theta) = 50\,\dfrac{\ln r - \ln r_2}{\ln r_1 - \ln r_2}$

$+ \displaystyle\sum_{\substack{n=1 \\ n \text{ odd}}}^{\infty} \dfrac{200}{n\pi}\left[\left(\dfrac{r}{r_2}\right)^n - \left(\dfrac{r_2}{r}\right)^n\right]\sin n\theta$

94. $u(r,z,t) = \displaystyle\sum_{n=1}^{\infty}\sin\dfrac{n\pi z}{h}\displaystyle\sum_{m=1}^{\infty}B_{nm}J_0$

$\cdot \left[\sqrt{\delta_{nm}^2 - \dfrac{n^2\pi^2}{h^2}}\,r\right] \times \exp\left(-\delta_{nm}^t t / a^2\right)$

$+ u_{ss}(r,z)$

where $B_{nm} = \dfrac{\displaystyle\int_0^b G_n(r)J_0\left[\sqrt{\delta_{nm}^2 - \frac{n^2\pi^2}{h^2}}\,r\right]r\,dr}{\dfrac{b^2}{2}J_1^2\left[\sqrt{\delta_{nm}^2 - \frac{n^2\pi^2}{h^2}}\,b\right]}$,

$G_n(r) = \dfrac{2}{h}\displaystyle\int_0^h\left[\phi(r,z) - u_{ss}(r,z)\right]\sin\dfrac{n\pi z}{h}dz$,

u_{ss} is the solution of the steady-state heat problem in Exercise 16, $\delta_{nm}^2 = \dfrac{n^2\pi^2}{h^2} + \dfrac{\rho_m^2}{b^2}$ and ρ_m is the mth root of the equation $J_0(\rho) = 0$.

Section 12.9

18. $f(x) = \displaystyle\sum_{n=0}^{\infty}a_n P_n(x)$ where

$a_n = \begin{cases} 0 & n \text{ even} \\ P_{n-1}(0) - P_{n+1}(0) & n \text{ odd} \end{cases}$

20. $f(x) = \displaystyle\sum_{n=0}^{\infty}a_n P_n(x)$ where $a_0 = \frac{1}{2}$ and

$a_n = \begin{cases} 0 & n \text{ odd} \\ \dfrac{n(2n+3)P_{n-2}(0) - (2n+1)P_n(0)}{(2n-1)(2n+3)} \\ \quad - \dfrac{(n+1)(2n-1)P_{n+2}(0)}{(2n-1)(2n+3)} & n \text{ even} \end{cases}$

26. $u(r,\theta) = \displaystyle\sum_{n=1}^{\infty}a_n r^n P_n(\cos\theta)$, where

$a_n = \begin{cases} 0 & n \text{ even} \\ \dfrac{50}{b^n}[P_{n-1}(0) - P_{n+1}(0)] & n \text{ odd} \end{cases}$

28. $u(r,\theta) = \displaystyle\sum_{n=1}^{\infty}a_{2n-1}r^{2n-1}P_{2n-1}(\cos\theta)$

where $a_{2n-1} = \dfrac{50}{b^{2n-1}}[P_{2n-2}(0) - P_{2n}(0)]$

30. $u(r,\theta) = \displaystyle\sum_{n=0}^{\infty}\left(A_n r^n + \dfrac{B_n}{r^{n+1}}\right)P_n(\cos\theta)$ where

A_n and B_n are determined by the equations

$A_n b_1^n + \dfrac{B_n}{b_1^{n+1}} = \dfrac{2n+1}{2}\displaystyle\int_0^{\pi}f_1(\theta)\sin\theta P_n(\cos\theta)d\theta$

$A_n b_2^n + \dfrac{B_n}{b_2^{n+1}} = \dfrac{2n+1}{2}\displaystyle\int_0^{\pi}f_2(\theta)\sin\theta P_n(\cos\theta)d\theta$

32. $v(r, \theta) = M \sum_{k=1}^{\infty} \frac{(-1)^{k+1} r^{2k+1}}{(2k+1)c^{2k+2}} P_{2k+1}(\cos\theta) \; r < c \quad v(r, \theta) = M \sum_{k=0}^{\infty} \frac{(-1)^k c^{2k}}{(2k+1)r^{2k+1}} P_{2k}(\cos\theta) \; r > c$

36. $P_1^{(1)}(x) = (x^2 - 1)^{1/2} \quad P_2^{(1)}(x) = 3x(x^2 - 1)^{1/2}, \quad P_3^{(1)}(x) = \frac{15x^2 - 3}{2}(x^2 - 1)^{1/2} \quad P_1^{(2)}(x) = 0$

$P_2^{(2)}(x) = 3(x^2 - 1) \quad P_3^{(2)}(x) = 15x(x^2 - 1)$

38. $H_{n0}(x) = a_0 \left[1 - \frac{2n}{2!} x^2 + \frac{2^2 n(n-2)}{4!} x^4 - \frac{2^3 n(n-2)(n-4)}{6!} x^6 + \ldots \right]$

$H_{n1}(x) = a_1 \left[x - \frac{2(n-1)}{3!} x^3 + \frac{2^2 (n-1)(n-3)}{5!} x^5 - \frac{2^3 (n-1)(n-3)(n-5)}{7!} x^7 + \ldots \right]$

$H_{n0}(x)$ is a polynomial if n is even, and $H_{n1}(x)$ is a polynomial if n is odd. The usual definitions are obtained by choosing a_0 and a_1 so that the coefficients of the highest power of x in each is equal to 2^n. The orthogonality of the H's follows from the fact that the given differential equation can be written in the

Sturm-Liouville form $\frac{d(e^{-x^2} y')}{dx} + 2n e^{-x^2} y = 0$

No boundary conditions are required since the weight function e^{-x^2} vanishes at $\pm\infty$.

40. $L_n(x) = a_0 \left[1 - \frac{n}{(1!)^2} x + \frac{n(n-1)}{(2!)^2} x^2 - \frac{n(n-1)(n-2)}{(3!)^2} x^3 + \ldots \right]$

where, customarily, a_0 is taken equal to 1. Since Laguerre's equation can be written in the form

$\left(xe^{-x} y' \right)' + n e^{-x} y = 0$, it follows from Theorem 4, Section 11.6, that solutions corresponding to different values of n are orthogonal with respect to xe^{-x} over the interval $[0, \infty)$, without the necessity of boundary conditions, since $r(x) = xe^{-x}$ vanishes at both $x = 0$ and $x = \infty$. Clearly, $L_n(x)$ is a polynomial for every integral value of n.

42. If n is even it is the term containing $x^{n/2}(2x - z)^{n/2}$. If n is odd, it is the term containing $x^{(n+1)/2}(2x - z)^{(n+1)/2}$.

Chapter 13

Section 13.1

2. **(a)** $(u, v) = 0$

(b) u and v are orthogonal on $\{1, 2, 3, 4, 5\}$.

4. **(a)** No

(b) No

(c) Yes

6. $\mathbf{w} = c(2, 1, -4)$, c arbitrary

8. $f_3(x) = 1 - 6x + 6x^2$

12. An arbitrary vector $\mathbf{v} = (a, b, c)$ is given by
$$\mathbf{v} = \frac{9a+4b-6c}{133}\mathbf{u}_1 + \frac{2a-3b+c}{14}\mathbf{u}_2 + \frac{2a+3b+5c}{38}\mathbf{u}_3$$

14. To expand $\mathbf{v} = (v_1, v_2, v_3)$, set
$\mathbf{v} = a_1\mathbf{u}_1 + a_2\mathbf{u}_2 + a_3\mathbf{u}_3$ and equate
components, with $\mathbf{u}_k = (u_{k1}, u_{k2}, u_{k3})$, to
obtain $v_j = a_1 u_{1j} + a_2 u_{2j} + a_3 u_{3j}$.
Multiply this equation through by $w_j u_{kj}$, sum
the result over j, an use the orthogonality of
the $\mathbf{u}_k$'s with respect to $\mathbf{w}$, to get
$$\sum_{j=1}^{3} w_j v_j u_{kj} = a_k \sum_{j=1}^{3} w_j u_{kj}^2, \quad \text{then}$$
$$a_k = \frac{\sum_{j=1}^{3} w_j v_j u_{kj}}{\sum_{j=1}^{3} w_j u_{kj}^2} \quad 1 \le k \le 3 \quad \text{which}$$
determines the a_j's. For the vector
$\mathbf{v} = (1, -2, 3)$ and the given $\mathbf{u}$'s,
$$\mathbf{v} = \frac{1}{4}\mathbf{u}_1 - \frac{3}{5}\mathbf{u}_2 + \frac{11}{20}\mathbf{u}_3$$

16. $a + bx + cx^2 = \left(a + \frac{c}{3}\right)P_0(x) + bP_1(x) + \frac{2c}{3}P_2(x)$

18. The expansion of $h(x) = x^4$ is
$\frac{1}{5}P_0(x) + \frac{4}{7}P_2(x) = -\frac{3}{35} + \frac{6}{7}x^2$ which does not
represent x^4. This proves that in the space of
quartic functions the set of P's is incomplete.

20. $(f, g) = 0$. Yes

22. $\{w_n\}$ is an orthogonal set on $(-\pi, \pi)$ in the
hermitian sense. No w_n is trivial on $(-\pi, \pi)$.

24. **(a)** $\|w\| = \sqrt{e - 1}$

(b) $\|w_n\| = \sqrt{2\pi}$, $n = 0, \pm 1, \pm 2, \ldots$

26. **(a)** $\begin{bmatrix} 3 & 7 \\ 13 & 3 \end{bmatrix}$

(b) $\begin{bmatrix} 5 & -10 \\ 7 & -6 \\ 4 & -4 \end{bmatrix}$

30. R^2: a Cartesian plane; R^3: Cartesian
3-dimensional space.

32. **(a)** $p(x) = -\frac{5}{3}x^3 - \frac{1}{3}x^2 + x$

(b) $p(x) = x^3 - 3x^2$

(c) $p(x) = 9 + 9x^2$

(d) $p(x) = 1 + 2x + 3x^2 + 4x^3$

34. **(a)** $\mathbf{D} = \{(i, j) \mid 1 \le i \le m, 1 \le j \le n\}$

(b) $\mathbf{D} = \{j \mid 1 \le j \le n\}$

36. Yes

38. Yes

40. No

42. Yes

44. Yes

46. Yes

48. Yes

50. Yes

52. Yes

54. Yes

56. (a) The line $x - y = 0$ in an xy plane

    (b) The line $2x + y = 0$ in an xy plane

    (c) The plane $x = 0$ in Cartesian three space

    (d) The line of intersection of the planes defined by $x + y = 0$ and $z = 0$ in Cartesian three space

    (e) The plane $x + y - z = 0$ in Cartesian three space

    (f) The plane $y = x$ in Cartesian three space

58. One solution is $M_3 = \begin{bmatrix} 0 & 0 \\ 1 & 0 \end{bmatrix}$,

$$M_4 = \begin{bmatrix} -1 & 1 \\ 0 & 1 \end{bmatrix}$$

Section 13.2

2. (a) Not necessarily

    (b) Yes

    (c) No

4. (a) Yes

    (b) No; not closed under scalar multiplication.

    (c) No; not closed under addition.

    (d) No; not closed under addition.

    (e) Yes

    (f) No; not closed under addition.

8. R^3 itself

12. (a) $2x - 6y - z = 0$; a plane

    (b) $6x = 4y = 3z$; a line

    (c) $2x + 2y - z = 0$; a plane

    (d) $9x + 7y + 6z = 0$; a plane

    (e) $10x = -5y = 2z$; a line

    (f) $5x + y - z = 0$; a plane

    (g) $-2x = y = -2z$; a line

    (h) $8x + 6y + 5z = 0$; a plane

14. No; one space is the plane $x - 5y - 3z = 0$; the other space is the plane $17x - 13y - 3z = 0$.

16. (a), (b), (e), and (f)

18. (a) Independent

    (b) Dependent

    (c) Independent

    (d) Independent

    (e) Dependent

    (f) Dependent

    (g) Dependent

    (h) Independent

    (i) Independent

    (j) Dependent

30. (a) Independent

    (b) Independent

    (c) Dependent

    (d) Independent

(f) Independent

(g) Dependent

(h) Independent

(i) Independent

(j) Independent

32. Impossible

38. **(a)** Yes

(b) Yes

40. At least 10

46. Delete all conjugate symbols in G.

50. $w(t) \equiv 0$

Section 13.3

2. $\theta = n\pi$, n an integer

4. Yes; the wronskian of
$1, x - a, \ldots, (x - a)^{n-1}$ is non zero and
these functions span P_n.

6. **(a)** Yes

(b) No

(c) No

(d) Yes

(e) No

(f) No

(g) Yes

(h) No

(i) No

(j) No

(k) Yes

(l) Yes

8. **(a)** Basis: $\{(2, 3, 0), (-5, 0, 3)\}$; dim = 2

(b) Basis: $(3, 1, 0)$; dim = 1

(c) Basis: $\{e^x, e^{2x}, e^{3x}\}$; dim = 3

(d) Basis: $\{\cosh x - \cos x, \sinh x - \sin x\}$; dim = 2

12. Yes

14. Yes

16. Basis: $\begin{bmatrix} 1 & 0 \\ 0 & 1 \end{bmatrix}, \begin{bmatrix} 0 & 1 \\ 0 & 0 \end{bmatrix}, \begin{bmatrix} 0 & 0 \\ 1 & 0 \end{bmatrix}, \begin{bmatrix} 0 & 0 \\ 0 & 1 \end{bmatrix}$; dim = 4

18. **(a)** $(1, 0, 0) = -\frac{1}{5}(1, 0, 2) + \frac{2}{5}(3, 0, 1)$

(b) $(0, 1, 0) = -\frac{4}{5}(1, 0, 2) + \frac{1}{10}(3, 0, 1) + \frac{1}{2}(1, 2, 3)$

(c) $(0, 0, 1) = \frac{3}{5}(1, 0, 2) - \frac{1}{5}(3, 0, 1)$

(d) $(1, -2, -4) = -(1, 0, 2) + (3, 0, 1) - (1, 2, 3)$

(e) $(3, -2, 0) = (1, 0, 2) + (3, 0, 1) - (1, 2, 3)$

(f) $(-5, 2, 1) = -2(3, 0, 1) + (1, 2, 3)$

22. **(a)** $\langle -1, -1, 8 \rangle$

(b) $\langle -1, -1, 4 \rangle$

(c) $\langle 0, -\frac{1}{2}, \frac{3}{2} \rangle$

(d) $\langle -\frac{1}{2}, 0, \frac{3}{2} \rangle$

(e) $\langle 2, -1, -3 \rangle$

(f) $\langle 5, -5, 10 \rangle$

24. Two bases are $\{2 + x, 1 + x, -x + x^2\}$ and $\{1 - 2x - x^2, 1 - x, 1 + 2x^2\}$

28. $\{1 - x^3, 2x + 3x^2, x^2, x^3\}$

32. No

34. Only $(\mathbf{u}, \mathbf{v})$ and $(\mathbf{u}, \mathbf{w})$ are defined by (2).

Section 13.4

2. Use of the principal inverse cosine function is justified because $0 \leqq \theta \leqq \pi$.

4. (a) $k = -3$

  (b) $k = 4/3$

6. Yes, if either vector is the zero vector.

8. $\cos(2\pi - \theta) = \dfrac{\mathbf{u} \cdot \mathbf{v}}{(\mathbf{u} \cdot \mathbf{u})^{1/2}(\mathbf{v} \cdot \mathbf{v})^{1/2}}$

12. (a) $1/\sqrt{2}$

  (b) $\sqrt{13}$

  (c) 10

  (d) $3/\sqrt{2}$

  (e) $1/\sqrt{5}$

  (f) $\sqrt{10}$

  (g) 1

  (h) 2

16. (b) Equality holds if and only if $\mathbf{u}$ and $\mathbf{v}$ are linearly dependent.

20. $u_1 = 1$, $u_2 = x$, $u_3 = (3x^2 - 1)/3$, and $u_4 = (5x^3 - 3x)/5$ are proportional to the respective Legendre polynomials P_0, P_1, P_2 and P_3; continuation of the process using $\{x^4, x^5, \ldots\}$ yields polynomials which are in turn proportional to successive Legendre polynomials of higher order.

22. (a) $\dfrac{2}{3}\mathbf{b}_1 + \dfrac{1}{3}\mathbf{b}_2 + \dfrac{2}{15}\mathbf{b}_3 + \dfrac{1}{15}\mathbf{b}_4$

  (b) $2\mathbf{b}_1 + \mathbf{b}_2 + \dfrac{6}{5}\mathbf{b}_3 + \dfrac{3}{5}\mathbf{b}_4$

  (c) $\mathbf{b}_1 + \mathbf{b}_2 + \mathbf{b}_3 + \mathbf{b}_4$

  (d) $-\dfrac{2}{3}\mathbf{b}_1 + \dfrac{4}{3}\mathbf{b}_2 - \dfrac{2}{3}\mathbf{b}_3 + \dfrac{1}{3}\mathbf{b}_4$

  (e) $\mathbf{b}_1 - \mathbf{b}_2$

  (f) $3\mathbf{b}_1 + \mathbf{b}_2 - \dfrac{1}{5}\mathbf{b}_3 + \dfrac{2}{5}\mathbf{b}_4$

24. (a) Yes

  (b) No, not closed under addition

  (c) Yes

  (d) Yes

  (e) No, not closed under addition

  (f) Yes

  (g) No, x and $\ln x$ have different domains

  (h) No, x and $\sqrt{x}$ have different domains

26. Euler's formula gives a value for a_0 twice that of Eq. (31a).

28. The scalar projections of Y give $a_0 = \pi/2$, for $n \geqq 1$,

$$a_n = 0, \quad b_n = \frac{\left[(-1)^{n+1} - 1\right]}{n} = \begin{cases} 0 & n \text{ odd} \\ \frac{-2}{n} & n \text{ even} \end{cases};$$

$$y(t) = \frac{\pi}{2} + \sum_{n=1}^{\infty} \frac{\left[(-1)^{n+1} - 1\right]}{n} \sin nt = \frac{\pi}{2} - \sum_{k=1}^{\infty} \frac{\sin 2kt}{k}$$

30. $y(t) = \pi - 2 \displaystyle\sum_{n=1}^{\infty} \frac{\sin nt}{n}$

Section 13.5

2. (a) $\begin{bmatrix} 0 \\ 1 \end{bmatrix}$

  (b) $K_A = \{\mathbf{0}\}$

2. (a) $\begin{bmatrix} 0 \\ 1 \end{bmatrix}$

(b) $K_A = \{ \mathbf{0} \}$

(c) Yes, since $K_A = \{ \mathbf{0} \}$

(d) Yes

(e) None are in K_A; all four are in R_A.

4. (a) $\begin{bmatrix} 3 \\ -2 \end{bmatrix}$

(b) K_A contains all vectors $c\begin{bmatrix} 3 \\ 1 \end{bmatrix}$ with c real; geometrically, K_A is the line $x - 3y = 0$

(c) No; $K_A \neq \{ \mathbf{0} \}$

(d) R_A contains all vectors $c\begin{bmatrix} 3 \\ -2 \end{bmatrix}$ with c real; R_A is the line $2x + 3y = 0$.

(e) $\mathbf{v}_2, \mathbf{v}_3$ belong to K_A; $\mathbf{v}_1, \mathbf{v}_4$ belong to R_A.

6. (a) $\begin{bmatrix} 0 \\ 0 \end{bmatrix}$

(b) all vectors $c\begin{bmatrix} 5 \\ 2 \\ -1 \end{bmatrix}$ with c real, or the line $\frac{x}{5} = \frac{y}{2} = -z.$

(c) No; $K_A \neq \{0\}$

(d) Yes

(e) $\mathbf{v}_2$ and $\mathbf{v}_3$ are in K_A

8. $(12, -6)$

10. (b) K_{T_1} is the set of all real sequences of the form $(0, x_2, 0, x_4, 0, \dots)$; K_{T_2} is the trivial subspace of R^∞.

(c) T_1, yes; T_2, no

(d) T_1, no; T_2, yes

12. (a), (b), and **(d)**

14. $m = 1, 3$

16. All linear combinations of a fundamental set of solutions of $Ly = 0$ on I.

20. (a) $A: R^2 \to R^2$; $A = \begin{bmatrix} 2 & -1 \\ 1 & 1 \end{bmatrix}$

(b) The columns of A

(c) $\dim R_A = 2$

22. (a) $A: R^3 \to R^2$; $A = \begin{bmatrix} 3 & 1 & 5 \\ -2 & 4 & 6 \end{bmatrix}$

(b) Any two columns of A

(c) $\dim R_A = 2$

24. (a) Yes

(b) No; $K_T \neq \{ \mathbf{0} \}$

28. $\dim K_A = n - r$

Section 13.6

2. (a) $T = \begin{bmatrix} 1 & -1 & 0 \\ 1 & 0 & 1 \end{bmatrix}$

(b) $-T = \begin{bmatrix} -1 & 1 & 0 \\ -1 & 0 & -1 \end{bmatrix}$

(d) $2T + A = 2\begin{bmatrix} 1 & 1 & 1 \\ 1 & 1 & 1 \end{bmatrix}$ has the plane $x + y + z = 0$ as its kernel.

4. No. If both cT_1 and cT_2 are to be linear transformations, V_1 and W_1 must be vector spaces over the same set of scalars as V_2 and W_2. If T_1 and T_2 is to be linear, or even defined, $T_1\mathbf{v}$ and $T_2\mathbf{v}$ must be vectors of the same linear space for all $\mathbf{v}$ in $V_1 \cap V_2$.

6. $T_1 T_2 = T_2 T_1 = \begin{bmatrix} 1 & 0 \\ 0 & -1 \end{bmatrix};$

$T_1 T_2 (x, y) = (x, -y)$

8. $T_1 T_2 = T_2 T_1 = \begin{bmatrix} 17 & -2 \\ 4 & 17 \end{bmatrix}$

$T_1 T_2 (x, y) = (17x - 2y, 4x + 17y)$

10. $T_1 T_2 = \begin{bmatrix} 0 & -1 \\ 0 & -1 \end{bmatrix};\ T_2 T_1 = \begin{bmatrix} 0 & 0 & 1 \\ 1 & -1 & 1 \\ -1 & 1 & 0 \end{bmatrix};$

$T_1 T_2 \neq T_2 T_1;\ T_1 T_2 (x, y) = (-y, -y);$
$T_2 T_1 (x, y, z) = (z, x - y + z, y - x)$

14. $T_1 T_2 p(x) = T_2 T_1 p(x) = 2p(x) - p(x - h)$
$\qquad\qquad - p(x + h);$
$T_1 T_2 (1 + x^2) = -2h^2$

16. $T_1 T_2 = xD^2 + (3x - 2)D - 6;$

$T_2 T_1 = xD^2 + (3x - 1)D - 6;$

$T_1 T_2 = (1 - 6x) = 18x + 6;$

$T_2 T_1 (1 - 6x) = 18x$

18. (a) $T_1 T_2 f(x) = \int_{-1}^{x} \int_{s}^{1} f(t)\,dt\,ds = \int_{-1}^{1} f(t)\,dt$
$\qquad\qquad + x \int_{x}^{1} f(t)\,dt + \int_{-1}^{x} tf(t)\,dt$

$T_2 T_1 f(x) = \int_{x}^{1} \int_{-1}^{s} f(t)\,dt\,ds = \int_{-1}^{1} f(t)\,dt$
$\qquad\qquad - x \int_{-1}^{x} f(t)\,dt - \int_{x}^{1} tf(t)\,dt$

(b) No

(c) $T_1 T_2 (1 / \{x + 2\}) = (x + 1)(1 + \ln 3)$
$\qquad - (x + 2)\ln(x + 2),\ -1 \leq x \leq 1$
$T_2 T_1 (1 / \{x + 2\}) = x + 3\ln 3$
$\qquad - (x + 2)\ln(x + 2) - 1\ \ -1 \leq x \leq 1$

(d) $(T_1 + T_2) f = \int_{-1}^{1} f(s)\,ds, f$ in $C[-1, 1]$

(e) The space of all constant functions on $[-1, 1]$

(f) $(T_1 + T_2)\mathrm{Sin}^{-1} x = 0$

20. (a) $T^{-1}(x, y) = (-x, -y, -x)$

(b) $T^{-1}(x, y) = (x + y, 2x + 3y)$

(c) $T^{-1}(x, y) = (x \cos \theta + y \sin \theta$
$\qquad\qquad -x \sin \theta + y \cos \theta)$

(d) No inverse

(e) No inverse

(f) $T^{-1}(x, y, z) = (x + y + z, y + z, z)$

(g) $A^{-1} = \begin{bmatrix} 1 & 1 & 1 \\ 1 & 1 & 0 \\ 0 & 1 & 0 \end{bmatrix}$

(h) $A^{-1} = \begin{bmatrix} 1 & 1 & -1 \\ 1 & -1 & 0 \\ 0 & 1 & -1 \end{bmatrix}$

26. Yes. Since T_1 and T_2 may be written as nonsingular matrices A_1 and A_2, respectively, both $A_1 A_2$ and $A_2 A_1$ are nonsingular.

Section 13.7

2. (a) R

(b) R itself

(c) The inverse $\mathrm{Tan}^{-1} x$ of $\mathrm{Tan}\ x$ is the **principal arc**, or **inverse, tangent function**. Its domain is $(-\infty, \infty)$; its range is $(-\pi/2, \pi/2)$.

4. (a) Take $V = C^{(n)}[a, b]$, $T = L$, and U to be the set of all functions in $C^{(n)}[a, b]$ that satisfy Eq. (12.ii).

(b) Note that det W is the wronskian $W(y_1, y_2, \ldots y_n)$.

(e) From (d), Y is of rank r if and only if $AW(a) + BW(b)$ is.

6. Incompatible

8. $k = 2$

10. $k = 2$

Chapter 14

Section 14.1

2. In the nth power of a transition matrix, $\left[p_{ij}^{(n)}\right]$ is the number of different communication-paths between P_i and P_k involving $n-1$ intermediaries.

4. $P = \begin{bmatrix} 1 & 0 & 0 & 0 & 0 \\ 1/3 & 1/3 & 1/3 & 0 & 0 \\ 0 & 1/3 & 1/3 & 1/3 & 0 \\ 0 & 0 & 1/3 & 1/3 & 1/3 \\ 0 & 0 & 0 & 0 & 1 \end{bmatrix}$

$9P^2 = \begin{bmatrix} 9 & 0 & 0 & 0 & 0 \\ 4 & 2 & 2 & 1 & 0 \\ 1 & 2 & 3 & 2 & 1 \\ 0 & 1 & 2 & 2 & 4 \\ 0 & 0 & 0 & 0 & 9 \end{bmatrix}$

$27P^3 = \begin{bmatrix} 27 & 0 & 0 & 0 & 0 \\ 14 & 4 & 5 & 3 & 1 \\ 5 & 5 & 7 & 5 & 5 \\ 1 & 3 & 5 & 4 & 14 \\ 0 & 0 & 0 & 0 & 27 \end{bmatrix}$

$81P^4 = \begin{bmatrix} 81 & 0 & 0 & 0 & 0 \\ 46 & 9 & 12 & 8 & 6 \\ 20 & 12 & 17 & 12 & 20 \\ 6 & 8 & 12 & 9 & 46 \\ 0 & 0 & 0 & 0 & 81 \end{bmatrix}$

The probability that A is ruined in exactly four turns is $p_{20}^{(4)} - p_{20}^{(3)} = \frac{5}{81}$. The probability that the game continues for more than 4 turns is $1 - p_{20}^{(4)} - p_{24}^{(4)} = \frac{41}{80}$.

8. $P = \frac{1}{8}\begin{bmatrix} 4 & 3 & 1 \\ 3 & 4 & 1 \\ 3 & 3 & 2 \end{bmatrix}$

$P^2 = \frac{1}{8^2}\begin{bmatrix} 28 & 27 & 9 \\ 27 & 28 & 9 \\ 27 & 27 & 10 \end{bmatrix}$

$P^3 = \frac{1}{8^3}\begin{bmatrix} 220 & 219 & 73 \\ 219 & 220 & 73 \\ 219 & 219 & 74 \end{bmatrix}$

$P^4 = \frac{1}{8^4}\begin{bmatrix} 1,756 & 1,755 & 585 \\ 1,755 & 1,756 & 585 \\ 1,755 & 1,755 & 586 \end{bmatrix}$

10.

$$K = \begin{bmatrix} -(k_1 + k_{12}) & k_{12} & 0 \\ k_{12} & -(k_{12} + k_{23} + k_2) & k_{23} \\ 0 & k_{23} & -(k_{23} + k_3) \end{bmatrix}$$

12. $PE = \frac{1}{2}k_1 x_1^2 + \frac{1}{2}k_{12}(x_1 - x_2)^2 + \frac{1}{2}k_{13}(x_1 - x_3)^2 + \frac{1}{2}k_{23}(x_2 - x_3)^2 + \frac{1}{2}k_3 x_3^2$

14. In a multi-loop RLC network, the current which flows in the jth loop when a voltage is inserted in the ith loop is equal to the current which flows in the ith loop when the same voltage is inserted in the jth loop.

16.

$$\begin{bmatrix} 1 & a & 0 & 0 & 0 & 0 \\ 1 & -a & 0 & 0 & 0 & 0 \\ 0 & 0 & 1 & b & 0 & 0 \\ 0 & 0 & 1 & -b & 0 & 0 \\ 0 & 0 & 0 & 0 & 1 & c \\ 0 & 0 & 0 & 0 & 1 & -c \end{bmatrix}$$

18.

$$\begin{bmatrix} 0 & 0 & 1 & 0 & 0 \\ 1 & 0 & 0 & 0 & 0 \\ 0 & 0 & 0 & 1 & 0 \\ 0 & 0 & 0 & 0 & 1 \\ 0 & 1 & 0 & 0 & 0 \end{bmatrix}$$

Section 14.2

2.

$$M_8 = \begin{bmatrix} 1 & 1 & 1 & 1 & 1 & 1 & 1 & 1 \\ 1 & \omega & \omega^2 & \omega^3 & \omega^4 & \omega^5 & \omega^6 & \omega^7 \\ 1 & \omega^2 & \omega^4 & \omega^6 & 1 & \omega^2 & \omega^4 & \omega^6 \\ 1 & \omega^3 & \omega^6 & \omega & \omega^4 & \omega^7 & \omega^2 & \omega^5 \\ 1 & \omega^4 & 1 & \omega^4 & 1 & \omega^4 & 1 & \omega^4 \\ 1 & \omega^5 & \omega^2 & \omega^7 & \omega^4 & \omega & \omega^6 & \omega^3 \\ 1 & \omega^6 & \omega^4 & \omega^2 & 1 & \omega^6 & \omega^4 & \omega^2 \\ 1 & \omega^7 & \omega^6 & \omega^5 & \omega^4 & \omega^3 & \omega^2 & \omega \end{bmatrix}$$

where $\omega = w_8$

4. Because of Theorem 1, the work is essentially the same for solving

$\mathbf{A} = M_n^{-1}\mathbf{F}$ and $\mathbf{F} = M_n\mathbf{A}$. For the first equation, the factor $1/n$ can be absorbed in $\mathbf{F}$ and then the process proceeds using negative rather than positive powers of w.

6.

$$\begin{bmatrix} 1 & 1 & 1 & 1 \\ 0 & 1 & 0 & -i \\ 1 & 0 & -1 & 0 \\ 0 & 1 & 0 & i \end{bmatrix} \times \begin{bmatrix} 1 & 1 & 0 & 0 \\ 1 & -1 & 0 & 0 \\ 0 & 0 & 1 & -1 \\ 0 & 0 & 1 & -1 \end{bmatrix}$$

$$\times \begin{bmatrix} 1 & 0 & 0 & 0 \\ 0 & 0 & 1 & 0 \\ 0 & 1 & 0 & 0 \\ 0 & 0 & 0 & 1 \end{bmatrix} = \begin{bmatrix} 1 & 1 & 1 & 11 \\ 1 & -i & -1 & i \\ 1 & -1 & 1 & -1 \\ 1 & i & -1 & -i \end{bmatrix}$$

8. $\mathbf{F} = [4 \quad 1+3i \quad 2 \quad 1-3i]^T$;
$f(t) = 2 + 2\cos t + \cos 2t - \cos 3t + i\,(2\sin t + \sin 2t - \sin 3t)$

12. Simply introduce a new variable by the substitution $t = \frac{\pi}{p}\tau$.

14. $\mathbf{A} = \frac{1}{4}[5 \quad -1 \quad 1 \quad -1]^T$;
$f(t) = \frac{1}{4}[5 - \cos\frac{\pi t}{2} + \cos\pi t - \cos\frac{3\pi t}{2}]$

16. (a) $\mathbf{F} = [4 \; 0 \; 0 \; 0 \; -4 \; 0 \; 0 \; 0]$
$f(t) = \cos t + \cos 3t + \cos 5t + \cos 7t$

(b) $f(t) = \cos\frac{t}{2} + \cos\frac{3t}{2} + \cos\frac{5t}{2} + \cos\frac{7t}{2}$

Section 14.3

4. No; since any matrix of order $r > \rho$ can itself be expanded in terms of minors of order ρ, and if all of the latter vanish, so must all of the former.

6. (a) Rank $= \begin{cases} 3 & \lambda \neq \frac{1}{2}, 1, 2 \\ 2 & \lambda = \frac{1}{2}, 1, 2 \end{cases}$

(b) Rank $= \begin{cases} 3 & \lambda \neq 1, 6 \\ 2 & \lambda = 1, 6 \end{cases}$

(c) Rank $= \begin{cases} 3 & \lambda \neq 1, \frac{19}{2} \\ 2 & \lambda = \frac{19}{2} \\ 1 & \lambda = 1 \end{cases}$

(d) Rank $= \begin{cases} 3 & \lambda \neq 1 \\ 1 & \lambda = 1 \end{cases}$

12. 1

14. $BQ_1Q_2Q_3Q_4Q_5Q_6 = I$, where

$$Q_1 = \begin{bmatrix} 1 & -2 & 0 \\ 0 & 1 & 0 \\ 0 & 0 & 1 \end{bmatrix}, \quad Q_2 = \begin{bmatrix} 1 & 0 & 0 \\ 0 & 1 & -1 \\ 0 & 0 & 1 \end{bmatrix},$$

$$Q_3 = \begin{bmatrix} 1 & 0 & 0 \\ 2 & 1 & 0 \\ 0 & 0 & 1 \end{bmatrix}, \quad Q_4 = \begin{bmatrix} 1 & 0 & 0 \\ 0 & 1 & 0 \\ -1 & 0 & 1 \end{bmatrix},$$

$$Q_5 = \begin{bmatrix} 1 & 0 & 0 \\ 0 & 1 & 0 \\ 0 & -1 & 0 \end{bmatrix}, \quad Q_6 = \begin{bmatrix} 1 & 0 & 0 \\ 0 & -1 & 0 \\ 0 & 0 & 1 \end{bmatrix}$$

16. Interchange Rows 1 and 4. Subtract Row 1 from Row 2. Subtract Row 3 from Row 2. Subtract Row 2 from Row 4. Subtract Row 2 from Row 3. Add four times Column 1 to

Column 4. Add twice Column 1 to Column 5. Subtract Column 2 from Column 3. Subtract three times Column 2 from Column 4. Subtract twice Column 2 from Column 5. Add Column 3 to Column 4. Add Column 3 to Column 5. This reduction shows that the rank of the given matrix is 3.

18. $PAQ = B$ where $P = \begin{bmatrix} 1 & 0 & 0 \\ -2 & 1 & 0 \\ 5 & -2 & 1 \end{bmatrix}$

and $Q = \begin{bmatrix} 0 & 1 & -1 \\ 1 & 1 & 0 \\ 0 & 0 & 2 \end{bmatrix}$

Since A is of rank 3 it follows that A^{-1} exists. Hence, more immediately, we may take $P = A^{-1}$ and $Q = B$, since $A^{-1}AB = B$.

20. (a) $(x_1, x_2, x_3) = k(-1, 1, 1)$

(b) $(x_1, x_2, x_3, x_4) = k(5, -3, 1, -4)$

22. (a) The set of points for which $|x| > 2$ and $|y| > 2$.

(b) The set of points for which the determinant is equal to zero is the hyperbola $y = (x + 1)/(3x - 1)$.

32. (a) $\begin{bmatrix} 0 & 0 & 1 & 0 \\ 0 & 1 & 0 & 0 \\ 1 & 0 & 0 & 0 \\ 0 & 0 & 0 & 1 \end{bmatrix}$

(b) $\begin{bmatrix} 0 & 0 & 0 & 1 \\ 1 & 0 & 0 & 0 \\ 0 & 1 & 0 & 0 \\ 0 & 0 & 1 & 0 \end{bmatrix}$

(c) $\begin{bmatrix} 0 & 0 & 0 & 5 \\ 0 & 0 & 4 & 0 \\ 0 & 3 & 0 & 0 \\ 2 & 0 & 0 & 0 \end{bmatrix}$

Section 14.4

2. (b) No; C cannot consist of the last two columns of $[A, B]$ because C must be nonsingular.

4. $u(x) = x^4$

6. $u(x) = 1 + x^2$

8. $u(x) = \frac{1}{70}(81x^2 - 167x^3 + 87x^4 - x^9)$

10. $\begin{bmatrix} y_1 \\ y_2 \end{bmatrix} = \frac{e}{e-1}\begin{bmatrix} 3 \\ 4 \end{bmatrix}e^{-2x} + \begin{bmatrix} 4 \\ 3 \end{bmatrix}e^{-3x}$

Section 14.5

2. (a) $x_1 = y_1 - 2y_2 + y_3$
$x_2 = y_2 - y_3$
$x_3 = y_3,$

(b) $x_1 = y_1 - 2y_2 + y_3 - \frac{4}{3}y_4$
$x_2 = y_3 + \frac{2}{3}y_4$
$x_3 = y_2 - y_3 + \frac{1}{3}y_4$
$x_4 = \frac{1}{3}y_4$

(c) $x_1 = \frac{1}{2}(2y_1 + y_2 - 5y_3 - y_4)$
$x_2 = \frac{1}{2}(y_2 - y_3 + y_4)$
$x_3 = y_3$
$x_4 = y_4$

(d) $x_1 = y_1 + y_2 - 3y_3 + 12y_4$
$x_2 = y_3 - 5y_4$
$x_3 = -y_2 + y_3 - 3y_4$
$x_4 = y_4$

(e) $x_1 = y_1 + y_2$
$x_2 = y_1 - y_2$
$x_3 = y_3 + y_4$
$x_4 = y_3 - y_4$

(f) $x_1 = y_1 + y_2$
$x_2 = y_1 - y_2$
$x_3 = y_3 + y_4 - y_5 - y_6$
$x_4 = y_3 - y_4$
$x_5 = y_5 + y_6$
$x_6 = y_5 - y_6$

12. (a) n

(b) $\mathbf{x}^T A_1 \mathbf{x} = 0$, $\mathbf{x}^T A_2 \mathbf{x} = 0$, $\mathbf{x}^T A_3 \mathbf{x} = 0$
where

$$A_1 = \begin{bmatrix} 1 & 1 & 1 \\ 1 & 0 & 0 \\ 1 & 0 & 0 \end{bmatrix}, \quad A_2 = \begin{bmatrix} 1 & -1 & -1 \\ -1 & 0 & 2 \\ -1 & 2 & 0 \end{bmatrix}$$

$$A_3 = \begin{bmatrix} 2 & 1 & 1 \\ 1 & 0 & 1 \\ 1 & 1 & 0 \end{bmatrix}$$

14. $PE = \frac{1}{2}k_1 x_1^2 + \frac{1}{2}k_{12}(x_2 - x_1)^2 + \frac{1}{2}k_2 x_2^2$
$\qquad + \frac{1}{2}k_{23}(x_3 - x_2)^2 + \frac{1}{2}k_3 x_3^2$

Clearly this is never negative and is equal to zero if and only if $x_1 = x_2 = x_3 = 0$.

16. $\mathbf{u}_1 = \begin{bmatrix} 1 \\ 0 \\ 0 \end{bmatrix}$, $\mathbf{u}_2 = \begin{bmatrix} -1 \\ 1 \\ 0 \end{bmatrix}$, $\mathbf{u}_3 = \frac{1}{\sqrt{2}}\begin{bmatrix} 0 \\ 0 \\ 1 \end{bmatrix}$

18. $(2, 0, -2, -2)$, $(\frac{2}{3}, \frac{4}{3}, -\frac{14}{3}, -\frac{2}{3})$

Section 14.6

2. (a) $\lambda_1 = \frac{1}{6}$, $\mathbf{x}_1 = \begin{bmatrix} 2 \\ 3 \\ 2 \end{bmatrix}$,

$\lambda_2 = \frac{2}{3}$, $\mathbf{x}_2 = \begin{bmatrix} 1 \\ 0 \\ -1 \end{bmatrix}$,

$\lambda_3 = 1$,

$\mathbf{x}_3 = \begin{bmatrix} 1 \\ -1 \\ 1 \end{bmatrix}$; $\mathbf{v} = \frac{4}{5}$, $\mathbf{x}_1 - \mathbf{x}_2 + \frac{2}{5}\mathbf{x}_3$

(b) $\lambda_1 = \frac{1}{4}$, $\mathbf{x}_1 = \begin{bmatrix} 2 \\ 3 \\ 3 \end{bmatrix}$; $\lambda_2 = 1$, $\mathbf{x}_2 = \begin{bmatrix} 1 \\ 0 \\ -1 \end{bmatrix}$;

$\lambda_3 = \frac{9}{4}$, $\mathbf{x}_3 = \begin{bmatrix} 2 \\ -5 \\ 3 \end{bmatrix}$;

$\mathbf{v} = \frac{3}{4}\mathbf{x}_1 - \frac{3}{5}\mathbf{x}_2 + \frac{1}{20}\mathbf{x}_3$

(c) $\lambda_1 = \frac{1}{4}$, $\mathbf{x}_1 = \begin{bmatrix} 2 \\ 4 \\ 1 \end{bmatrix}$; $\lambda_2 = 1$, $\mathbf{x}_2 = \begin{bmatrix} -1 \\ 1 \\ 1 \end{bmatrix}$;

$\lambda_3 = \frac{7}{4}$, $\mathbf{x}_3 = \begin{bmatrix} 1 \\ -4 \\ 2 \end{bmatrix}$;

$\mathbf{v} = \frac{7}{9}\mathbf{x}_1 + \frac{10}{9}\mathbf{x}_2 + \frac{5}{9}\mathbf{x}_3$

8. If the characteristic equation vanishes identically, as it does, for instance, for the matrices

$$\mathbf{A} = \begin{bmatrix} 1 & 2 & 3 \\ 2 & 3 & 1 \\ 1 & 1 & -2 \end{bmatrix} \text{ and } \mathbf{B} = \begin{bmatrix} 1 & 2 & 3 \\ 1 & 2 & 1 \\ 1 & 2 & 1 \end{bmatrix}$$

14. $\begin{bmatrix} 1 & i \\ i & -1 \end{bmatrix}$ has only the one characteristic root $\lambda = 0$.

18. $\lambda \doteq 6.58$, $\mathbf{x} \doteq \begin{bmatrix} 1.83 \\ 1.00 \\ -9.78 \end{bmatrix}$

24. (a) 3.41; the exact value of the root is $2 + \sqrt{2}$.

(b) The iterative process does not converge, since the root of largest absolute value is not unique. There are in fact two conjugate complex roots whose absolute value is greater than the absolute value of the real root of this equation. However, if the constant term in the equation is changed from –5 to –7, the process converges to the root $\lambda = 3.33$.

(c) $\lambda = -3.20$

28. (b) When normalized with respect to B, the characteristic vectors are

$$(\mathbf{a}_1)_N = \frac{1}{4\sqrt{6}}\begin{bmatrix}2\\3\\3\end{bmatrix}; \quad (\mathbf{a}_2)_N = \frac{1}{\sqrt{10}}\begin{bmatrix}1\\0\\-1\end{bmatrix};$$

$$(\mathbf{a}_3)_N = \frac{1}{4\sqrt{10}}\begin{bmatrix}2\\-5\\3\end{bmatrix}$$

(c) When normalized with respect to A, the characteristic vectors are

$$(\mathbf{a}_1)_N = \frac{1}{2\sqrt{6}}\begin{bmatrix}2\\3\\3\end{bmatrix}; \quad (\mathbf{a}_2)_N = \frac{1}{\sqrt{10}}\begin{bmatrix}1\\0\\-1\end{bmatrix};$$

$$(\mathbf{a}_3)_N = \frac{1}{6\sqrt{10}}\begin{bmatrix}2\\-5\\3\end{bmatrix}$$

30. $\mathbf{x}(t) = \frac{1}{2}\begin{bmatrix}1\\0\\-1\end{bmatrix}(1 - \cos t)$

32. (a) $\lambda_1 = 1,\ \mathbf{x_1} = \begin{bmatrix}1\\1\end{bmatrix};\ \lambda_2 = 2,\ \mathbf{x_2} = \begin{bmatrix}2\\-1\end{bmatrix}$

(b) $\mathbf{x} = \frac{5}{3}\begin{bmatrix}1\\1\end{bmatrix}\cos t - \frac{1}{3}\begin{bmatrix}2\\-1\end{bmatrix}\cos 2t$

$$+ \frac{1}{2}\begin{bmatrix}2\\-1\end{bmatrix}\sin 2t$$

(c) $\mathbf{x} = \frac{1}{8}\begin{bmatrix}1\\1\end{bmatrix}[3\sin t - \sin 3t]$

34. $\mathbf{x}_{ss} = \left\{-\frac{1}{42}\begin{bmatrix}1\\2\\2\end{bmatrix} + \frac{1}{24}\begin{bmatrix}1\\0\\-2\end{bmatrix} - \frac{1}{48}\begin{bmatrix}1\\-4\\2\end{bmatrix}\right\}\cos 2t$

36. $\omega_1^2 = \frac{7}{4},\ \mathbf{a}_1 = \begin{bmatrix}1\\4\\4\end{bmatrix};\ \omega_2^2 = 4,\ (\mathbf{a}_2)_1 = \begin{bmatrix}1\\-1\\0\end{bmatrix},$

$$(\mathbf{a}_2)_2 = \begin{bmatrix}1\\0\\-1\end{bmatrix}$$

44. No, unless A is symmetric. For example, both $A = \begin{bmatrix}3 & 1\\2 & 2\end{bmatrix}$ and $B = \begin{bmatrix}3 & 2\\1 & 2\end{bmatrix}$ have the characteristic values 1, 4. However, for A the corresponding characteristics vectors are $\begin{bmatrix}1\\-2\end{bmatrix}$ and $\begin{bmatrix}1\\1\end{bmatrix}$ and for B they are $\begin{bmatrix}1\\-1\end{bmatrix}$ and $\begin{bmatrix}2\\1\end{bmatrix}$

46. Yes, since $B^{-1}A$ satisfies all the necessary conditions in Theorem 11 if B is nonsingular.

Section 14.7

2. (a) $Q_1 = \begin{bmatrix}1 & -2\\0 & 1\end{bmatrix},\ Q_2 = \begin{bmatrix}0 & 1\\1 & -2/3\end{bmatrix}$

(b) $Q_1 = \begin{bmatrix}1 & 1\\0 & 1\end{bmatrix},\ Q_2 = \begin{bmatrix}1 & 2\\0 & 2\end{bmatrix}$

(c) $Q_1 = \begin{bmatrix}1 & -1 & -2\\0 & 1 & 1\\0 & 0 & 1\end{bmatrix},\ Q_2 = \begin{bmatrix}0 & 0 & 1\\1 & 0 & -1/2\\0 & 1 & -1/3\end{bmatrix}$

(d) $Q_1 = \begin{bmatrix} 1 & -2 & 4 \\ 0 & 1 & -2 \\ 0 & 0 & 1 \end{bmatrix}$,

$$Q_2 = \begin{bmatrix} -1 & 0 & 2 \\ 1 & 0 & -1 \\ -1/2 & 1/2 & 1/2 \end{bmatrix}$$

4. (b) $M = \begin{bmatrix} 1 & 1 \\ 2 & 1 \end{bmatrix}$

   (c) $M = \begin{bmatrix} 1 & 1 \\ -1 & 2 \end{bmatrix}$

6. $y_1 = \frac{1}{\sqrt{3}} x_1 + \frac{2}{\sqrt{6}} x_2, \quad y_2 = \frac{\sqrt{6}}{3} x_1 - \frac{\sqrt{6}}{3} x_2$

8. Consider the three scalar equations implied by the given matrix equation. Multiply these, respectively, by the arbitrary constants $\alpha_1, \alpha_2, \alpha_3$ and then, in turn, determine two of these three parameters so that two of the three periodic terms are eliminated from the expression $\alpha_1 x_1 + \alpha_2 x_2 + \alpha_3 x_3$. This will give three linear combinations of the x's, each of which varies with a single frequency. These, then, are proportional to the required normal coordinates y_1, y_2, and y_3. Finally, the three proportionality constants can be determined by requiring that
$$y_1^2 + y_2^2 + y_3^2 \equiv \mathbf{x}^T B \mathbf{x} \text{ and}$$
$$\lambda_1^2 y_1^2 + \lambda_2^2 y_2^2 + \lambda_3^2 y_3^2 \equiv \mathbf{x}^T A \mathbf{x}$$

Section 14.8

2. (a) $A = \begin{bmatrix} 0 & -2 \\ 1 & 3 \end{bmatrix}, p(x) = x^2 + 3x + 4$

   (b) $A = \begin{bmatrix} 0 & -2 \\ 1 & 3 \end{bmatrix}, p(x) = x^2 + x - 2$

   (c) $A = \begin{bmatrix} 1 & 2 \\ 2 & 4 \end{bmatrix}, p(x) = x^2 + x + 1$

   (d) $A = \begin{bmatrix} 1 & 2 \\ 2 & 4 \end{bmatrix}, p(x) = x^2 - 6x + 5$

6. For all values of x, $\begin{bmatrix} x & 1+x \\ 1-x & -x \end{bmatrix}^2 = I_2$

10. An arbitrary polynomial equation of degree n in an $n \times n$ matrix variable has infinitely many solutions.

14. All

16. (a) $\frac{1}{3} \begin{bmatrix} 7 & -16 \\ 8 & -17 \end{bmatrix}$

    (b) $\frac{1}{15} \begin{bmatrix} 9 & -2 \\ 12 & -1 \end{bmatrix}$

    (c) $\frac{1}{5} \begin{bmatrix} 3 & -2 \\ 8 & -7 \end{bmatrix}$

    (d) $\begin{bmatrix} 1 & -4 & 0 \\ -4 & 5 & 0 \\ 0 & 0 & 5 \end{bmatrix}$

    (e) $\frac{1}{15} \begin{bmatrix} -5 & 8 & 8 \\ 8 & -5 & -8 \\ -8 & 8 & 11 \end{bmatrix}$

18. The characteristic values of the three matrices are **i.** $-1, -3$ **ii.** $1, 2$ **iii.** $1, 3$
    In the various cases, $f(A)$ is

    (a, i) $\begin{bmatrix} -6 & 24 \\ -12 & 30 \end{bmatrix}$, (b, i) $\begin{bmatrix} -8 & 32 \\ -16 & 40 \end{bmatrix}$

    (c, i) $\begin{bmatrix} 20 & -40 \\ 20 & -40 \end{bmatrix}$

    (a, ii) $\begin{bmatrix} 5 & -1 \\ 6 & 0 \end{bmatrix}$, (b, ii) $\begin{bmatrix} -3 & 1 \\ -6 & 2 \end{bmatrix}$

    (c, ii) $\begin{bmatrix} 37 & -11 \\ 66 & -18 \end{bmatrix}$

    (a, iii) $\begin{bmatrix} 4 & 2 \\ 2 & 4 \end{bmatrix}$, (b, iii) $\begin{bmatrix} 0 & 0 \\ 0 & 0 \end{bmatrix}$

    (c, iii) $\begin{bmatrix} 22 & 18 \\ 18 & 22 \end{bmatrix}$

20. Yes. For instance, the matrix $A = \begin{bmatrix} 1 & 1 \\ -4 & 5 \end{bmatrix}$ has $\lambda = 3$ as a repeated characteristic value and $\begin{bmatrix} 1 \\ 2 \end{bmatrix}$ as its only characteristic vector. On the other hand, $p(A) = A^2 - 6A + 8I \equiv -I$ has -1 as a repeated characteristic value and any vector $\begin{bmatrix} a \\ b \end{bmatrix}$ as a characteristic vector. More generally, if A is an asymmetric matrix with a repeated characteristic value, this will not in general be a regular characteristic value. However, $p(A)$ may be symmetric and hence its corresponding repeated characteristic value will be regular, and therefore will have characteristic vectors corresponding to it which are not characteristic vectors of A.

22. Let $P(\lambda) = \begin{bmatrix} 1 & 2 \\ 4 & 3 \end{bmatrix} + \begin{bmatrix} 1 & 4 \\ 3 & 2 \end{bmatrix}\lambda + \begin{bmatrix} 1 & 2 \\ 3 & 4 \end{bmatrix}\lambda^2$,

and $A = \begin{bmatrix} 1 & 1 \\ 0 & 1 \end{bmatrix}$

Evaluate the identity

$(A - \lambda I)(A + \lambda I) = A^2 - \lambda^2 I$ for

$A = \begin{bmatrix} 1 & 2 \\ 4 & 3 \end{bmatrix}$ and $\lambda = \begin{bmatrix} 1 & 1 \\ 0 & 1 \end{bmatrix}$

24. **(a)** $2A^2 = 2A + I$

(b) Multiply the characteristic equation, evaluated for the matrix A, by A^{-1} and then solve for A^{-1}. In the present exercise this gives

$$A^{-1} = -A^2 + A + I = \begin{bmatrix} -1 & 2 & 2 \\ 2 & -1 & -2 \\ -2 & 2 & 3 \end{bmatrix}$$

In this special case, A is its own inverse. In other words, not only does A satisfy its own characteristic equation but it also satisfies the simpler equation $A^2 = I$.

26. $A^n = (2^n - 1)A - (2^n - 2)I$

28. $\lambda_1 = -1$, $\mathbf{v}_1 = \begin{bmatrix} 1 \\ 1 \end{bmatrix}$, $\lambda_2 = -2$, $\mathbf{v}_2 = \begin{bmatrix} 2 \\ 3 \end{bmatrix}$

30. $\frac{1}{5}\begin{bmatrix} 2e^5 + 3 & 6e^5 - 6 \\ e^5 - 1 & 3e^5 + 2 \end{bmatrix}$

32. **(a)** $\sin A = (\sin 1)A$

(b) $\cos A = I - (1 - \cos 1)A$

Chapter 15

Section 15.1

2. (a) 7, 15, 11

   (b) $\frac{1}{7}(2, -3, 6)$, $\frac{1}{11}(2, -9, -6)$

   (c) 80

   (d) −64/15

   (e) $\frac{80}{49}(2, -3, 6)$

   (f) $\mathrm{Cos}^{-1}(16/21)$

4. No, because two vectors can have the same projection in a given direction without being equal. The vectors **A** and **X** − **Y** are perpendicular.

6. **A** + **B** by the parallelogram law.

8. −1, 3

10. (a) 2

    (b) $-4\mathbf{j} + 2\mathbf{k}$

    (c) $5\sqrt{2}$

12. $\mathbf{v} = 0, \pm(3\mathbf{i} + 4\mathbf{j} + 12\mathbf{k})$

14. $\pi/4$

16. $\pi - \mathrm{Cos}^{-1}(-4/33) \doteq 96°56'$

20. (b) the sphere with center $\frac{1}{2}\mathbf{A}$ and radius $\frac{1}{2}|\mathbf{A}|$,

    (c) the point (a_1, a_2, a_3).

32. The wind is out of the northwest at a speed of $3\sqrt{2}$ mi/hr.

Section 15.2

2. $4\mathbf{i} - 7\mathbf{j} - 5\mathbf{k}$, $3\sqrt{10}$, $\theta = \mathrm{Cos}^{-1}(-\sqrt{2/7})$

4. $0, 0, \theta = 0$

6. $6\mathbf{i} - 4\mathbf{j} - 4\mathbf{k}$, $2\sqrt{17}$, $\theta = \mathrm{Sin}^{-1}\left(\frac{2}{3}\sqrt{17/21}\right)$

8. $72\mathbf{i} + 24\mathbf{j} - 12\mathbf{k}$

10. $-2\mathbf{i} + 2\mathbf{j} - \mathbf{k}$

12. $11\mathbf{i} + \mathbf{j} - 7\mathbf{k}$

14. There is no such vector.

16. (a) $6\sqrt{2}$

    (b) $2\sqrt{21}$

18. $y = -1, 3$

20. 7, Yes

26. $x = -2$ $\quad \frac{y-5}{1} = \frac{z+1}{2}$

28. (a) $\mathbf{R} = 4\mathbf{i} - 2\mathbf{j} + t(\mathbf{i} - \mathbf{j} - 3\mathbf{k})$

    (b) $\frac{x-4}{1} = \frac{y+2}{-1} = \frac{z}{-3}$

30. (b) $(\mathbf{R} - \mathbf{i} - 3\mathbf{j} - 4\mathbf{k}) \cdot (\mathbf{i} + 2\mathbf{j} - 4\mathbf{k}) = 0$; $x + 2y - 4z + 9 = 0$

32. $(0, 3, 0)$

34. Yes, because the replacement simply introduces a new parameter proportional to t.

36. $x + 3y + 2z = 6$

38. $2x + y + z = 3$

42. 8/3

44. $d = \sqrt{26}$

46. $x - 2y - 2z = 19$
$x - 2y - 2z = 1$

48. $5\sqrt{13/14}$

50. $\pm(17\mathbf{i} - 13\mathbf{j} + 18\mathbf{k})/\sqrt{522}$

52. No. In fact if $\mathbf{A} = \mathbf{0}$ and $\mathbf{B} = \mathbf{C} \neq \mathbf{0}$, then
$\mathbf{A} \times \mathbf{B} = \mathbf{B} \times \mathbf{C} = \mathbf{C} \times \mathbf{A} = \mathbf{0}$ whereas
$\mathbf{A} + \mathbf{B} + \mathbf{C} = 2\mathbf{C} \neq \mathbf{0}$

Section 15.3

2. (a) -636

  (b) $-210\mathbf{i} + 710\mathbf{j} + 425\mathbf{k}$

  (c) $78\mathbf{i} - 202\mathbf{j} + 329\,\mathbf{k}$

  (d) $-1,272$

  (e) 0

  (f) 892

  (g) $1,774\mathbf{i} + 603\mathbf{j} + 1,674\mathbf{k}$

4. $b = -3$

6. 10, 3/4

10. $x + 3y + 2z = 6$

12. No. For instance, for arbitrary, non coplanar vectors $\mathbf{A}$, $\mathbf{B}$, $\mathbf{C}$ we have
$(\mathbf{A} \times \mathbf{B}) \times (\mathbf{C} \times \mathbf{C}) = (\mathbf{A} \times \mathbf{B}) \times \mathbf{0} = \mathbf{0}$.

24. $\mathbf{i} + 2\mathbf{j} + 3\mathbf{k} = (-17\mathbf{A} + 14\mathbf{B} + 3\mathbf{C})/33 =$
$(-11\mathbf{U} + 319\mathbf{V} + 143\mathbf{W})/11$

Section 15.4

4. No. For instance, if $\mathbf{V} = \mathbf{i} + \mathbf{j} + t\mathbf{k}$, then
$|\mathbf{V}| = \sqrt{2 + t^2}$ and $d|\mathbf{V}| = t / \sqrt{2 + t^2}\, dt$,
whereas $|d\mathbf{V}| = |dt|$.

6. (a) Not necessarily

  (b) Yes

  (c) $R^3[\mathbf{u}\ \dot{\mathbf{u}},\ \ddot{\mathbf{u}}]$

8. (a) $\mathbf{k}$

  (b) $\frac{1}{\sqrt{2}}(-\mathbf{i} + \mathbf{j})$

10. $\pi / 2$

12. (a) $x = 4 + 6s, y = 4 + 4s, z = 1 + s$

  (b) $\frac{x-4}{6} = \frac{y-4}{4} = z - 1$

  (c) $\mathbf{R} = (4, 4, 1) + s(6, 4, 1)$

14. $x + 4y - 3z = 12$

16. (a) $t = 1$

  (b) $t = -1/8$

18. (a) $t = 1/4$

  (b) $t = \pm 1/8$

20. (a) $\mathbf{R} = (1, -2, 1) + s(1, -1, 2)$

(b) $\frac{x-1}{1} = \frac{y+2}{-1} = \frac{z-1}{2}$

(c) $t = 1$

(d) Never happens

(e) $-2/\sqrt{3}$

22. $\mathbf{r} = \left(1 + \frac{t^2}{2} + \frac{t^3}{3}\right)\mathbf{i} + \left(2 + \frac{t^5}{20}\right)\mathbf{j} + \left(3 + \frac{t^3}{3} - \frac{t^4}{12}\right)\mathbf{k}$

24. (a) $t = 1/3$

(b) Never happens

(c) $\sqrt{2/7}$

(d) At $(1, 1, 0)$

26. $\mathbf{V} = \mathbf{C}e^{\int \lambda(t)\,dt}$

28. $a_T = \frac{t}{\sqrt{2+t^2}}, \quad a_n = \sqrt{\frac{2}{(2+t)}}$

30. $a_T = 0, \quad a_n = a\omega^2$

32. 10π

38. $\kappa = 2/3$

40. $\kappa(t) = 2[(t^4 + 7t^2 + 16)/(t^2 + 4)^3]^{1/2}$,
$\tau(t) = 2\sqrt{3}(t^2 + 6)/(t^4 + 7t^2 + 16), \quad 0 \le t$

44. $3x - 3y + z$; $\mathbf{T}(1) = (\mathbf{i} + 2\mathbf{j} + 3\mathbf{k})/\sqrt{14}$
$\mathbf{N}(1) = (-11\mathbf{i} - 8\mathbf{j} + 9\mathbf{k})/\sqrt{266}$;
$\mathbf{B}(1) = (3\mathbf{i} - 3\mathbf{j} + \mathbf{k})/\sqrt{19}$

46. normal plane: $(\mathbf{r} - \mathbf{r}_0) \cdot \mathbf{T} = 0$;
rectifying plane: $(\mathbf{r} - \mathbf{r}_0) \cdot \mathbf{N} = 0$;
osculating plane: $(\mathbf{r} - \mathbf{r}_0) \cdot \mathbf{B} = 0$;
where $\mathbf{r}$ is the position vector of an arbitrary point in any particular plane.

48. $\mathbf{T} = (2\mathbf{i} + 2\mathbf{j} - \mathbf{k})/3, \mathbf{N} = (-4\mathbf{i} + 5\mathbf{j} + 2\mathbf{k})/3\sqrt{5}$,
$\mathbf{B} = (\mathbf{i} + 2\mathbf{k})/\sqrt{5}$;
normal plane: $2x + 2y - z = 4$,
rectifying plane: $4x - 5y - 2z = 3$,
osculating plane: $x + 2z = 2$.

50. $\mathbf{T} = (3\mathbf{i} + 4\mathbf{k})/5, \mathbf{N} = \mathbf{j}, \mathbf{B} = (-4\mathbf{i} + 3\mathbf{k})/5$;
normal plane: $3x + 4z = 0$,
rectifying plane: $y = 5$,
osculating plane: $4x - 3y = 0$.

54. $\kappa(s) = \frac{2}{s^2 + a^2}, \quad \tau(s) \equiv 0$

56. $\kappa(s) = \frac{2[t^4(s) + 7t^2(s) + 16]^{1/2}}{[t^2(s) + 4]^{3/2}}$,

$\tau(s) = \frac{2\sqrt{3}[t^2(s) + 6]}{[t^4(s) + 7t^2(s) + 16]}$

where $t(s)$ represents the inverse of the arc length function represented by

$s(t) = t\left(1 + \frac{t^2}{4}\right) + \ln\left[\frac{t + \sqrt{t^2 + 4}}{2}\right], \quad 0 \le t$

68. $\mathbf{c} = \int_{x_0}^{x} (\mathbf{e}_3 \times \mathbf{u})(f/a_0 W_{12})\,dt, \quad x_0, x \text{ in } I.$

70. C_{12} satisfies $(E - p_2)C_{12} = 0$,
$[\mathbf{Y}_1, \mathbf{Y}_2, \mathbf{Y}_3] = 0$, and if $\mathbf{Y}_1 \times \mathbf{Y}_2 \ne \mathbf{0}$,
$y_3 = ay_1 + by_2$.

72. (c) To form the determinant, take
$\mathbf{r}_1, \mathbf{r}_2, \cdots \mathbf{r}_n$ in succession as its first
$n - 1$ rows and the standard basis vectors
$\mathbf{e}_1, \mathbf{e}_2, \cdots \mathbf{e}_n$ of R^n as successive column entries of row n.

(d) $|A|$

(e) $\mathbf{c} = \int_{x_0}^{x} \left[\prod_{i=0}^{n-2} \mathbf{u}^{(i)} \right] [f / a_0 W] dt$, x_0, x in I, where W is the wronskian of the components of $\mathbf{u}$.

Section 15.5

2. **(a)** $(\mathbf{i}+\mathbf{j}-\mathbf{k})/\sqrt{3}, (-3\mathbf{i}-\mathbf{j}+\sqrt{2}\mathbf{k})2\sqrt{3}$

   (b) $(2\mathbf{i}-4\mathbf{j}-\mathbf{k})/\sqrt{21}, (-2\mathbf{i}+2\mathbf{j}-\mathbf{k})/3$

   (c) $(3\mathbf{j}+2\mathbf{k})/\sqrt{13}, [3\sqrt{2}(\mathbf{i}+\mathbf{j})-4\mathbf{k}]/2\sqrt{13}$

4. **(a)** $\dfrac{b x \mathbf{i} + a(a^2 - x^2)^{1/2} \mathbf{j}}{\sqrt{a^4 + (b^2 - a^2) x^2}}$

   (b) $\theta = \text{Cos}^{-1} \dfrac{b a^3}{\sqrt{a^4 + (b^2 - a^2) x^2} \sqrt{a^2 b^2 + (a^2 - b^2) x^2}}$

   (c) If $a = b$, the ellipse is a circle and $\theta = 0$, which shows that the radii of a circle are normal to the circle. If $x = 0$ or $x = \pm a$, then $\theta = 0$ which shows that the major and minor axes of an ellipse are normal to it.

6. **(a)** $14/3$

   (b) -4

   (c) $1/\sqrt{3}$

   (d) $-29/11$

8. $-2/5, 2\sqrt{41}$

10. In the direction of $-\nabla\phi(\mathbf{R})$, $-|\nabla\phi(\mathbf{R})|$

12. A proof

16. $\dfrac{\partial \phi}{\partial x}, \dfrac{\partial \phi}{\partial y}, \dfrac{\partial \phi}{\partial z}$, respectively

18. $36°$ C, In the direction of $-4\mathbf{i} - 9\mathbf{j}$.

20. $\phi_x(x_0, y_0, z_0)[x - x_0]$
    $+ \phi_y(x_0, y_0, z_0)[y - y_0]$
    $+ \phi_z(x_0, y_0, z_0)[z - z_0] = 0$

22. $2x + y - 2z = 4$

24. $2x - 4y - z = 5$

26. $4x + 11y - 4z = 19$, $\dfrac{x-1}{-4} = \dfrac{y-1}{-11} = \dfrac{z+1}{4}$

28. **(a)** $2x\mathbf{i} - 2(y-z)\mathbf{j} + 2y\mathbf{k}$

    (b) $-2/\sqrt{5}$

    (c) $(\mathbf{i}+\mathbf{j}+\mathbf{k})/\sqrt{3}$

    (d) $0, 0$

30. (a) 0

    (b) 0

    (c) $-e^{-y}(x\cos x + 3y\sin y) + 10z$

42. 3

48. 0

52. $\nabla \cdot (\rho\mathbf{v}) + \dfrac{\partial \rho}{\partial t} = 0$

60. $\nabla^2 \mathbf{v} = (\nabla^2 v_1)\mathbf{i} + (\nabla^2 v_2)\mathbf{j} + (\nabla^2 v_3)\mathbf{k}$

Section 15.6

2. Yes, its length

$$\frac{1}{2}\left[\frac{\pi\sqrt{4+\pi^2}}{4} + \ln\frac{1}{2}(\pi + \sqrt{4+\pi^2})\right] \text{ is finite.}$$

4. Along the parabola, $2\ln\frac{3}{2}$; along AB, $\frac{3}{4}\ln 3$; along APB, $\ln\frac{5}{2}$; along AQB, $\ln 2$.

6. (a) 0

    (b) –8/15

8. $\pi/4$

10. $k = 5/4$

12. 0

14. $W = 328/15$

18. The point P is the terminus of $\mathbf{R}(t)$ for distinct values t_1, t_2 of t such that $a < t_1$, $t_2 < b$, where $\mathbf{R}$ is defined by (9).

22. 10

24. $\cosh 2 - 3$

26. 1

28. 0

30. 3

32. $\dfrac{\pi a^3}{24}$

34. The common value of the integrals is –4/3.

36. The common value of the integrals is $3\pi a^2$.

38. $\dfrac{k}{n+1}\left[(x_1^2 + y_1^2)^{(n+1)/2} - (x_0^2 + y_0^2)^{(n+1)/2}\right]$

40. $2A$

44. The nature of the right-hand members of (13) and (14) are not altered by adding line integrals along segments of C parallel to the x-axis or y-axis, respectively.

46. The reason for the failure of Green's lemma is that U and V are not continuous at all points of $\Re$, since they are undefined at the origin.

48. $\displaystyle\iint_{\Re}\left[\frac{\partial g}{\partial x}\frac{\partial f}{\partial y} - \frac{\partial g}{\partial y}\frac{\partial f}{\partial x}\right]dx$

Section 15.7

2. (a) 2

(b) 3

(c) $8\pi/3$

(d) $8\pi/3$

4. $\iint_S (u\cos\alpha + v\cos\beta + w\cos\gamma)dS$

$= \iiint_V \left[\dfrac{\partial u}{\partial x} + \dfrac{\partial v}{\partial y} + \dfrac{\partial w}{\partial z}\right]dV$, where α, β, γ are the direction angles of the normal to the surface S.

6. The common value of the integrals is πa^4.

8. The common value of the integrals is $-1/2$.

12. The common value of the integrals is πa^2.

14. $\iint_S \dfrac{x\cos\alpha + y\cos\beta + z\cos\gamma}{(x^2 + y^2 + z^2)^{3/2}}dS = \begin{cases} 0, & O \text{ outside } S \\ 4\pi, & O \text{ inside } S \end{cases}$

where α, β, γ are the direction angles of the normal to the surface S.

16. 0

18. 0

22. No, since the divergence of $\mathbf{F}$ may vanish identically. Yes.

26. $-2\iint_S \mathbf{N}dS$

38. Yes; because of **c**, Theorem 5.

42. (a) $\phi = xy + xz + yz$

(b) 3

44. $\phi = xyz$, 1

46. $\phi = x^3 + x^2y + xz^2 + y^3 + y^2z + z^3$, 53

48. $\phi = \cosh x + \sin y + \ln z$, $2 + \cosh 10$

50. Yes; $\phi = x^2yz$, disregarding the additive constant.

Section 15.8

2. $\dfrac{m(x^2 + y^2)\omega^2}{2}$

4. $\begin{cases} \dfrac{3M}{2a} - \dfrac{Mr^2}{2a^3} & r \le a \\ \dfrac{M}{r} & r > a \end{cases}$

6. $\displaystyle\sum_{i \ne j} \dfrac{q_i q_j}{r_{ij}}$

16. $\mathbf{F}$ represents the rate at which fluid mass flows per unit time through a unit area placed normal to the direction of flow.

18. $\iiint_V \nabla \cdot \mathbf{F}dV = \iiint_V \nabla \cdot (\rho\mathbf{v})dV$

20. (a) Yes, it is the special case for which $\dot{\rho} = 0$ or $\rho = $ constant.

(b) Laplace's equation $\nabla^2\phi = 0$.

Chapter 16

Section 16.1

2. $y = x^{-2} + \frac{1}{4}x^2$

4. $y = e^{-x}\left(e^{1-x} - 2\right)$

6. $y = 1 - 2x - 2e^{-x}$

8. $y = 4\sinh x - \sin 4x$

10. $y = c_1\cos x + c_2\sin x + (\cosh x)/2$

12. $I = e(e-1)$ independent of the solution y.

14. $y = 2x;\ I = -\dfrac{104}{81}$

16. All twice-differentiable functions on $[x_1, x_2]$; $\frac{d}{dx}(xy + \cos xy)$ gives the integrand.

18. $c = 100 + 10\left[x_2^2 y_2^2 - x_1^1 y_1^2\right]$

22. $y = 12\left(x - x^{-2}\right)$, $I_{min} = 1{,}260 + 21\cos 4$

24. $2y' - y = 0$ at $x = 0$ and $x = 1$; $y'' - y = 0$;
$y = \dfrac{\sinh(1-x) + 2\sinh x}{\sinh 1}$;
$y = \dfrac{\sinh(1-x) - 2\cosh(1-x)}{\sinh 1 - 2\cosh 1}$;
$y = \dfrac{4\cosh x + 2\sinh x}{2\cosh 1 + \sinh 1}$; $y = 0$

26. $y = c\cosh^{-1}\left(\dfrac{1+x}{c}\right) + d$

28. The arc of a cycloid with a cusp at the origin, and with parametric equations
$x = a(\theta - \sin\theta),\ y = a(1 - \cos\theta)$, where $a \doteq 0.5729$ and, for the arc,
$0 \le \theta \le \theta_2 \doteq 138°11'$

30. (a) The brachistochrone is the arc of a cycloid with parametric equations
$x = a(\theta - \sin\theta),\ y = a(1 - \cos\theta)$;
where $0 \le \theta \le \theta_2 = \mathrm{Cos}^{-1}\frac{3}{5}$ and
$a = 2/\mathrm{Cos}^{-1}\frac{3}{5}$; the arc meets the given
line in the point $(x_2, y_2) = \left(2, -\frac{4a}{5}, \frac{2a}{5}\right)$.

(b) $T = \sqrt{\dfrac{2}{g}}\left[\mathrm{Cos}^{-1}\frac{3}{5}\right]^{1/2}$

(c) $F = \sqrt{\dfrac{2}{g}}$

32. (a) Parametric equations of the brachistochrone are $x = 2(\theta - \sin\theta)$, $y = 2(1 - \cos\theta)$; $0 \le \theta \le \pi/2$; $(x_2, y_2) = (\pi - 2, 2)$

(b) $T = \pi/\sqrt{2g}$

(c) $F = \sqrt{2\pi/g}$

34. (a) Parametric equations of the brachistochrone are $x = 2(\theta - \sin\theta)$, $y = 2(1 - \cos\theta)$; $0 \le \theta \le \pi/2$; $(x_2, y_2) = \left(\frac{3\pi - 6}{2}, 3\right)$

(b) $T = \frac{\pi}{2}\sqrt{3/g}$

(c) $F = \sqrt{3\pi/g}$

36. (a) $(x_2, y_2) = \left(\frac{1}{4}, \frac{1}{2}\right)$

(b) $(x_1, y_1) = \left[\dfrac{1 + (2-\pi)(2b-1)}{2\pi}, \dfrac{4b + \pi - 1}{2\pi}\right]$

(c) $T = \frac{\sqrt{\pi}}{2}\sqrt{\frac{4b-1}{2g}}$

(d) $F = \sqrt{\frac{4b-1}{2g}}$

40. $T = \int_{x_1}^{x_2} \frac{\sqrt{1+(y')^2}}{u(x,y)}\,dx$

42. (a) $(x+1)^2 + \left(y-\frac{17}{6}\right)^2 = \frac{325}{36}$

(b) The circle is intersected by the vertical line $x = 2$ at $\left(2, \frac{8}{3}\right)$ and $(2, 3)$, and twice by every vertical line $x = a$ for which $2 < a < -1 + \frac{5\sqrt{13}}{6}$.

44. The arc of a helix with parametric equations:
$x = a\cos\theta,\, z = \theta/3;\, 0 \leqq \theta \leqq \frac{\pi}{2}$.

46. The arc of helix with parametric equations;
$x = a\cos\theta,\, y = a\sin\theta,\, z = \frac{2\theta}{3}$:
$0 \leqq \theta \leqq \frac{\pi}{2}$.

48. (a) $I = \int_{u_1}^{u_2}\sqrt{P + 2Qv' + Rv'^2}\,du$, where

$P = x_u^2 + y_u^2 + z_u^2$,

$Q = x_u x_v + y_u y_v + z_u z_v$, and

$R = x_v^2 + y_v^2 + z_v^2$

(b) In such cases $Q \equiv 0$

52. $\sum_{k=0}^{n}(-1)^k d^k / dx^k \left[\partial f / \partial y^{(k)}\right] = 0 \quad n \geq 1$

Section 16.2

2. $\begin{bmatrix} x \\ y \end{bmatrix} = c_1\begin{bmatrix} 1 \\ 0 \end{bmatrix}\cosh t + c_2\begin{bmatrix} 1 \\ 0 \end{bmatrix}\sinh t$

$\quad + c_3\begin{bmatrix} 0 \\ 1 \end{bmatrix}\cosh t + c_4\begin{bmatrix} 0 \\ 1 \end{bmatrix}\sinh t$

4. $\begin{bmatrix} x \\ y \end{bmatrix} = c_1\begin{bmatrix} 1 \\ 2 \end{bmatrix}\cos t + c_2\begin{bmatrix} 1 \\ 2 \end{bmatrix}\sin t$

$\quad + c_3\begin{bmatrix} 1 \\ -1 \end{bmatrix}\cos 2t + c_4\begin{bmatrix} 1 \\ -1 \end{bmatrix}\sin 2t$

10. $\frac{\partial f}{\partial x} - \frac{d}{dt}\left[\frac{\partial f}{\partial \dot{x}}\right] + \frac{d^2}{dt^2}\left[\frac{\partial f}{\partial \ddot{x}}\right] = 0$

$\frac{\partial f}{\partial y} - \frac{d}{dt}\left[\frac{\partial f}{\partial \dot{y}}\right] + \frac{d^2}{dt^2}\left[\frac{\partial f}{\partial \ddot{y}}\right] = 0$

12. (a) $\frac{d}{dt}(m\mathbf{v}) + \dot{m}_1(\mathbf{V}_1 + \mathbf{v}) + \dot{m}_2(\mathbf{V}_2 + \mathbf{v})$

$\quad = \sum \mathbf{F}_i$

14. $\dot{\mathbf{v}} + g\frac{\mathbf{r}}{r} + \frac{\kappa e^{-\gamma r}}{m}\mathbf{v} = \frac{\dot{m}}{m}\mathbf{V}$,

$\kappa, \gamma > 0$ proportionality constants

16. $\dot{\mathbf{v}} + g\frac{f(r)}{r}\mathbf{r} + \frac{\kappa v}{m}\mathbf{v} = \frac{\dot{m}}{m}\mathbf{V}$,

$\kappa > 0$ a proportionality constant

18. $2R + h$ which is the sum of the radii of the two circles.

Section 16.3

2. $y = 12x - 3x^2$

4. $(ry')' + (q + \lambda p)y = 0;\ (ry')\big|_{x=x_1} = 0$

6. $(x-h)^2+(y+k)^2=\lambda^2$ where
$h=\frac{1}{2}(x_1+x_2)$, $k^2=\lambda^2-a^2$,
$a=\frac{1}{2}(x_2-x_1)$ and λ is to be determined so
that the required area is cut off.

8. $y=\dfrac{3\left[x_2(y_1+y_2)-2A\right]}{x_2^3}x^2$
$\quad+\dfrac{2\left[3A-x_2(2y_1+y_2)\right]}{x_2^2}x+y_1$

10. (a) $y_n(x)=\pm\sin\dfrac{n(x+\pi)}{2}$; $n=1,2,3...$

    (b) $y(x)\equiv 0$

12. (a) The curve is an arc of the circle
$x^2+\left(y+\dfrac{k}{\lambda}\right)^2=\dfrac{1}{\lambda^2}$ where $\lambda^2+k^2=1$,
$4(1-\lambda^2)$
$=\left(2\lambda A+\sqrt{1-\lambda^2}+\dfrac{1}{\lambda}\text{Sin}^{-1}\lambda\right)^2$,
$0<|\lambda|\leqq 1$.

    (b) The quarter circle defined by
$y=\sqrt{1-x^2}$; $0\leqq x\leqq 1$.

14. (a) Minimize $\displaystyle\int_0^1 2\pi y\sqrt{1+(y')^2}\,dx$ with
$\ell=\displaystyle\int_0^1\sqrt{1+(y')^2}\,dx$ and $A=\displaystyle\int_0^1 y\,dx$
fixed in value.

    (b) $(y+\lambda_1)+(\lambda_2 y+k)\sqrt{1+(y')^2}=0$

    (c) $x=\pm\displaystyle\int\dfrac{u\,du}{\sqrt{au^2+2bu+b^2}}$ where
$a=1-\lambda_2^2, b=\lambda_1\lambda_2-k, u=\lambda_2 y+k$

16. $y=b\cosh\dfrac{x}{b}-\sqrt{b^2+\dfrac{l^2}{4}}$ where $\dfrac{l}{2b}=\sinh\dfrac{1}{b}$
and $-1\leq x\leq 1$

18. A parabola: $y=\dfrac{wx^2}{4\rho\lambda}+ax+b$, where w and ρ
denote the weight per unit length with respect
to the horizontal and along the cable,
respectively; a, b, and λ are constants.

20. (a) Minimize $\displaystyle\int_{t_1}^{t_2}\sqrt{\dot{X}^2+\dot{Y}^2}\,dt$ with
$\displaystyle\int_{t_1}^{t_2}Y\,dt=h+\dfrac{g}{2}\left(t_2^2-t_1^2\right)=$ fixed constant

22. (a) A circle $(x-h)^2+(y-k)^2=(l/2\pi)^2$

26. (a) A proof
    (b) $(1-z^2)\left[1-(1-a^2)z^2\right]\ddot{z}+a^2 z\dot{z}^2=0$
$\quad z(0)=1$, $z(T)=-1$

28. $x=\cos\dfrac{\pi(T-t)}{2T}$, $y=\sin\dfrac{\pi(T-t)}{2T}$, $z=\dfrac{T-2t}{T}$,
$0\leqq t\leqq T$

30. See Section 16.1, Exercise 50.

Section 16.4

2. $I=\displaystyle\int_0^{\pi/2}e^{-2x}\left[(y')^2-2y^2\right]dx$, all
comparison functions must have the values 1
and 0 at $x=0$ and $x=\pi/2$, respectively.

4. $I=\displaystyle\int_0^\pi(y')^2\,dx$, $J=\displaystyle\int_0^\pi y^2\,dx$, all comparison
functions must satisfy $\dfrac{\partial f}{\partial y'}=0$ at $x=0$ and
vanish at $x=\pi$.

6. $I=\displaystyle\int_1^2\left[x^2(y')^2-xy^2+2xy\right]dx$; all
comparison functions must have the values 2
and 4 at $x=1$ and at $x=2$, respectively.

8. $I = \int_2^3 \left\{ x(y')^2 - \frac{1}{x} y^2 + 2xy + \frac{d}{dx} \left[g(x)y^2 \right] \right\} dx$, $J = \int_2^3 y^2 dx$, $g(2) = 3$, $g(3) = 2$,
all comparison functions must satisfy natural boundary conditions at $x = 2$ and $x = 3$.

10. $I = \int_0^1 \left\{ e^{-x}(y')^2 - y^2 \cos x + 2y \sin x + \frac{d}{dx} \left[g(x)y^2 \right] \right\} dx$, $J = \int_0^1 y^2 \cosh x dx, g(0) = 2$, all comparison
functions must have the value 5 at $x = 1$; at $x = 2$ they must satisfy a natural boundary condition.

12. $I = \int_0^1 \left[x^2(y')^2 - xy^2 - 2xy \right] dx$, $y = \frac{5}{6}(1-x)^2$

14. $I = \int_0^1 \left[x^2(y')^2 - xy^2 - 2xy \right] dx$, $y = \frac{25x(x-2)}{14}$, No.

16. $I = \int_0^\pi (y')^2 dx$, $1 = \int_0^\pi y^2 dx$, $\lambda_1 \doteq \sqrt{10}/\pi \doteq 1.007$, the exact value is $\lambda_1 = 1$.

18. (a) $\lambda_k = k\pi / 3$, $y_k = B_k \sin k\pi \ln x$, $k = 1, 2, 3, ...$; $B_k \neq 0$

    (b) $(xy')' + \frac{9\lambda^2}{x} y = 0$, $y(1) = y(e) = 0$; $p(x) = 9/x$

    (c) $y_k = \frac{\sqrt{2}}{3} \sin k\pi \ln x$

    (d) $I = \int_1^e x(y')^2 dx$, $1 = \int_1^e 9y^2 /x \, dx$

    (e) $\Lambda_1 \doteq 1.1222$, $\lambda_1 = \pi / 3 \doteq 1.0472$
    (f) $y'(e) = 0$

20. Apply the conservation of energy law.

22. (b) $\partial f * / \partial y'' = 0$
    (c) $\partial f * / \partial y' - \frac{d}{dx}(\partial f * / \partial y'') = 0$

24. No. Although $y(x)$ satisfies the differential equation and the condition $y(-1) = 2$, it does not satisfy
$y'(1) = -2$ because it must satisfy the natural boundary condition $y'(1) = 0$.

Section 16.5

2. $\delta F = \left[3y^2\,\eta(x) + x\eta'(x)\right]\varepsilon,\ \triangle F = \delta F + 3y\eta^2(x)\varepsilon^2 + \eta^3(x)\varepsilon^3$

4. $\delta F = 2\left[e^y\,\eta(x) - 3xy'\eta'(x)\right]\varepsilon,\ \triangle F = \delta F + \left\{e^y\eta^2(x) - 3x[\eta'(x)]^2\right\}\varepsilon^2 + 2e^y\sum_{k=3}^{\infty}\frac{\eta^k(x)}{k!}\varepsilon^k$

6. $\delta F = \left[e^y\,\eta(x) + e^{y'}\,\eta'(x)\right]\varepsilon,\ \triangle F = \delta F + \sum_{k=2}^{\infty}\left\{e^y\eta^k(x) + e^{y'}[\eta'(x)]^k\right\}\varepsilon^k\,/k!$

8. $\delta F = x\left[u\eta(x) + v\varepsilon(x) - \varepsilon'(x)\right]\varepsilon,\ \Delta F = \delta F + x\varepsilon(x)\eta(x)\varepsilon^2$

10. **(b)** $\delta(dy/dx) = 2\varepsilon t^2,\ d(\delta y)/dx = 10\varepsilon t^2/3$

Section 16.6

2. $\ddot{y} + \dfrac{k}{m}y = 0$

4. **(a)** $m\ddot{x} = a\mu,\ m\ddot{y} = -mg - \mu$ where $\mu = -mg/(1+a^2)$

    (b) $\dfrac{ma\,g}{\sqrt{1+a^2}}$

6. **(a)** $a\ddot{\theta} + g\cos\theta = 0$

    (b) $\dot{\theta}^2 = \dfrac{-2g}{a}\sin\theta,\ \pi \leqq \theta \leqq 2\pi$

8. **(a)** $m\ddot{y} + \left(k_1 + k_2\right)y - \tfrac{1}{2}l\left(k_1 + k_2\right)\sin\theta = 0,$

       $I\ddot{\theta} - \tfrac{1}{2}ly\left(k_1 - k_2\right)\cos\theta + \tfrac{1}{4}l^2\left(k_1 + k_2\right)\sin\theta\cos\theta = 0$

    (b) $m\ddot{y} + (k_1 + k_2)y - \tfrac{1}{2}l(k_1 - k_2)\theta = 0$

       $I\ddot{\theta} - \tfrac{1}{2}l(k_1 - k_2)y + \tfrac{1}{4}l^2(k_1 + k_2)\theta = 0$

10. $T = \frac{m}{2}(\dot{s}^2 + 2\ell\dot{s}\dot{\theta}\cos\theta + \ell^2\dot{\theta}^2)$, $V = mg\ell(1 - \cos\theta)$, $\ddot{\theta} + \frac{g}{\ell}\sin\theta = \frac{a}{\ell}\omega^2\cos\theta\sin\omega t$.

As $\omega \to \infty$, is appears that to keep the equation meaningful, $\cos\theta$ must approach 0, i.e., θ must approach 90°.

12. $\left(m_1 + m_2 + \frac{W}{2g}\right)\ddot{q} = (m_1 - m_2)g$, $\ddot{q} = 0$ if $m_1 = m_2$

14. $m\ddot{r} - mr(\dot{\theta})^2 + f'(r) = 0$, $\frac{d}{dt}(mr^2\dot{\theta}) = 0$

16. With $L = \frac{1}{2}(\dot{y}_1^2 + \dot{y}_2^2 + \dot{y}_3^2) - \frac{1}{2}\left(\frac{1}{4}y_1^2 + y_2^2 + \frac{9}{4}y_3^2\right)$, Lagrange's equations are:

$\ddot{y}_1 + \frac{1}{4}y_1 = 0$, $\ddot{y}_2 + y_2 = 0$, $\ddot{y}_3 + \frac{9}{4}y = 0$

18. $m\ell\ddot{\theta}_1 + \left(mg - \frac{k\ell}{4}\right)\theta_1 + \frac{k\ell}{4}\theta_2 = -ak$

$\frac{k\ell}{4}\theta_1 + m\ell\ddot{\theta}_2 + \left(mg - \frac{k\ell}{4}\right)\theta_2 = ak$ where $2a$ is the distance between the points from which pendulums are suspended. $= \frac{g}{\ell} - \frac{k}{2m}$, $\omega_2^2 = \frac{g}{\ell}$

22. (a) $\ddot{x}_1 = -3x_1 + x_2$ $f_1 = 1/2\pi$

        $\ddot{x}_2 = 2x_1 - 2x_2$ $f_2 = 1/\pi$

(b) $\begin{bmatrix} \ddot{x}_1 \\ \ddot{x}_2 \end{bmatrix} = \begin{bmatrix} -5 & 3 \\ \frac{3}{2} & -\frac{3}{2} \end{bmatrix}\begin{bmatrix} x_1 \\ x_2 \end{bmatrix}$ $f_1 = \sqrt{2}/4\pi$

                                          $f_2 = \sqrt{6}/2\pi$

(c) $2\ddot{x}_1 = -13x_1 + 5x_2$ $f_1 = 1/\pi$

       $2\ddot{x}_2 = 5x_1 - 13x_2$ $f_2 = 3/2\pi$

24. $\frac{d}{dt}(\dot{\theta}\sin^2\phi) = 0$, $\ddot{\phi} = \left(\dot{\theta}^2\cos\phi + \frac{g}{a}\right)\sin\phi$. The motion takes place in a plane $\theta = \theta_0$ and for $\delta = \pi - \phi$ small, $\delta = \alpha\cos\sqrt{\frac{g}{a}}t$. The reactive force of the sphere on P has magnitude $mg\left(\alpha^2\sin^2\sqrt{\frac{g}{a}}t + \cos\delta\right)$ and its direction is opposite that of r.

26. (a) $L = \frac{m}{2}(\dot{q}_1^2 + \dot{q}_2^2) - \frac{mg}{2\ell}(q_1^2 + q_2^2) - \frac{e^2}{a + q_2 - q_1}$, $\begin{cases} m\ddot{q}_1 + \frac{mg}{\ell}q_1 + \frac{e^2}{(a + q_2 - q_1)^2} = 0 \\ m\ddot{q}_2 + \frac{mg}{\ell}q_2 - \frac{e^2}{(a + q_2 - q_1)^2} = 0 \end{cases}$

(b) $m\ddot{q}_1 + \left(\dfrac{mg}{\ell} + \dfrac{2e^2}{a^3}\right)q_1 - \dfrac{2e^2}{a^3}q_2 = -\dfrac{e^2}{a^2}, \quad m\ddot{q}_2 + \left(\dfrac{mg}{\ell} + \dfrac{2e^2}{a^3}\right)q_2 - \dfrac{2e^2}{a^3}q_1 = \dfrac{e^2}{a^2}$

With $\omega_1 = \sqrt{\dfrac{g}{\ell}}$ and $\omega_2 = \sqrt{\dfrac{g}{\ell} + \dfrac{4e^2}{ma^3}}$,

$q_1 = A\cos(\omega_1 t - \alpha) - B\cos(\omega_2 t - \beta) - \dfrac{e^2}{ma^2\omega_2^2}$

$q_2 = A\cos(\omega_1 t - \alpha) + B\cos(\omega_2 t - \beta) + \dfrac{e^2}{ma^2\omega_2^2}$

$A,\ B,\ \alpha$ and β parameters

(c) Replace $q_1 + \dfrac{e^2}{ma^2\omega_2^2}$ and $q_2 - \dfrac{e^2}{ma^2\omega_2^2}$ by new variables.

Section 16.7

2. (a) $L = \frac{1}{2}m\ell^2\dot{\theta}^2 + mg\ell\cos\theta, \quad \ddot{\theta} + \frac{g}{\ell}\sin\theta = 0$

(b) $H = \frac{1}{2}\dfrac{p^2}{m\ell^2} - mg\ell\cos\theta$

(c) $\dot{\theta} = \dfrac{p}{m\ell^2}, \quad \dot{p} = -mg\ell\sin\theta$

4. (a) $H = \frac{1}{2m}(p_r^2 + p_\theta^2/r^2) + V(r)$

(b) $\dot{r} = p_r/m, \quad \dot{\theta} = p_\theta/(mr^2), \quad \dot{p}_r = p_\theta^2/(mr^3) - V'(r), \quad \dot{p}_\theta = 0$

(c) $m\ddot{r} = mr\dot{\theta}^2 - V'(r), \quad \dfrac{d}{dt}(r^2\dot{\theta}) = 0$

8. (a) $H = \dfrac{\ell^2 p_x^2 - 2\ell p_x p_\theta\cos\theta + p_\theta^2}{2m\ell^2\sin^2\theta} + mg\ell(1 - \cos\theta) + \frac{1}{2}(k_1 + k_2)x^2$

(b) $\dot{x} = \dfrac{\ell p_x - p_\theta\cos\theta}{m\ell\sin^2\theta}, \quad \dot{\theta} = \dfrac{p - \ell p_x\cos\theta}{m\ell^2\sin^2\theta}, \quad \dot{p}_x = -(k_1 + k_2)x,$

$\dot{p}_\theta = \dfrac{(\ell^2 p_x^2 + p_\theta^2)\cos\theta - \ell p_x p_\theta(1 + \cos^2\theta)}{m\ell^2\sin^3\theta} - mg\ell\sin\theta$

(c) $x = 0, \quad \theta = 0$

10. (a) $p_1 = (m_1 + m_2)\ell_1^2 \dot\theta_1 + [m_2 \ell_1 \ell_2 \cos(\theta_1 - \theta_2)]\dot\theta_2$, $\;p_2 = [m_2 \ell_1 \ell_2 \cos(\theta_1 - \theta_2)]\dot\theta_1 + m_2 \ell_2^2 \dot\theta_2$

(b) $\dot\theta_1 = \dfrac{\ell_2 p_1 - \ell_1 p_2 \cos(\theta_1 - \theta_2)}{\ell_1^2 \ell_2 [m_1 + m_2 \sin^2(\theta_1 - \theta_2)]}$, $\;\dot\theta_2 = \dfrac{(m_1 + m_2)\ell_1 p_2 - m_2 \ell_2 p_1 \cos(\theta_1 - \theta_2)}{m_2 \ell_1 \ell_2^2 [m_1 + m_2 \sin^2(\theta_1 - \theta_2)]}$

(c) $H = \dfrac{m_2 \ell_2^2 p_1^2 - 2m_2 \ell_1 \ell_2 p_1 p_2 \cos(\theta_1 - \theta_2) + (m_1 + m_2)\ell_1^2 p_2^2}{2m_2 \ell_1^2 \ell_2^2 [m_1 + m_2 \sin^2(\theta_1 - \theta_2)]} - (m_1 + m_2)g\ell_1 \cos\theta_1 - m_2 g \ell_2 \cos\theta$

Chapter 17

Section 17.2

2. $7 + 11i$

4. $\frac{4-3i}{5}$

6. $z^3 + iz$

8. $-iz^2 + 2z - 1$

10. (a) Open, simply-connected, unbounded (upper half plane excluding $y = 0$).

(b) Closed, multiply-connected, bounded (an annulus).

(c) Open, multiply-connected, unbounded (exterior of a circle).

(d) Closed, simply-connected, unbounded (a vertical strip).

(e) Neither open nor closed, simply-connected, unbounded (a sector).

(f) Open, simply-connected, unbounded (exterior of a parabola).

(g) Closed, simply-connected, unbounded (interior of a parabola).

(h) Closed, simply-connected, unbounded (quarter plane: boundaries $y = \pm x, x \geqq 0$).

(i) Closed, simply-connected, unbounded (connected quarter planes: boundaries $y = \pm x$, containing $y = 0$).

18. $z = \pm i$. The function is undefined at these points.

20. The function is everywhere continuous.

22. $z = i$. $\underset{z \to i}{\text{Lim}} f(z) \neq f(i)$.

30. (a) The annulus bounded by two circles centered at $z = 4 - 3i$ of radii 3 and 5. Points of the outer circle belong to S, points on the inner circle do not.

(b) No. Points of the circle $|z - (4 - 3i)| = 5$ belong to S but are not interior points of S.

(c) Yes. S consists of the domain $D = \{ z \mid 3 < |z - (4 - 3i)| < 5 \}$ together with some boundary points of S.

(d) 0 is a boundary point and a limit point; 1 is an interior point and a limit point; 4 is a boundary point and a limit point; $-3i$ is an interior point and a limit point; $4 - 3i$ is an exterior point.

Section 17.3

6. At $z = -1, \pm i$

8. Only if u and v are constants.

14. For $u + iv = (x^2 - y^2) + 0i$, both u and v satisfy Laplace's equation and the formula of the exercise yields $2i(x + iy)$ which is analytic, even thought $u + iv$ is not.

18. $v = -e^x \cos y$

20. $u = -x^2 + y^2 - 6y, u + iv = -z^2 + 6iz$

34. (a) Only at $z = i$

(b) Only at $z = i$; $f'(z) = 0$

(c) Nowhere, because there is no neighborhood throughout which $f'(z)$ exists.

36. u is harmonic in any region R which does not contain the point $z = 0$.

$$f(z) = \ln(x^2 + y^2) + 2i \tan^{-1}\frac{y}{x} + c.$$

$$f'(z) = \frac{2}{z}, z \neq 0$$

Section 17.4

2. **(a)** $\ln 5 + i\tan^{-1}\frac{4}{-3} \doteq 1.609 + 2.214\,i$

   (b) $\cos(\ln 2) + i\sin(\ln 2) \doteq 0.769 + 0.639\,i$

   (c) $\frac{i\sinh 1}{\cosh 1} = i\tanh 1 \doteq 0.762\,i$

   (d) $\frac{1}{2}\ln(-3) = \frac{1}{2}(\ln 3 + i\pi) \doteq 0.549 + 1.571\,i$

   (e) $e^{(\ln 2 + \pi/4)} + i(\ln\sqrt{2} - \pi/2)$
   $\doteq 1.490 - 4.123\,i$

   (f) $e^{(1-i)[\ln\sqrt{5} + i\tan^{-1}(1/2)]} \doteq 3.350 - 1.189\,i$

4. c must be an integer

24. 1

26. $z = (\frac{\pi}{2} + 2n\pi) + i\cosh^{-1} 3$

30. Yes

32. The complex numbers are not ordered (See Exercise 40, Section 3.1), and hence the inequalities involved in Rolle's theorem for real functions are meaningless for functions of a complex variable.

34. **(b)** $|\cos z|^2 = \cos^2 x + \sinh^2 y$

38. $|\cos z| \leq 5/3$

42. $\tanh z = i$ has no solutions.

50. The points of the line $y = -k$, $k > 0$.

52. The images of the lines $x = c$ are the hyperbolas $\dfrac{u^2}{\sin^2 c} - \dfrac{v^2}{\cos^2 c} = 1$

The images of the lines $y = k$ are ellipses
$$\frac{u^2}{\cosh^2 k} + \frac{v^2}{\sinh^2 k} = 1$$

54. The images of the lines $x = c$ are the ellipses
$\dfrac{u^2}{\sinh^2 c} + \dfrac{v^2}{\cosh^2 c} = 1$ The images of the lines $y = k$ are the hyperbolas $\dfrac{v^2}{\sin^2 k} + \dfrac{u^2}{\cos^2 k} = 1$

58. $\frac{1}{2}[(2n+1)\pi + i\ln 3]$

Section 17.5

2. Along each path the value of the integral is i.

4. **(a)** 1

   (b) i

   (c) $2i$

6. **(a)** $12 - 26/3i$

   (b) $10 - 10/3i$

   (c) $6 - 28/3i$

8. $1/2 - \cosh 1$

10. $-(\cos 1 + \sin 1) + i(\cos 1 - \sin 1)$

12. $-i/2$

14. The integral is different from zero around the contours a, b, c, and d, although around the contours b and d it has the same (non zero) value. It is zero around the contours e and f.

16. $v = 2y - 3x$, $f(z) = (2 - 3i)z$

18. $v = -e^x \sin y$, $f(z) = -ie^z$

20. $v = -\sin x \cosh y, \ f(z) = -i \sin z$

22. $v = 2xy + y^2 - x^2, \ f(z) = (1 - i)z^2$

26. $\frac{1}{3} - \pi^2 + \frac{\sinh 2}{2} + \frac{i\pi}{3}(3 - \pi^2)$

28. (a) $\sqrt{2}$

   (b) $\sqrt{5}$

   (c) 2

Section 17.6

2. (a) 0

   (b) $\frac{3+2i}{2}\pi$

   (c) $\frac{-3+2i}{2}\pi$

4. (a) $2\pi i/e$

   (b) $2\pi i/e$

6. Maximum: 2 at $z = 1$; minimum: 0 at $z = -1$.

8. Maxima: 3 at $z = 1$, 1 at $z = -1$; minima: 0 at $z = \left(1 - \pm i\sqrt{3}\right)/2$.

10. Maxima: 2 at $z = 0$ and 1; minima: $\sqrt{7/2}$ at $z = \frac{1}{2}, \frac{3}{4}$ at $z = \frac{1}{2} + i$.

Section 17.7

2. $u(x, y) = \frac{50}{3}xy + 50$

4. As families of curves, the two sets are identical, although congruent curves will correspond to different parameters.

6. The curves on which $|f'(z)|$ is a constant.

8. $f(z) = 20iz - 20; \ u(y) = 20y - 20.$

10. A constant equal to the flow across any curve joining O and O' is added to the stream function.

12. $f(z) = -\dfrac{\mu(1+im)}{2\pi\sqrt{1+m^2}\,z}$

14. $f(z) = \frac{1}{2\pi}[\ln(z - 1) - \ln(z + 1)]$

   $\phi(z) = \frac{1}{2\pi}\ln\left|\frac{z-1}{z+1}\right|$

   $\psi(z) = \frac{1}{2\pi}[\arg(z-1) - \arg(z+1)]$

   The equipotential curves are circles on the points –1 and 1. The streamlines are the circles which are the orthogonal trajectories of the equipotential curves.

18. $f(z) = -iz - 2i \ln z,$
   $\Phi = y + 2\theta, \ \psi = -x - 2\ln r.$

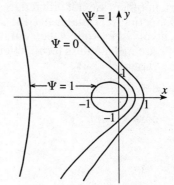

20. $f(z) = -\frac{iK}{2\pi}[\ln(z-1) - \ln(z+1)]$

   $\Phi(z) = \frac{K}{2\pi}[\arg(z-1) - \arg(z+1)]$

   $\psi(z) = \frac{K}{2\pi}[\ln|z+1|z - \ln|z-1|]$

   The streamlines are circles on the points –1, 1.

22. $f(z) = -iUz - \frac{\mu}{2\pi z}$ There is no circular
streamline.

24. $\Phi = \arg(z \pm \sqrt{z^2 - 1})$, $\quad \psi = -\ln(z \pm \sqrt{z^2 - 1})$

Chapter 18

Section 18.1

2. **(a)** The series converges to the sum $(z+1)/(z-3)$ in the interior of the circle whose radius is 4/3 and whose center is the point $(\frac{5}{3},0)$.

   (b) The series converges to the sum $1/(2z-1+2i)$ in the interior of the circle $|z+i|=\frac{1}{2}$.

4. **(a)** The open half-plane $x>0$;
   $$S=e^{-z}/(1-e^{-z})$$

   (b) The vertical angles where $x^2-y^2>0$;
   $$S=e^{-z^2}/(1-e^{-z^2})$$

   (c) The exterior of the hyperbola $x^2-y^2+1=0$;
   $$S=e^{-(z^2+1)}/[1-e^{-(z^2+1)}]$$

   (d) The exterior of the hyperbola $(x-\frac{1}{2})^2-y^2=\frac{1}{4}$; $S=e^{z^2}/(e^z-e^{z^2})$.

6. The exterior. Only at the origin.

8. **(a)** Throughout the exterior of the circle $|1+z|=1$ and at the origin.

   (b) The sum is $\begin{cases} 0, & z=0 \\ 1+z, & z\neq 0 \end{cases}$

   (c) The convergence is uniform on and in the exterior of any circle of the family $|1+z|=1+\delta,\ \delta>0$.

10. **(a)** The series converges in the interior of the lemniscate $\left|1-z^2\right|=1$.

    (b) The sum is $\frac{1}{z^2}$.

(c) The convergence is uniform within and on the boundary of either of the lobes of the curve $\left|1-z^2\right|=1-\delta,\ \delta>0$.

12. **(a)** The series converges for all values of z .

    (b) The convergence is uniform over any region of the z plane.

14. The series converges to the sum 1 for all values of z except $z=-1/n$. $n=1,2,3,\dots$

16. **(a)** The x axis and the upper half-plane.

    (b) The series converges uniformly at all points of the region of convergence.

18. The convergence is clearly not uniform. Around the origin the plots of S_n will jump from 0 to $1+x^2$ more and more abruptly over shorter and shorter intervals.

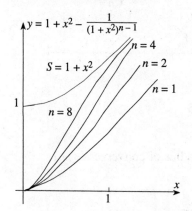

24. The y axis and the left half-plane. The series converges uniformly at all points of the region of convergence.

Section 18.2

2. **(a) (b)** Both the series and its derivative converge in the interior of the lemniscate $\left|1-z^2\right|=1$.

4. **(a) (b) (c)** The three series converge in the open half-plane $|x-1|<0$.

8. The series converges to the sum $e^z/(e^z-1)^2$ in the half plane $x>0$.

12. The terms of a real series are not analytic functions of a complex variable.

16. The convergence is clearly not uniform. The maxima of the S_n's never decrease to zero, but are "pinched off" over a shorter and shorter interval around $x=0$.

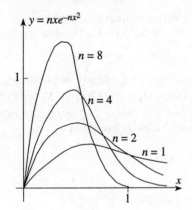

Section 18.3

2. The radius of convergence is 1.

4. **(a)** $\displaystyle\sum_{n=0}^{\infty} z^n/n! = e^z$

(b) $\displaystyle\sum_{n=0}^{\infty} n!z^n$

6. **(a)** $R=\frac{1}{4}$

(b) $R=1$

(c) $R=1$

(d) $R=1$

(e) $R=1$

Section 18.4

2. **(a)** $f(z)=\frac{1}{2}-\frac{3}{4}z+\frac{7}{8}z^2-\frac{15}{16}z^3+\ldots, R=1$

(b) $\displaystyle\sum_{n=1}^{\infty}\left[\frac{1}{3^n}-\frac{1}{4^n}\right](z-2)^{n-1},\ R=3$

4. **(a)** $e^z=i\displaystyle\sum_{n=0}^{\infty}\left(z-\frac{i\pi}{2}\right)^n/n!,\ R=\infty$

(b) $e^z=-\displaystyle\sum_{n=0}^{\infty}(z-i\pi)^n/n!,\ R=\infty$

(c) $e^z=-i\displaystyle\sum_{n=0}^{\infty}\left(z-\frac{3i\pi}{2}\right)^n/n!,\ R=\infty$

6. **(a)** $\tan z=z+\frac{1}{3}z^3+\frac{2}{15}z^5+\ldots\ |z|<\frac{\pi}{2}$

(b) $\sec z=1+\frac{1}{2!}z^2+\frac{5}{4!}z^4+\ldots\ |z|<\frac{\pi}{2}$

8. **(a)** 15

(b) $-43760/243$

(c) $-3805/972$

12. **(b)** Each series converges to $1/(2-z)$ within the lens-shaped region common to the two circles $|z|=2$ and $|z-i|=\sqrt{5}$.

14. $f(z)=2\pi i$

16. **(a)** $e^z=\displaystyle\sum_{n=0}^{\infty}z^n/n!,\ |z|<\infty$

(b) $e^x=\displaystyle\sum_{n=0}^{\infty}z^x/n!,\ |x|<\infty$

18. (a) (b) $1/z = \sum\limits_{n=0}^{\infty}(-1)^n(z-1)^n, \quad |z-1|<1$

20. $|z|=1$

Section 18.5

2. $f(z) = \dfrac{2}{z-1} + \dfrac{1}{2} - \dfrac{z-1}{4} + \dfrac{(z-1)^2}{8} - \dfrac{(z-1)^3}{16} + \ldots, \quad 0<|z-1|<2$

$f(z) = \ldots - \dfrac{8}{(z-1)^4} + \dfrac{4}{(z-1)^3} - \dfrac{2}{(z-1)^2} + \dfrac{3}{z-1}, \quad |z-1|>2$

4. $f(z) = \ldots + \dfrac{1}{2(z+1)^3} + \dfrac{1}{2(z+1)^2} + \dfrac{1}{2(z+1)} + \dfrac{1}{3} + \dfrac{7(z+1)}{36} + \dfrac{23}{216}(z+1)^2 + \ldots +$

$\dfrac{1}{2}\left[\dfrac{1}{2^n} - \dfrac{1}{3^{n+1}}\right](z+1)^n + \ldots; \quad 1<|z+1|<2$

$f(z) = \ldots + \left[-2^{n-2} + \dfrac{1}{2}\right]\dfrac{1}{(z+1)^n} - \ldots - \dfrac{1}{2(z+1)^2} - \dfrac{1}{6} - \dfrac{z+1}{18} - \ldots - \dfrac{(z+1)^n}{6\cdot 3^n} - \ldots; \quad 2<|z+1|<3$

$f(z) = \ldots + \left[\dfrac{1}{2} - 2^{n-1} + \dfrac{3^{n-1}}{2}\right]\dfrac{1}{(z+1)^n} + \ldots + \dfrac{1}{(z+1)^3}; \quad |z+1|>3$

6. Since the first term is undefined for $z = 0$, the series cannot have a sum for this value of z.

10. (c) $a_n = \dfrac{1}{2\pi}\displaystyle\int_0^{2\pi}\cosh(2\cos\theta)\cos n\theta\, d\theta$

  (d) $a_n = \dfrac{1}{2\pi}\displaystyle\int_0^{2\pi}\cosh(2\cos\theta)\cos n\theta\, d\theta$

14. $z^{-2} + z^{-1} + \sum\limits_{n=0}^{\infty}z^n; \quad 0<|z|<1, -\sum\limits_{n=0}^{\infty}1/z^{n+3}; \quad 1<|z|$

Chapter 19

Section 19.1

2. (a) $-3/4$

    (b) $3/4$

4. 0

6. 1

8. 1

10. (a) $i\pi$

    (b) $i\pi/2$

    (c) $i\pi/4$

    (d) 0

    (e) 0

    (f) $i\pi/2$

12. (a) $-2i\pi$

    (b) 0

    (c) 0

    (d) $-2i\pi$

    (e) $i\pi$

    (f) $-i\pi^2$

22. (a) $\dfrac{\pi \operatorname{csch} \pi a}{a}$

    (b) $\dfrac{\pi^2 \cos \pi a}{\sin^2 \pi a}$

    (c) $-\dfrac{\pi}{6a}\Big[\csc 2\pi a$

    $+2\,\dfrac{\sin \pi a \cosh \sqrt{3}\pi a - \cos \pi a \sinh \sqrt{3}\pi a}{\cosh 2\sqrt{3}\pi a - \cos 2\pi a}\Big]$

24. (a) $-3i\pi/2$

    (b) $3i\pi/2$

    (c) 0

Section 19.2

2. $2\pi a/(a^2 - b^2)^3$

4. $\pi/3$

6. $\pi/12$

8. $3\pi/8$

10. $\pi/4\sqrt{2}$

12. $\pi/3$

14. $\pi\left[\dfrac{a(b^2-c^2)+b(c^2-a^2)+c(a^2-b^2)}{(a^2-b^2)(b^2-c^2)(c^2-a^2)}\right]$

16. No. Yes, its value is 0.

18. $\dfrac{\pi e^{-mb}\sin ma}{b}$

20. $\dfrac{\pi e^{-m\sqrt{2}}}{2\sqrt{2}}(\cos\frac{m}{\sqrt{2}} + \sin\frac{m}{\sqrt{2}})$

22. $\dfrac{\pi(e^{-mb}-e^{-ma})}{a^2-b^2}$

24. $\dfrac{\pi(b^{a-1}-c^{a-1})}{(c-b)\sin a\pi}$

26. $\dfrac{\pi}{\sin a\pi}\left[\dfrac{b^{a-1}}{(b-c)(b-d)} + \dfrac{c^{a-1}}{(c-b)(c-d)} + \dfrac{d^{a-1}}{(d-b)(d-c)}\right]$

28. $\dfrac{\pi}{4\sin(\pi a/4)}$

38. $\dfrac{\pi^3}{8a}+\dfrac{\pi\ln^2 a}{2a}\,,\dfrac{\pi\ln a}{2a}$

40. $5\pi/12$

42. $\dfrac{\pi e^{-a}}{a}$

44. 0

Section 19.3

2. te^{-2t}

4. $e^{-2t}\cos 3t-\dfrac{2}{3}e^{-2t}\sin 3t$

6. $-\dfrac{e^{-t}}{3}+\dfrac{e^{t/2}}{3}(\cos\dfrac{\sqrt{3}t}{2}+3\sin\dfrac{\sqrt{3}t}{2})$

8. $\dfrac{\sin 2t}{10}-\dfrac{\sin 3t}{15}$

10. $\dfrac{e^{-t}(-2t\cos 2t+\sin 2t)}{16}$

12. $\theta(x,t)=\dfrac{T_0}{E_s J}\left[x+\dfrac{8\ell}{\pi^2}\sum_{n=1}^{\infty}\dfrac{(-1)^n}{(2n-1)^2}\sin\dfrac{(2n-1)\pi x}{2\ell}\cos\dfrac{(2n-1)\pi axt}{2\ell}\right]$

14. $\dfrac{e^{-bt}}{\cosh ab}+4\sum_{n=1}^{\infty}\left[\dfrac{(-1)^n(2n-1)\pi}{(2n-1)^2\pi^2+4a^2b^2}\cos\dfrac{(2n-1)\pi t}{2a}-\dfrac{(-1)^n 4ab}{(2n-1)^2\pi^2+4a^2b^2}\sin\dfrac{(2n-1)\pi t}{2a}\right]$

16. $1-2\sum_{n=1}^{\infty}\dfrac{J_0(\rho_n r)}{nJ_1(\rho_n)}\exp(-\rho_n^2 t)$ where ρ_n is the nth one of the roots of the equation $J_0(r)=0$.

Section 19.4

2. $D_1 = 0$, $D_2 = -9$, $D_3 = -81$; therefore there is at least one root with nonnegative real part. (Actually, the roots are, approximately, -1.92 and $0.86 \pm 1.94i$.)

4. $D_1 = 2$, $D_2 = 10$, $D_3 = D_4 = 0$; therefore there is at least one root with nonnegative real part. (Actually the roots are $\pm i\sqrt{2} \equiv 0 \pm i\sqrt{2}$ and $-1 \pm 2i$)

10. Apply Rouché's theorem to the circle $|z| = 1$ with $f(z) = 12$ and $g(z) = z^7 - 5z^3$. Then apply Rouché's theorem to the circle $|z| = 2$ with $f(z) = z^7$ and $g(z) = 12 - 5z^3$.

12. $s \doteq -1.74, \ 0.37 \pm 1.47i$.

14. Quadrants I and II.

Chapter 20

Section 20.1

2. The circle $u^2 + v^2 = a^6$. As a point traverses the upper half of the circle $x^2 + y^2 = a^2$ in the counterclockwise direction, its image starts at $(a^3, 0)$ and traverses in the counterclockwise direction the image circle and its upper semicircle.

4. The mapping is equivalent to the mapping defined by the function $w = z^2$ followed by a reflection in the real axis.

6. The equations of the transformation are $u = 1 - 2y$, $v = 2x$. Lines parallel to the x axis go into lines parallel to the v axis. Lines parallel to the y axis go into lines parallel to the u axis.

8. Yes. The lines $y = \pm x$ go into the line $u = 0$; the lines $xy = 0$ go into the line $v = 0$.

10. The equations of the transformation are
$$u = 1 - \frac{y}{x^2 + y^2}, v = \frac{-x}{x^2 + y^2}$$

12. $u = x^3 - 3xy^2$, $v = 3x^2y - y^3$. The circle $x^2 + y^2 = a^6$. The cubic curve whose parametric equations are
$$u = 1 - 3y^2, v = 3y - y^3.$$

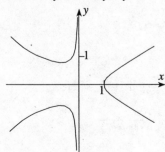

14. $a = \pm b$, c unrestricted.

18. The equations of the transformation are
$u = \sin x \cosh y$, $v = \cos x \sinh y$
The lines $y = c$ map into the ellipses
$$\frac{u^2}{\cosh^2 c} + \frac{v^2}{\sinh^2 c} = 1$$
The lines $x = k$ map into the hyperbolas
$$\frac{u^2}{\sin^2 k} + \frac{v^2}{\cos^2 k} = 1$$

20. The entire first quadrant exterior to the circle $(u - \frac{1}{2})^2 + v^2 = \frac{1}{4}$

Section 20.2

2. (a) $a^2 + b^2$

   (b) 28/5

4. (a) At $z = \frac{1}{2} - i$. At $z = -\frac{1}{2} - i$ segments are left unchanged in length but are rotated through $180°$

   (b) At $z = -1$ and at $z = \frac{1}{3}$. At $z = \frac{-1 + \sqrt{2}i}{3}$ segments are left unchanged in length but are rotated through $180°$.

6. The images of the perpendicular lines $x = 1$ and $y = 0$ intersect at an angle of $45°$.

Section 20.3

2. -1

4. $z = \frac{-dw + b}{cw - d}$

6. $w = \frac{iz + (1 + 2i)}{(3 + 2i)z + (2 - i)}$

10. If $(d - a)^2 + 4bc = 0$, the transformation $z' = \frac{az + b}{cz + d}$ leaves only one point, $z = \frac{a - d}{2c}$, invariant. A transformation of the

form $z' = z + k$ leaves no point invariant, although it is conventional to say that it leaves the "point at infinity" invariant.

12. The only invariant point is $z = i$.

14. $w = \frac{iz-2}{z+2}$; $3(u^2 + v^2) + 8u + 2v + 3 = 0$.

16. $x' = \frac{x}{x^2+y^2}$, $y' = \frac{y}{x^2+y^2}$

18. The line $u = -\frac{1}{2}$.

20. Inside the circle, the lengths are increased; outside the circle, lengths are decreased. The locus of points where segments are not rotated is the line $\arg(cz + d) = \frac{1}{2}\arg(ad - bc)$.

22. $w = \frac{(z-1)^2 + i(z+1)^2}{(z-1)^2 - i(z+1)^2}$

26. $T = \frac{100}{\pi}\tan^{-1}\left[2y/(x^2 + y^2 - 1)\right]$

28. $T = \frac{100}{\pi}\tan^{-1}\frac{3x^2y - y^3}{x^3 - 3xy^2}$

30. $T = \frac{100}{\pi}\tan^{-1}\frac{x^2 + y^2 - 1}{2y}$

32. $T = \frac{100}{\pi}\tan^{-1}\frac{4y(1 - x^2 - y^2)}{(x^2+y^2)^2 - 2x^2 - 6y^2 + 1}$

34. $w = -\left(\frac{z^{1/2}-1}{z^{1/2}+1}\right)^2$

36. (a) $w = e^{i\theta}\frac{z+1}{z-1}$

(b) Taking $e^{i\theta} = -1$, the temperature in the w plane is $T = \frac{100}{\pi}\tan^{-1}\frac{v}{u}$. In the z plane the isotherms are defined parametrically by the equations

$x = \frac{1 - u^2 - v^2}{u^2 + v^2 - 2v + 1}$, $y = \frac{-2u}{u^2 + v^2 - 2u + 1}$ where $v = u\tan\frac{\pi T}{100}$.

38. $w = \frac{8z + 8i}{5z + 2i}$

Section 20.4

2. $T = \frac{100}{\pi}\tan^{-1}\frac{y}{x}$

4. $T = \frac{100}{\pi}\tan^{-1}\left[\frac{4\sinh u\sin v}{\cos^2 v + \sinh^2 u - 4}\right]$

8. $T = 100 - \frac{100v}{\pi}$

10. $w = iz^{3/2}$

12. $w = \sqrt{z^2 - 1}$

14. $w = -\sqrt{z^2 - 1} + \cosh^{-1}z$

16. $w = -\frac{1}{2}\ln(z^2 - 1) + i\pi$

18. $w = A\int_0^z \frac{t^{2\alpha/\pi}}{(1-t^2)^{\alpha/\pi}}dt + ai$ where $A = \frac{(b+ai)\sqrt{\pi}}{\Gamma(\alpha/\pi + 1/2)\Gamma(1 - \alpha/\pi)}$

20. $w = \frac{\sqrt{\pi}}{\Gamma^2(3/4)}\int_0^z [t(1-t)]^{-1/4}dt - 1$